BEST

LOOP HIKES
Arizona

BEST LOOP HIKES
Arizona

Bruce Grubbs

THE MOUNTAINEERS BOOKS

THE MOUNTAINEERS BOOKS
is the nonprofit publishing arm of The Mountaineers Club, an organization founded in 1906 and dedicated to the exploration, preservation, and enjoyment of outdoor and wilderness areas.

1001 SW Klickitat Way, Suite 201, Seattle, WA 98134

Published simultaneously in Great Britain by Cordee, 3a DeMontfort Street, Leicester, England, LE1 7HD

Manufactured in Canada

Acquiring Editor: Cassandra Conyers
Project Editor: Mary Metz
Copy Editor: Paula Thurman
Cover and Book Design: The Mountaineers Books
Layout: Mayumi Thompson
Cartographers: Moore Creative Designs and Steve Cherkas
All photographs by Bruce Grubbs unless otherwise indicated.

Cover photograph: *Saguaro cactus are the symbol of the Sonoran Desert.*
Frontispiece: *Pinnacle Balanced Rock, Heart of Rocks Trail*

Maps shown in this book were produced using National Geographic's *TOPO!* software. For more information, go to *www.nationalgeographic.com/topo.*

Library of Congress Cataloging-in-Publication Data
Grubbs, Bruce (Bruce O.)
  Best loop hikes, Arizona / by Bruce Grubbs.— 1st ed.
     p. cm.
  Includes index.
  1. Hiking—Arizona—Guidebooks. 2. Arizona—Guidebooks. I. Title.
  GV199.42.A95G78 2004
  917.9104'54—dc22
                              2004020871

CONTENTS

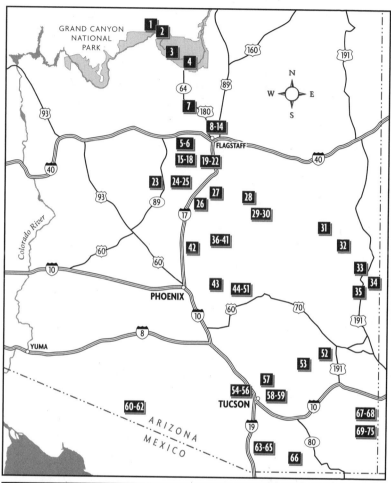

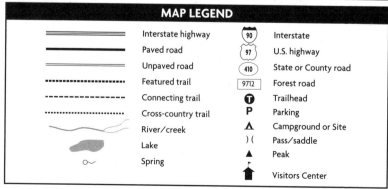

MAP LEGEND

═══════	Interstate highway
━━━━━━	Paved road
───────	Unpaved road
■■■■■■	Featured trail
─ ─ ─ ─	Connecting trail
••••••	Cross-country trail
～～～	River/creek
▬	Lake
～	Spring

(90)	Interstate
(97)	U.S. highway
(410)	State or County road
9712	Forest road
T	Trailhead
P	Parking
▲	Campground or Site
) (	Pass/saddle
▲	Peak
↑	Visitors Center

ACKNOWLEDGMENTS

I'd like to thank the following people who reviewed the manuscript and made valuable suggestions: Steve Bridgehouse, Grand Canyon National Park; Sharlot Minor, Kaibab National Forest; Suzanne Moody, Chiricahua National Monument; and Betsy D. Warner, The Nature Conservancy. Thanks also to my many hiking companions over the years, who have not only made the backcountry more enjoyable but who have also patiently endured my photographic and trail mapping efforts. Special thanks to Duart Martin, who as always encouraged this book every step of the way.

PREFACE

Wilderness is our lifeline to the past. Without it, we have no record of how humans have changed the face of the earth. Our wild lands are sentries of a bygone era when Nature thrived in its most intact, undamaged state—the epitome of balance. Save for small patches here and there, gone are the vast swaths of tall grass prairie that bore great herds of bison; gone are the rambling, undeveloped coastlines of the Eastern and Western United States; gone are the giant hardwood forests of Appalachia, great tracts of Adirondack spruce, and millions of acres of old-growth ponderosa pine in the Southwest. Vanished, too, are many of the cultures that lived in harmony with our wild lands. What we have left are fragments of our nation's identity that—without adequate protection from mining, off-road vehicle use, logging, invasive species, climate change, and development—will also disappear without so much as a whisper.

In Arizona, the threat of losing our wilderness is greater than ever. Arizona has risen on U.S. census charts to the second-fastest growing state in the nation. Ironically, one of the most enticing lures for those moving to Arizona is access to the outdoors. Here one can find snow-capped mountains and deep rugged canyons; blooming desert and spring-fed streams; verdant conifer forests and fiery orange sunsets. This wild natural symphony is open to hikers, campers, boaters, horseback riders, hunters, photographers, fishermen, and other nature lovers to enjoy. Yet Arizona guards only 6 percent of its public lands under the protective mantle of wilderness.

The Arizona Wilderness Coalition (AWC) is a statewide alliance of concerned groups and individuals working to protect and restore Arizona's wild lands and waters. The Coalition conducts wilderness inventories and educates citizens and Congress about the unique features of Arizona's landscape. Gaining the support of local communities, businesses, civic groups, and government agencies, we advocate for the congressional legislation necessary to ensure lasting wilderness protection. The Coalition has identified an additional 6 million acres of public lands in Arizona that are suitable for wilderness designation, including spectacular wild lands in lush, high-elevation forests, in the secluded Sonoran and Western deserts, and within the treasured Grand Canyon.

This year marks the fortieth anniversary of the 1964 Wilderness Act—a landmark piece of legislation that won bipartisan support in Congress and established our National Wilderness Preservation System, a network of wild lands that now protects approximately 106 million acres of America's most remarkable landscapes. Today, our strongest allies for safeguarding wild lands are the people who get out into them, hike them, breathe them, and sleep in them. But even if we travel to wilderness only in books—"even if we never do more than drive to its edge and look in," as Wallace Stegner wrote in 1960—we will be more complete as a nation and more fulfilled as individuals.

We cannot put a price tag on wilderness. Once it is lost, we cannot re-create or rebuild it, no matter how advanced our engineering skills. Wilderness is natural perfection of the kind no human can ever copy, and preservation is our only hope for sustaining it.

—*Katurah Mackay, Arizona Wilderness Coalition*

INTRODUCTION

I'm always surprised how many trails are described as one-way hikes. Either you hike out a ways and turn around, seeing the same country again, or you do a long car shuttle—time better spent hiking. Although most trails were originally planned as transportation routes, from point A to point B, there are often connecting trails that make loops possible. And as recreation becomes a more and more important use of public lands, rangers and managers are designing loop trails on purpose.

Arizona has an incredible variety of terrain, from stark deserts to lush alpine meadows. Scattered across the state are a large number of excellent and enjoyable loop hikes—far more than could fit in this book. I've selected seventy-five of the best loops, based on my more than thirty-five years of exploring Arizona, which represent a cross section of Arizona hiking. You'll find loops through alpine forests and meadows atop the state's highest mountains, loops through immense desert canyons, and rambles on historic routes. The loops range from easy, level hikes that take only an hour to demanding multiday backpack trips.

Desert bighorn sheep, Arizona Sonora Desert Museum

PERMITS AND REGULATIONS

Arizona hikers are lucky in that there are still many areas of public land that may be freely enjoyed, without any requirements for permits or fees. A few places do require permits and/or fees, and all public lands have rules and regulations which the hiker should follow. Most of the rules are based on common sense and are intended to minimize impacts on fragile backcountry from an increasing amount of human use.

Specific requirements are noted in each loop's description, but here's a general summary. National parks, such as Grand Canyon and Saguaro, charge an entrance fee. Both parks require permits for overnight hiking and backcountry camping, and charge a fee for this service. A few of the loops are on private preserves, which usually charge an entrance fee. Some of the national forests charge parking fees at trailheads, although as of this writing there are no fees or permits required for National Forest wilderness areas. The fee situation is changing rapidly, primarily because of the "temporary" Fee Demo program that somehow gets extended for another two years each time it expires. This program allows selected recreation areas to charge access fees.

Remember that backcountry permits for popular areas, such as South Rim trails at Grand Canyon National Park, may be difficult to obtain at the time of your trip, and you may have to get advance reservations. It's always a good idea to check the agency's website and call for the latest information before planning your trip (see the Appendix).

TRAIL ETIQUETTE

Hikers are only one group that uses the trails. Where permitted, you may encounter mountain bikers, horseback riders, runners, and people hiking with dogs. Everyone should recognize the other groups that have equal right to the trails and use common sense and courtesy in dealing with other people and the backcountry environment in order to preserve trails and backcountry opportunities for all.

When hikers meet other hikers, the group hiking uphill has the right of way, because uphill hikers tend to watch the trail immediately in front of them and may not see the downhill group coming, and also because it's easier for the downhill group to break their pace and resume it than it is for the uphill group. Of course, the uphill hikers may decide to take a rest stop and let the downhill hikers pass, but that is their prerogative.

When faster hikers catch up to slower hikers, it's only courteous to let the faster group pass. It shouldn't be necessary for the faster hikers to start yelling at the slow hikers when still dozens of feet behind, as I've heard some self-proclaimed "fast packers" do. The slow hikers can hear you as you come up behind; if they don't, a quiet, polite word is all that's needed.

Hikers should yield the right of way to trail runners so that the runner doesn't have to break his or her pace. Also, it's easier for slower hikers to find a place to step off the trail. Technically, mountain bikers are supposed to yield to hikers, but in practice it's better for the more maneuverable hikers to step off the trail and let the cyclists pass, rather than forcing the riders to go off trail.

Horses definitely have the right of way over hikers. When you encounter horses, step off the trail on the downhill side and stand quietly in an open spot. Talk to the riders as they approach, so the animals will have time to recognize you as humans. Avoid making sudden moves or noises.

Never roll rocks off cliffs. Not only does rock rolling make an obnoxious amount of noise, you never know who or what is below.

I have to put in a word for dirt road courtesy also. Many of Arizona's trailheads can be reached only by long dirt roads. It is standard dirt road practice to pull off and let overtaking vehicles pass, rather than forcing them to choke in your dust as you meander along. The passing vehicle and its dust cloud will soon be well ahead of the slower vehicle, and such courteous behavior removes the dangerous temptation to pass on dirt roads, which are seldom wide enough.

On back roads, leave all gates as you find them, open or closed. Failure to close a gate may allow cattle into closed or sensitive areas, or onto highways, possibly disrupting wildlife or causing a fatal vehicle accident. Failure to leave a gate open may deprive domestic or wild animals of access to water.

Leave No Trace

Leave No Trace is a set of seven principles for minimizing our impact on the land. The backpacking boom of the 1970s showed that even hikers and backpackers can severely degrade the backcountry. Leave No Trace is a joint partnership between the National Outdoor Leadership School and the U.S. Forest Service, Bureau of Land Management, National Park Service, and U.S. Fish and Wildlife Service.

1. **Plan ahead and prepare.** Advance planning and preparation for your trip is important. For example, having a comfortable sleeping pad means that you can sleep on sand, gravel, or rock, rather than seeking out fragile patches of grass or duff. Having a good tent or other shelter means that you won't feel the need to dig drainage ditches to keep water from getting into leaky seams.

2. **Travel and camp on durable surfaces.** Stay on trails and never cut switchbacks or take shortcuts. Leaving the trail always costs you more energy than staying on it and causes erosion and damage to the trail and surroundings. It's especially important to stay on the trail if it is wet or muddy to avoid making multiple trails and scarring fragile meadows. Wear waterproof boots—either leather or lightweight hiking boots constructed with waterproof/breathable fabric—when hiking after snowmelt or during the rainy seasons.

   When cross-country hiking, watch where and how you walk. In the

Opposite: Desert wash in flood

high deserts of the Colorado Plateau in northern Arizona, a black crust is often found on top of the sandy soil. This *cryptobiotic* soil is actually a microscopic community of plants which act together to protect the underlying soil from erosion. Once disturbed, it can take decades for the crust to re-form. Similar soils are found in many desert areas. *Desert pavement* is a layer of stones left on the surface by the dissolving and leaching away of the underlying soil, and by the action of wind removing loose particles. Desert pavement is easily destroyed by off-road vehicle tires, which greatly accelerates erosion. It can take hundreds of years to re-form. Stay on existing trails and roads, and when you have to walk cross-country, stay on sand, gravel, bedrock, or animal trails. On fragile surfaces, spread out, if possible, to avoid creating a trail.

Wilderness camping can cause serious impacts, but most can be eliminated by camping on hard surfaces or in previously used sites. Sand, gravel, and deep duff are certainly acceptable, but some of the best campsites are to be found on bare rock. The impact is zero and all you need is a good sleeping pad to make a rock campsite comfortable. You'll have to be careful of your tent floor, and anchoring your shelter requires different techniques from forest camping, but the rewards can be immense.

Use common sense in picking your campsite. For example, don't camp at a scenic viewpoint just off the trail, thus depriving all other hikers of the chance to enjoy it.

3. **Dispose of waste properly.** In other words, carry everything out. All trash and food scraps must be carried out. Animals will always dig up buried food, and human food is never good for them. Even if they do eat your leavings, they'll make a mess doing it. Such practices attract even more scavengers, which become nuisances or even dangers for the next campers. Wash yourself, and your dishes, well away from open water and seasonal water courses, and pour the waste water on the ground so that the soil's natural filtering and purifying action will clean it before it reaches the water table. Use the absolute minimum of biodegradable soap for washing. Most backcountry dirt comes off nicely with plain warm water. If you're worried that your cook gear isn't clean enough, rinse everything in boiling water.

Human waste is a serious problem in dry country. Dispose of human waste by selecting a spot at least 200 feet from springs, creeks, lakes, and other open water. Dig a small pit 6 to 8 inches deep, into but not below, the organic layers of the soil. Avoid sandy, barren soil whenever possible. Pack out your toilet paper. Don't burn it—many Arizona wildfires have been started this way. When finished, replace the soil and the ground cover as much as possible. Don't cover the site with a rock—that inhibits natural decay.

4. **Leave what you find.** This principle should be easy for a wilderness traveler to apply. After all, presumably you're there to enjoy the

Gray fox, Arizona Sonora Desert Museum

backcountry in a wild, untouched state. Common sense and courtesy means you would leave everything as you found it for the next visitor to enjoy. It's especially important to leave archaeological ruins and artifacts undisturbed. Moving, let alone removing, an artifact destroys its context, which is a major piece of the prehistoric puzzle. Federal and state laws prohibit disturbing archaeological and historical sites, and all natural features are protected in national parks and monuments.

5. **Minimize campfire impacts.** Campfires are prohibited in some areas, such as Grand Canyon National Park, because there's not much wood to burn, and because campfire scars last for hundreds of years. Campfire scars are still visible from the Anasazi people who lived in the Grand Canyon more than a thousand years ago! In Arizona, you should avoid building campfires except in an emergency. With good equipment and clothing, you'll have no trouble staying warm without one. If you must build a campfire, select a site where the ground is free of any flammable material. Then dig a pit into mineral soil, using the dirt to form a berm. Keep your fire small—it's easier to cook on small fires and they don't have as much tendency to throw sparks. Before leaving camp, even temporarily, put your fire out by stirring in dirt and mixing until the fire is cool to the touch. That means you should be able to put your hand into the fire—if you can't, the fire *is not out.* Fires can escape from under a layer of dirt, so never bury a fire before it is out. Before you leave your campsite, use the remaining dirt from the pit to cover the pit and restore the surface to as natural a condition as you can. Never use rocks to construct a fireplace. The fire scars on

the rocks last just about forever, and some rocks explode when heated in a campfire.

6. **Respect wildlife.** Never feed or disturb wildlife. Human food is bad for wild animals and causes them to become dependent on it and lose their natural fear of people. At best such animals may become pesky camp robbers; at worst they can become a safety hazard. In the case of larger animals, such as bears, the animal usually has to be killed. Observe wildlife from a distance to avoid disturbing mating or nesting activities. Use binoculars for viewing and a long telephoto lens for photographing wildlife. Arizona wilderness areas are the last refuge for many animals and plants whose habitat is being steadily destroyed by human development. Treat the backcountry as you would someone else's home.

In Arizona, it is illegal to camp within one quarter mile of a spring or other source of water so that wildlife can drink freely. Especially during the summer, many animals go to springs to drink only at night to avoid predators and daytime heat. There's also much less chance of contaminating springs and natural tanks if you camp well away. When backpacking, make sure you have enough water capacity so that you can fill up at a spring, then hike on for some time before camping.

7. **Be considerate of other visitors.** Other visitors to the wilderness are there for the same reasons as you—to enjoy a primitive experience away from the pressures of modern life. Avoid overcrowded places and times as much as possible. Camp well out of sight of trails, avoid the use of camp lanterns, and pick muted colors for your tent, pack, and outerwear. Don't make unnecessary noise while hiking or in camp.

Most national parks and monuments do not allow dogs on trails, and most state parks require dogs to be on a leash. National forests generally allow dogs to be off leash, but only if they are under voice control. When camped, keep your dog under control and quiet, to avoid disturbing other campers and wildlife. Remember that wildlife may be a danger to your dog—coyotes have been known to lure dogs away from their owners. Never allow your dog to chase wildlife. Such practices are the reason more and more areas are closed to dogs.

WATER

All backcountry water sources should be filtered or purified before drinking. Even the clearest mountain streams or desert springs may harbor microorganisms capable of making you seriously ill. Dangerous organisms include viruses, bacteria, and cysts. Bringing water to a boil kills all dangerous organisms at any altitude, but uses large amounts of stove fuel and leaves you with hot, flat-tasting water. You can both cool it and restore the dissolved air, improving the taste, by pouring it back and forth between two containers. Iodine water purification tablets are lightweight and fast, but do not kill *cryptosporidium*. Newer chemical treatments such as chlorine dioxide promise to be effective against all dangerous organisms. Pump filters remove cysts such as *giardia* as well as bacteria, but do not remove viruses, which are too small to be caught by the filter. A few pump filters are labeled as purifiers, and these use active chemical elements to kill viruses.

HAZARDS

Hiking in Arizona is a very safe activity, but you should be award of certain hazards.

Bears

Grizzly bears have been extinct in Arizona for many decades. Black bears, while found in the forested mountains of northern and eastern Arizona, are generally very shy of people. In recent years, there have been problems with bears raiding vehicle campgrounds and summer home communities in the mountains. If you see bear tracks or signs near your camp, take precautions with your food. Store it well away from your camp, hung from a tree at least 12 feet in the air and 10 feet from the trunk, or preferably in a bear-proof food container. Don't cook or store food in or near your tent. Avoid scented deodorant or lotions. If you do spot a bear, give it a wide berth, especially if it has cubs.

Another useful technique is what Ray Jardine calls "stealth camping," which is similar to the desert technique of dry camping. If you pick up water an hour or two before you plan to camp, you could also stop to make dinner at the same time (remember not to clean your dishes in or near a water source). Then when you camp, you can pick an undisturbed, waterless, and scenic site where bears and camp robbers haven't learned to think of backpackers as walking supermarkets.

Camp Robbers

Mice, skunks, and ringtail cats are nocturnal and can keep you up all night as they cleverly try to get into your food supply. In desert areas where there are no trees, you can hang your food from a walking stick tripod, or from a stick projecting from the top of a boulder, but the only sure solution is a rodent-proof container, such as a bear canister.

Mountain Lions

Mountain lions (also known as cougars) are fairly common in the mountainous portions of Arizona, but with rare exceptions are not dangerous to humans. An exception seems to be people who run or mountain bike, which apparently rouses the cat's predator instinct. As far as I know, no Arizona hiker or backpacker has ever been attacked, but people have reported "threatening" encounters. Most of these encounters seem to involve dogs. Experts advise that mountain lions are normally curious but not aggressive toward humans. You should stand your ground, make yourself as large as possible by opening your jacket or waving your arms, and maintain eye contact with the cat so that you appear to be another predator.

Ocelot, a denizen of the southeast mountains and Mexico, Arizona Sonora Desert Museum

Don't approach the cat and don't run—running may mark you as prey in the cat's eyes. Back away slowly if you can but don't turn your back on the animal. If the mountain lion becomes aggressive, fight back aggressively. Shout, throw things, and hit the cat hard with your hiking stick, if you have one.

Standard advice for avoiding mountain lion problems include never hiking alone, not running or jogging, keeping children close, keeping dogs on leash and under control, being alert to your surroundings, and using a walking stick.

Snakes and Other Reptiles

North American deserts are home to many species of snakes, some poisonous, most not. The two most common rattlesnakes are the Western Diamondback and the Mohave. Western Diamondbacks are the largest desert rattlesnakes and may reach seven feet in length. They are found throughout the southwestern deserts, tending to favor lower country. The Mohave rattlesnake is smaller and ranges from low desert to rocky mountain ridges.

Rattlesnakes strike fear into the hearts of many novice hikers, but hikers and outdoor recreationists are rarely bitten—most rattlesnake victims are bitten when working around places such as woodpiles, where rattle-snakes tend to hide, or when attempting to handle or catch a snake. Rattle-snakes are probably more frightened of you than you are of them. You'll never see most of the snakes that you pass because they sense you first and move quietly away. Only if surprised or cornered will a rattlesnake rattle. When you hear this unmistakable sound, stop where you are and locate the snake before moving away.

As you hike, watch the ground about ten to twenty feet in front of you. If you want to look at the scenery, stop first. Keep an especially sharp eye on hidden spots, such as deep shade under rocks and bushes. Rattlesnakes can strike about one half their body length, and most rattlesnakes are four feet long or less. So don't walk or place a hand or foot within several feet of blind spots. Go around or step up on large rocks or logs and see what's on the far side before stepping down.

During the summer, when daytime temperatures are too hot for them, rattlesnakes become nocturnal. Always use a flashlight or headlamp when walking around camp or along a trail at night in warm weather. Other poisonous desert creatures such as scorpions are nocturnal during hot weather as well, so you might want to use a net tent or sleep off the ground during the summer.

Rattlesnake bites are a serious medical emergency but generally not life-threatening. The victim should be kept calm and transported to a hospital as soon as possible. The only effective treatment is rattlesnake antivenin, which must be administered under a doctor's care because of possible severe side effects. All of the field treatments that have been proposed over the years, including antivenin, tourniquets, cutting and sucking, and application of cold packs, have been shown to cause more harm than good.

Arizona coral snakes are found in the Sonoran Desert, ranging into southern Arizona. Their venom is more dangerous than that of rattle-snakes, but the snake is so small that it could probably only bite a finger. You'll be lucky if you ever see one. Sonoran coral snakes are marked with bright yellow or cream, red, and black bands, and the colored bands completely encircle the snake. There are several nonpoisonous snakes that have similar colors but the bands do not encircle the snake's body.

The only other poisonous reptile in the North American deserts is the Gila monster, found primarily in the saguaro forests of the Sonoran Desert. This large black, orange, pink, and yellow lizard grows to about 18 inches, including its thick tail. Gila monsters appear to be torpid and slow moving, but react very fast when disturbed. They can inflict a very painful bite and are hard to dislodge. Gila monster bites are a medical emergency. Gila monsters are rare and are protected by Arizona state law.

Scorpions

Scorpions have been responsible for more deaths in North America than any reptile. Most scorpion stings are no worse than that of a yellow jacket,

but one species can be lethal. *Centruroides sculpturatus* is found in southern California, Arizona, Southwest New Mexico, Mexico, and Baja California. Smaller than many of the nonlethal scorpions, it is greenish yellow to straw-colored, averages about two inches in length, and prefers to cling upside down to the underside of rocks and loose bark. Most of the nonlethal scorpions, while they do hide under rocks and logs, stay upright on the ground. Nonlethal scorpions produce a painful sting with swelling and discoloration at the site. A sting from *C. sculpturatus* causes immediate severe pain but no swelling or discoloration at the site. Any sting from *C. sculpturatus* is a medical emergency. Luckily, antivenin is available.

A few simple practices can greatly reduce the danger from scorpions. The primary one is the age-old desert rule of never putting your hands or feet in places you can't see. When picking up rocks, sticks, bark, or logs, kick them over with your shod foot before picking them up. Shake out any footwear, socks, clothing, and other gear that's been on the ground or where scorpions could reach it. Keep your sleeping bag stuffed until you intend to use it, or keep it in a closed tent.

Bees

Africanized bees have attacked humans and killed several dogs since they reached Arizona a few years ago. Avoid all bees, and especially avoid hives (wild or domestic) and swarms. If attacked, seek shelter in a vehicle or building. In the backcountry, run and try to get into heavy brush. Africanized bees won't pursue more than half a mile, and brush confuses all bees. Protect your eyes and don't swat at the bees.

Spiders

The female black widow (the male is not venomous) is about one inch long and can be recognized by the hourglass-shaped red mark on the underside of its abdomen. Although the bite from a black widow is not very painful, it can be life-threatening to small children, the elderly, and those with preexisting health problems. Victims should be transported to medical care as soon as possible, where antivenin can be administered. Black widow spiders are more likely to be found around man-made structures than in the open desert.

Brown recluse spiders have a small, violin-shaped mark on their upper body. The bite is not life-threatening, but medical care should be sought. As with the black widow, brown recluse spiders are found mostly around human structures.

Tarantulas are fierce-looking, large, hairy spiders that grow to six or seven inches, but they rarely bite humans unless aggravated. Even then, their venom is no worse than a bee or wasp sting. Tarantulas are most commonly seen crossing desert roads on summer nights.

Opposite: Lenticular, or wave, clouds topping the peaks are often the first sign of an approaching storm

Centipedes

Centipedes grow as long as eight inches in the American deserts. They look fearsome and do have a pair of poison claws, but their venom is only dangerous to the insects that are their prey. Their many pairs of legs are sharp-tipped and might scratch you as they run across bare skin—and it would certainly be startling. Centipedes are primarily active at night during the summer.

Cactus

Teddy bear cholla is commonly known as jumping cholla. Fuzzy-looking light yellow branches and stems make up the bulk of the plant, which grows about three or four feet high. The "fuzz" is actually thousands of slender, razor-sharp spines, each of which is covered with microscopic barbs. These barbed spines grab and don't let go. The real hazard to hikers (and air-filled sleeping pads) is not the standing plants, which are easily avoided, but the burrs that litter the ground around the cactus. It's easy to pick up a cholla burr on your foot and then transfer it to some other part of your anatomy—usually painfully. Dogs are especially good at this. Burrs that are only lightly attached are easy to remove by inserting a comb under the burr and then carefully flicking it away. A burr that is more seriously embedded may require pliers to remove the spines.

Other species of cholla, such as chain fruit and Christmas tree cholla, like to litter the ground with small clusters of nearly invisible spines. These specialize in puncturing air mattresses and self-inflating pads. Other cactus to watch out for include several species of pincushions. These plants grow in small clusters, and blend into the desert ground. Their tiny spines are just as efficient as cholla at puncturing air mattresses.

Not all spine-toting desert plants are members of the cactus family. Agave, a member of the lily family, has a series of daggerlike leaves growing outward from the base. Each thick, stiff leaf has a series of large, curved barbs growing along the edges and is tipped with a very sharp spine. You'll want to be especially careful when edging past agaves on steep or loose terrain.

Poison Ivy

You will encounter poison ivy in moist canyon bottoms and drainages at intermediate elevations in Arizona. The leaves and stems of the low-growing plant contain an organic acid that causes a skin reaction in many people. Prevention is the best cure—learn to recognize the plant by its glossy leaves, which grow in groups of three, and by recognizing the places where you can expect to see it. Poison ivy can be expected when there's flowing water, but it also grows without nearby surface water. Remember that the acid in the sap can adhere to walking sticks, boots, clothing, and dogs, so be careful handling any of these items if you suspect a previous encounter with poison ivy. Soap and water removes the acid from human skin, clothing, and dogs. Even plain water is effective.

Old Mines

Arizona has always attracted prospectors and miners. Some mountain ranges are literally honeycombed with mine shafts and tunnels, and nearly all show some signs of past mining activity. Mine shafts and tunnels are unstable and extremely dangerous. Besides the obvious dangers of cave-ins and unexpected vertical shafts, mines also tend to collect poisonous or radioactive gases. Abandoned mine shafts are supposed to be sealed or barricaded, but in practice many are not. Vertical shafts and prospect holes are especially dangerous in brushy country and at night.

WEATHER HAZARDS

Although Arizona weather is usually stable, it also has extremes, which can be dangerous to unprepared hikers.

Floods

Steady, winter rains and sudden summer thunderstorms can produce flooding. Winter rains tend to be light but persistent. If the rainfall continues for several days, the ground becomes saturated and runoff may increase rapidly. Rain falling on the highest mountains also melts what snow may have accumulated. Creek- and riverbeds that have been dry for years may carry large volumes of water, sometimes for weeks on end.

Violent summer thunderstorms can cause flash floods miles from the storm. Heavy rain falling on bare soil or rock runs off much faster than it can be absorbed, and it quickly collects in tributary drainages. As the drainages combine, the flood gathers force and volume, and often takes the form of a wall of water moving down a dry wash. Because of the carrying capacity of fast-moving water, flash floods usually contain a large amount of soil, sand, gravel, and even boulders. Rapid erosion of the streambed takes place and paved roads and stream crossings can be destroyed in minutes. Never try to cross a flooding wash on foot or in a vehicle. The roadbed may be gone and the water is usually deeper than you expect. Just one foot of fast-moving water is enough to wash away a vehicle.

Never park a vehicle or camp in a dry wash. Every year vehicles are swept away and people lose their lives in desert washes.

Heat-Related Illnesses

Summer is the serious season in Arizona. Hikers out in the desert and lower elevations during the hottest time of the year must be prepared and experienced. Even during the fall, winter, and spring, the air is often dry and warm and heat injury is a possibility.

Sweating is the body's mechanism for keeping cool under heat stress. In an arid environment, skin moisture evaporates rapidly and a hot weather hiker can lose significant amounts of moisture insensibly, without sweating. That's why you must be aware of your environment and make sure you consume plenty of water, even if you're not sweating. Mild dehydration impairs body function; severe dehydration results in death. Water, of course, is the primary treatment for dehydration, and if the dehydration isn't too serious, recovery is rapid. Serious cases must be moved to a cool environment, if possible, and transported to medical care as soon as possible.

Other heat hazards are heat exhaustion and sunstroke. Heat exhaustion occurs when the body moves excessive amounts of blood from the core to the extremities in an attempt to keep the core at normal temperature. Heat exhaustion victims are weak, pale, and sweat profusely. Treatment consists of moving the victim to a cool place, providing electrolyte replacement drinks, and providing ventilation to aid the sweating process.

Sunstroke (also known as heatstroke) occurs when the brain loses control of the body's heat regulating system. Sunstroke is a medical emergency and can result in death. Sunstroke comes on suddenly and the primary symptom is hot, dry skin. The victim must be promptly treated by moving them to a cool location, removing as much clothing as possible, making certain the airway is open, reducing body temperature by wrapping the victim with wet cloths or dousing with water, and transporting to medical care as soon as possible.

Hypothermia

Hypothermia is a medical emergency caused by the loss of the body's ability to keep warm. Even in the low-elevation deserts, nights are usually cool

Javelina, or peccary, which travel in herds throughout Arizona, Arizona Sonora Desert Museum

because the dry, clear atmosphere allows the earth to rapidly radiate heat to the dark sky. In addition, the open desert often lacks natural shelter from wind-driven rain. Hypothermia is often thought of as something that only happens in subzero conditions in snow and ice, but actually the most dangerous conditions are the subtle ones—cool temperatures, light wind, and rain or mist.

The body produces heat by metabolizing food and water, so the key to preventing hypothermia is to stay hydrated, eat high-energy foods, and wear the right amount of protective clothing. It's especially important to choose clothing made of fibers that shed water and retain their insulating ability when wet.

The early stages of hypothermia can be treated by wrapping the victim in insulating clothing or sleeping bags and providing warm drinks and food. Once the body's temperature regulating system breaks down, hypothermia becomes a medical emergency. External heat must be provided, preferably in the form of other people, or in the form of warm water bottles, and the victim must be transported to medical care immediately.

Dust Storms

Dust storms are fairly common in the southwest deserts of Arizona and occur when strong high winds (generally 20 mph or higher) blow across large areas of loose soil and dust. These high winds can be caused either by winter and spring cold fronts or the outflow from summer thunderstorms. Dust storms striking a highway or freeway are a frequent cause of multiple car accidents, when drivers abruptly slow down and are rear-ended by oncoming vehicles. The safest action is to get completely off the road and stop. Don't park on the shoulder, and don't leave lights or flashers on. Another vehicle may see your lights and attempt to follow you, not realizing you've stopped.

Sand Storms

Similar to dust storms, sand storms occur with wind of 30 mph or greater. Sand storms can restrict visibility on freeways and highways. The highly abrasive sand can cause severe damage to vehicles by sandblasting paint and pitting windshields. Get to shelter as soon as you can.

Wildfires

Arizona is a dry state, notwithstanding the fact that large areas are forested. In recent years, a prolonged drought, coupled with forests that have grown too thick from poor management practices, have combined to create severe fire seasons. Some of the hikes in this book pass through burned areas, and more of the forested hikes will burn in the future. In the long term, these fires are good for the forest, as dense stands of trees are thinned or removed. In the short term, fires can create problems for hikers in the form of deadfall across trails and erosion. Dead standing trees are a hazard—never camp under one. While trails through burned areas are generally reopened by the next season, it's always a good idea to check with the land management agency listed with the hike for current conditions.

GEAR

Although you don't need much equipment for a casual day hike, on longer treks your gear can make or break the trip. And even on short hikes a few good items of gear can make the hike a lot more fun, as well as safer. On all Arizona hikes, you should carry The Mountaineers' Ten Essentials at a minimum.

1. **Navigation (map and compass).** Always carry a topographic map of the area you'll be in because without one, you're at the mercy of trail signs, which are sometimes missing or erroneous. In Arizona's open terrain, you won't need a compass often, but when you do, you'll need it badly. A Global Positioning System (GPS) receiver can be a great help, but satellite-based navigation is not a substitute for map and compass skills.
2. **Sun protection (sunglasses and sunscreen).** An effective sun hat is important in the intense Arizona sun, even at higher elevations where the air is cool. During spring, summer, and fall use a sunscreen with an SPF of at least 15, preferably higher. Good sunglasses are a must because the Arizona sun can produce glare comparable to that of high-altitude snowfields, especially in areas of light-colored stone or sand.
3. **Insulation (extra clothing).** Carry an insulating layer, such as a synthetic fleece or down vest or jacket, in case the weather changes or you're caught out overnight. Even hot desert days turn into surprisingly cool nights. Also bring a rain jacket, which doubles as a wind shell.
4. **Illumination (headlamp or flashlight).** Bring along a headlamp or flashlight, even if you don't plan to make a full day of it. It's easy to miscalculate the time that a hike or ride will take, and even a minor problem can extend your trek into the dark.
5. **First-aid supplies.** A first-aid kit should always be in your pack. There are commercial first-aid kits for hikers, or you can make up your own.
6. **Fire (firestarter and matches or lighter).** A disposable lighter or matches in a waterproof, metal match container allow you to start a fire in an emergency. Having a fire on a cold and windy night can save your life if you don't have a sleeping bag and shelter.
7. **Repair kit and tools (including knife).** Carry repair items that you may need to fix a critical item of gear. A sturdy pocketknife can be used to make tinder for an emergency campfire and has many other uses.
8. **Nutrition (extra food).** Carry extra food, beyond what you plan to eat, so that you can keep your energy up if your trip is longer than you expect.
9. **Hydration (extra water).** In the dry Arizona climate, the most important item in your pack is water. Each person may need anywhere from a quart to a gallon per day, depending on the temperature. Use several smaller containers so that if one leaks, you won't lose your entire supply.

Desert flowers

10. **Emergency shelter.** An aluminized emergency space blanket is a good choice because it keeps wind and rain off while reflecting back your body's heat. In hot weather, a space blanket can be used to create shade.

Several other items are worth considering. A watch lets you accurately gauge your progress toward important goals, such as the turnaround point, the next spring, or the planned campsite. Toilet paper, insect repellent, spare car keys, eyeglasses or contact lenses, medications, and personal hygiene items are also useful.

USING THIS BOOK

Each hike has a summary section, description, map, and elevation profile.

Round trip: This is the total distance of the hike in miles, including any out-and-back (cherry stem) sections, but not including optional side hikes. The length of optional side hikes is mentioned in the description. Distances were measured using topo mapping software for consistency, and they don't always agree with trail signs and official mileages.

Loop direction: Some loops can be hiked in either direction, while others are more enjoyable if hiked counterclockwise or clockwise.

Hiking time: This is the total time required for an average hiker to hike the loop. I assume reasonable fitness on the part of the reader but try to err on the conservative side, so some hikers will be able to complete the hike in less time. Others, especially those distracted by extra-hiking activities, such as photography or bird watching, will need more time.

Starting elevation: This is the elevation of the trailhead in feet.

High point: The highest point in the hike. Some hikes start at their highest point and descend into a canyon, in which case I'll give the lowest point instead or in addition to the high point.

Elevation gain: A rough total of the elevation gain while hiking the loop. This doesn't include minor ups and downs, so total elevation gain is always more than this number. Since the hike is a loop, you'll have just as much elevation loss as gain. Not all hikes start with a climb and end with a descent. Canyon hikes typically involve a descent at the beginning and a climb at the end.

Seasonal water availability: Since water sources are so critical in Arizona, especially on extended backpack trips, I list all known water sources along the hike such as springs, creeks, water pockets, and natural tanks. **Except where noted, all water sources should be considered seasonal, meaning that they may dry up during extended dry periods.** As of this writing, the ongoing drought in the Southwest has dried up many springs once considered permanent. **More than ever, this means you should never depend on a single source of water.** All backcountry water sources should be filtered or purified before use.

Best hiking time: You can hike year-round in Arizona, but some seasons are better than others for any given hike.

Maps: All of Arizona is covered by USGS 7.5-minute series topographic maps. Some areas have recreation maps published by the land management agency or private companies and these are often more up-to-date than the USGS maps.

Contact: The agency and unit that manages the area of the hike. Refer to the Appendix for phone numbers and Web addresses.

Driving directions: The approach roads from the nearest town on a highway. Many of Arizona's trailheads are located on dirt roads. Most of these are passable to an ordinary car if it is driven with care. A few approach roads require high-clearance and/or four-wheel-drive vehicles.

For a few locations where critical landmarks, springs, or routes are difficult to find, I supplement the usual landmark-based directions with GPS coordinates. These are always given in the UTM coordinate system and based on the WGS84/NAD83 datum. Because it is easy to make a mistake keying in GPS coordinates, always double-check all coordinates. The UTM coordinates in this book were generated from National Geographic's Topo! mapping software.

A NOTE ABOUT SAFETY

Safety is an important concern in all outdoor activities. No book can alert you to every hazard or anticipate the limitations of every reader. The descriptions of techniques and procedures in this book are intended to provide general information. Nothing substitutes for formal instruction, routine practice, and plenty of experience. When you follow any of the procedures here, you assume responsibility for your own safety. Use this book as a general guide to further information. Under normal conditions, excursions into the backcountry require attention to traffic, road and trail conditions, weather, terrain, the capabilities of your party, and other factors. Keeping informed on current conditions and exercising common sense are the keys to a safe, enjoyable outing.

—*The Mountaineers Books*

HIKE SUMMARY TABLE

Hike Number and Name	Distance (miles)	Hiking Time (hours or days)	Elevation Gain (feet)	Season	Highlight
1 Kanab Canyon Loop	52.8	7 days	10,000	March through mid-May and mid-September through November	Kanab Canyon, Deer Creek Falls, Thunder River
2 Powell Plateau Loop	54.7	9 days	10,000	Mid-September through November	Very remote portion of Grand Canyon
3 Boucher-Hermit Loop	19.1	3 to 5 days	7100	October-November, March-April	Boucher Creek, Hermit Canyon and Hermit Rapid
4 Horseshoe Mesa Loop	11.3	9-10 hours	6100	October-April	Historic mine, Colorado River side trips
5 Dogtown Reservoir Trail	2.3	1 hour	0	April-November	Very easy trail around a lake
6 Sycamore Rim Trail	10.9	4 hours	1130	May-November	Scenic trail on rim of Sycamore Canyon
7 Pumpkin Loop	10.4	7 hours	3380	May-October	Loop over 10,418-foot peak
8 Abineau-Bear Jaw Loop	7.1	4-5 hours	1980	June-October	Scenic views of Arizona's highest peak
9 Inner Basin Loop	4.3	2-3 hours	920	June-October	Loop through a glacial valley
10 Kachina Loop	16.9	10-11 hours or 2 days	4350	July-October	Alpine forests and meadows on Arizona's highest mountain
11 Schultz Peak	6.2	4 hours	2120	May-October	Historic trail and seldom-visited peak
12 Little Bear-Heart Loop	6.3	4 -5 hours	1820	April-October	Alpine forests and Painted Desert views
13 Sunset-Brookbank Loop	5.5	4 hours	1100	April-November	Alpine meadows and seasonal lake
14 Fatmans Loop	2.2	1.5 hours	500	March-November	Complex volcanic rock formations
15 Kelsey-Dorsey Loop	6.5	4 hours	1370	April-November	Views of Sycamore Canyon Wilderness

Hike Number and Name	Distance (miles)	Hiking Time (hours or days)	Elevation Gain (feet)	Season	Highlight
16 Winter Cabin Loop	14.5	9-10 hours or 2 days	3730	April-November	Upper Sycamore Canyon
17 Taylor Cabin Loop	19	11 hours or 2 days	4450	April-November	Red rock formations, historic cabin, scenic ridge
18 Sycamore Canyon Loop	22.3	12 hours or 2 days	3540	April-May, October through mid-December	Permanent stream in lower Sycamore Canyon
19 Bear Sign-Secret Canyon Loop	5.1	3-4 hours	1170	April-November	Rare stands of Arizona cypress, red rock canyons
20 Eagles Nest-Apache Fire Loop	2.4	1 hour	370	All year	Very easy loop along Oak Creek
21 Courthouse Butte	3.9	2 hours	400	All year	Towering rock formations and cliffs
22 Hot Loop	16.9	10 hours	2610	April-November	Views of Mogollon Rim and red rock country
23 Little Granite Mountain Loop	6.1	4 hours	1220	April-November	Granite rock formations
24 Mingus Rim Loop	3.8	3 hours	1470	April-November	Views of Verde and Mogollon Rims
25 Yaeger Canyon Loop	5.6	4 hours	1560	April-November	Loop over forested Mingus Mountain
26 Pine Mountain Loop	13.4	8-9 hours	3270	April-November	Historic ranch site, views of remote Verde River
27 West Clear Creek Loop	12.8	8 hours	3470	April-November	West Clear Creek canyon, permanent stream
28 Cabin Loop	21.6	12 hours or 2 days	2940	May-November	Historic cabins and trails
29 Horton Creek Loop	7.1	4-5 hours	1600	April-November	Permanent stream, ponderosa pine glades
30 Rim Lakes Vista Loop	4.2	2 hours	0	May-November	Easy trail along Mogollon Rim, historic military trail
31 Blue Ridge Mountain Loop	7.8	4-5 hours	780	May-November	Blue Ridge Mountain, permanent stream along Billy Creek

HIKE SUMMARY TABLE (CONTINUED)

Hike Number and Name	Distance (miles)	Hiking Time (hours or days)	Elevation Gain (feet)	Season	Highlight
32 Mount Baldy	15.6	10 hours or 2 days	3180	June–October	Alpine forests and meadows, Arizona's second highest mountain
33 KP Creek	21.4	13–14 hours or 2 days	4750	June–October	Alpine meadows, waterfall, little-visited area
34 Bear Mountain	23.4	15 hours or 2 days	5360	May–November	Remote Blue Range and eastern Mogollon Rim country
35 Strayhorse-Squaw Creek Loop	36.6	3 days	6840	April–November	Seldom-visited area, Blue River
36 Wet Bottom Loop	43	5 -7 days	9950	March–May, October–November	Wild and Scenic Verde River
37 Midnight Mesa Loop	40.8	6–7 days	10,080	March–May, October–November	Sonoran Desert, pine-forested mountains, little-visited country
38 Deadman Creek Loop	43.1	6–7 days	10,040	March–May, October–November	Historic ranching cabins, portion of Arizona Trail
39 Barnhardt-Rock Creek Loop	17.3	11–12 hours or 2 days	4970	April–November	Best trail in Mazatzal Mountains, seasonal waterfalls
40 Y Bar-Barnhardt Loop	13.8	9–10 hours or 2 days	4110	April–November	Loop around highest peak in range
41 Gold Ridge Loop	15.8	9–10 hours or 2 days	3810	April–November	Permanent creek, scenic ridge, easy trailhead
42 Go John Trail	4.3	2–3 hours	780	October–April	Sonoran Desert views
43 Pass Mountain Trail	6.3	3–4 hours	1030	October–April	Views of Four Peaks and Goldfield Mountains
44 Garden Valley	8.6	5 hours	1190	October–April	Accessible trailhead, Sonoran cactus desert
45 Lower La Barge Box	12	8 hours or 2 days	3600	October–April	Narrow canyon

Hike Number and Name	Distance (miles)	Hiking Time (hours or days)	Elevation Gain (feet)	Season	Highlight
46 Superstition Crest	19	12-14 hours or 2 days	6510	October-April	Hike along western skyline of Superstition Mountains
47 Barks Canyon	5	4 hours	1610	October-April	Easy hike through dramatic scenery
48 Dutchmans Trail	15.5	9-10 hours or 2 days	2860	October-April	Scenic Sonoran Desert loop on excellent trail
49 Fire Line Loop	15.1	10 hours or 2 days	3480	September-November, April-May	Remote eastern Superstition canyon, pioneer ranch site
50 Angel Basin Loop	18	11 hours or 2 days	3060	September-November, April-May	Remote central Superstition canyons
51 West Pinto Creek	17.4	11 hours or 2 days	4070	September-November, April-May	Seldom-visited eastern Superstition trails
52 Webb Peak	3.9	2-3 hours	990	June-October	"Sky Island" 10,000-foot peak, waterfall
53 Deer Creek Loop	25.1	3 days	7030	September-November, April-May	Little-used trails, historic ranch site
54 Coyote Pass Loop	5.3	3 hours	460	October-April	Easy Sonoran Desert loop in Saguaro National Park
55 Wasson Peak Loop	7	5 hours	2340	October-April	Less-used route to highest peak in Tucson Mountains
56 Brown Mountain Loop	3.6	2 hours	820	October-April	Scenic ridge, saguaro cactus "forest"
57 Sabino Basin Loop	11.7	8-9 hours	4410	April-November	Granite canyons with seasonal waterfalls
58 Three Tanks Loop	7.7	6 hours	1320	October-April	Seasonal waterfall, Rincon Mountain foothills
59 Mica Peak Loop	19.9	2-3 days	5990	April-November	Desert to alpine forest, highest peak in Saguaro National Park
60 Senita Basin Loop	2.6	1 hour	90	October-April	Very easy loop through stands of rare Senita cactus

HIKE SUMMARY TABLE (CONTINUED)

Hike Number and Name	Distance (miles)	Hiking Time (hours or days)	Elevation Gain (feet)	Season	Highlight
61 Grass Canyon Loop	6.3	4-5 hours	1230	October-April	Rugged desert canyons
62 Bull Pasture	3.1	2 hours	1070	October-April	Easy hike with views of rugged Ajo Mountain crest
63 Mount Wrightson	10.8	8-9 hours	4720	April-November	Loop over the highest peak in the Santa Rita Mountains
64 Bog Springs Loop	4.5	3 hours	1830	April-November	Two springs, views of Madera Canyon and rugged Santa Rita crest
65 Sonoita Creek Loop	1.7	2 hours	0	All year	Riparian corridor through nature preserve
66 Ramsey Canyon Loop	8.4	6 hours	3450	May-November	World-famous birding area
67 Heart of Rocks	7.3	5 hours	2200	September-November, March-May	Stone hoodoos, volcanic canyons
68 Echo Canyon	2.6	2 hours	800	September-November, March-May	Easy hike through weird rock formations
69 Round Park	6.8	4 hours	2140	May-November	Easy hike along Chiricahua Crest
70 Mormon Canyon Loop	6.2	4-5 hours	2660	May-November	Scenic ridge, highest peak in range
71 Chiricahua Crest Loop	11.5	8 hours	4240	May-November	Hike along Chiricahua Crest with the best views
72 Monte Vista Peak	13.4	9 hours	3780	May-November	Alternate route to most scenic Chiricahua summit
73 Raspberry Ridge	14.7	10 hours	4610	May-November	Beautiful Chiricahua ridges and canyons
74 Snowshed Loop	8.8	6 hours	3050	May-November	Ridge hike in the spectacular Portal Basin
75 Greenhouse Loop	13	8 hours	4640	May-November	Central Chiricahua Crest and deep, forested canyon

HIKES BY INTEREST

Hike Number and Name	Easy	Moderate	Difficult	Very Difficult	Day Hike	Overnight	Multiday	Peak Bagging	Desert	Forest	Family Friendly	Rough Access Road
1 Kanab Canyon Loop				•			•		•			
2 Powell Plateau Loop				•			•		•			•
3 Boucher-Hermit Loop			•				•		•			
4 Horseshoe Mesa Loop			•		•	•			•			
5 Dogtown Reservoir Trail	•				•					•	•	
6 Sycamore Rim Trail		•			•					•		
7 Pumpkin Loop		•			•			•		•		
8 Abineau-Bear Jaw Loop		•			•					•		
9 Inner Basin Loop	•				•					•	•	
10 Kachina Loop			•		•	•		•		•		
11 Schultz Peak		•			•			•		•		
12 Little Bear-Heart Loop		•			•					•		
13 Sunset-Brookbank Loop		•			•					•		
14 Fatmans Loop	•				•					•	•	
15 Kelsey-Dorsey Loop		•			•					•		•
16 Winter Cabin Loop		•			•	•			•	•		•
17 Taylor Cabin Loop		•				•			•	•		•
18 Sycamore Canyon Loop			•			•				•		
19 Bear Sign-Secret Canyon Loop	•				•					•		
20 Eagles Nest-Apache Fire Loop	•				•					•	•	
21 Courthouse Butte	•				•					•		
22 Hot Loop		•			•					•	•	
23 Little Granite Mountain Loop		•			•			•	•	•		
24 Mingus Rim Loop		•			•					•		
25 Yaeger Canyon Loop		•			•					•		
26 Pine Mountain Loop		•			•			•		•		•
27 West Clear Creek Loop		•			•				•			
28 Cabin Loop		•			•	•				•		
29 Horton Creek Loop		•			•					•		
30 Rim Lakes Vista Loop	•				•					•	•	
31 Blue Ridge Mountain Loop		•			•			•		•		
32 Mount Baldy		•			•	•	•	•		•		
33 KP Creek			•			•	•			•		
34 Bear Mountain			•			•	•			•		
35 Strayhorse-Squaw Creek Loop				•			•		•	•		
36 Wet Bottom Loop			•				•	•	•	•		•
37 Midnight Mesa Loop		•					•	•	•	•		•

37

Hike Number and Name	Easy	Moderate	Difficult	Very Difficult	Day Hike	Overnight	Multiday	Peak Bagging	Desert	Forest	Family Friendly	Rough Access Road
38 Deadman Creek Loop			•				•	•	•	•		•
39 Barnhardt-Rock Creek Loop		•			•	•			•	•		
40 Y Bar-Barnhardt Loop		•			•	•			•	•		
41 Gold Ridge Loop		•			•	•			•	•		
42 Go John Trail	•				•				•		•	
43 Pass Mountain Trail		•			•				•			
44 Garden Valley		•			•				•			
45 Lower La Barge Box			•		•	•			•			
46 Superstition Crest			•		•	•			•			
47 Barks Canyon	•				•				•		•	
48 Dutchmans Trail		•			•	•	•		•			
49 Fire Line Loop			•		•	•			•	•		•
50 Angel Basin Loop			•		•	•			•	•		•
51 West Pinto Creek			•		•	•			•	•		•
52 Webb Peak	•				•			•	•	•		•
53 Deer Creek Loop		•			•		•		•	•		•
54 Coyote Pass Loop	•				•				•		•	
55 Wasson Peak		•			•			•	•			
56 Brown Mountain Loop	•				•				•			
57 Sabino Basin Loop			•		•	•			•			
58 Three Tanks Loop		•			•				•			
59 Mica Peak Loop		•				•	•	•	•			
60 Senita Basin Loop	•				•				•		•	
61 Grass Canyon Loop		•			•				•			
62 Bull Pasture	•				•				•			
63 Mount Wrightson			•		•	•		•		•		
64 Bog Springs Loop		•			•					•		
65 Sonoita Creek Loop	•				•					•	•	
66 Ramsey Canyon Loop			•		•					•		
67 Heart of Rocks		•			•					•		
68 Echo Canyon	•				•					•	•	
69 Round Park	•				•					•		
70 Mormon Canyon Loop		•			•					•		
71 Chiricahua Crest Loop			•		•	•				•		
72 Monte Vista Peak			•		•	•		•		•		
73 Raspberry Ridge			•		•					•		
74 Snowshed Loop			•		•					•		
75 Greenhouse Loop			•		•	•				•		

GRAND CANYON

1 KANAB CANYON LOOP

Round trip ■	52.8 miles
Loop direction ■	Counterclockwise
Hiking time ■	7 days, or longer for exploration
Starting elevation ■	6300 feet
Lowest point ■	1910 feet
Elevation gain ■	10,000 feet
Seasonal water availability ■	Indian Hollow, Mountain Sheep Spring, and Jumpup Canyon. Kanab Creek, the Colorado River, and Deer Creek are permanent sources.
Best hiking time ■	March through mid-May and mid-September through November
Maps ■	Sowats Spring, Jumpup Point, Kanab Point, Fishtail, Tapeats Amphitheater USGS
Contact ■	Grand Canyon National Park. Permits required.

Driving directions: Starting from Jacob Lake on US 89A, drive 0.4 mile south on Arizona 67 and then turn right on Forest Road 461. Follow this dirt road 5.1 miles and then turn right on Forest Road 462. Continue 3.3 miles and then turn left on Big Springs Road (Forest Road 22). (During the spring, when the route from Jacob Lake may still be snowed in, you can reach the north end of Forest Road 22 from Arizona 89A on the east side of Fredonia.) Go south on Forest Road 22 for 11.9 miles, then turn right on Forest Road 425. Continue 8.3 miles and turn right on Forest Road 232. Follow this unmaintained road to its end at the Indian Hollow Campground and Trailhead.

This classic Grand Canyon loop takes you through spectacular Jumpup and Kanab Canyons, along the Colorado River, past the beauty of Deer Creek Falls and Thunder River, and along a gorgeous section of the Esplanade. Hiking this loop counterclockwise gets you through Jumpup and Kanab Canyons at the start of the hike, when your weather forecast is still reasonably current. Neither canyon is a place to be during a flood, although escape from rising water is possible most of the time. Going counterclockwise also lets

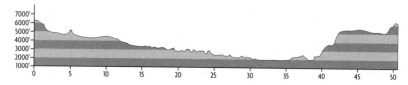

you finish the hike, which is mostly cross-country, on the Deer Creek and Thunder River Trails.

Much of the hiking is strenuous cross-country, and this hike should be attempted only by those with previous experience hiking on Grand Canyon trails. The Horseshoe Mesa and Boucher-Hermit Loops are good preparation for this hike. At least one member of the group should have Grand Canyon cross-country hiking experience. Do not underestimate this hike—cross-country hiking in the Grand Canyon can be as slow as 0.5 mile per hour.

Backpackers must have a permit for camping in Grand Canyon National Park. Campfires are not allowed in the park, and dogs are not allowed on trails or in the backcountry.

At Indian Hollow Campground, there's no hint of the nearby Grand Canyon. Follow the Thunder River Trail down Indian Hollow and up to Little Saddle, where the Grand Canyon, dominated by the red terrace of the Esplanade in the foreground, spreads out before you. Descend into the Canyon on the trail via one long switchback. When the trail comes out on the Esplanade 1.8 miles from the trailhead, it turns east. Leave the Thunder River Trail here (it will be the return route) and head west cross-country.

The Esplanade is the dominant terrace in the central and western Grand Canyon. Most road-bound tourists only see the eastern Grand Canyon, where the Tonto Plateau is the dominant terrace, so the Esplanade comes as a surprise to many. Formed on the top of the reddish Supai formation, the Esplanade is about 1500 feet below the rim. From a distance, it looks smooth, but close up you'll find that the Esplanade is broken by dozens of side canyons and their tributaries. Travel along the Esplanade is a matter of hiking around the heads of these side canyons while trying to avoid elevation gain and loss. Sometimes sandstone terraces provide easy walking even across side canyons, but often they peter out, forcing you to choose a new level.

On this section of the Esplanade, it pays to stay fairly high, about the same level as the point where you left the Thunder River Trail. After you pass the head of the western arm of Deer Creek, you'll come out onto a large point. Watch for an old cowboy camp under the overhang of a large boulder near the 4811 elevation point on the topographic map. This camp was apparently used in the days before the national park, when cattle were grazed on the Esplanade. The boulder's shade is welcome on a warm day, since the Esplanade is mostly covered with low brush and a few sparse juniper trees. Next, you'll contour around the head of the east arm of Fishtail Canyon and onto the point between the east and west arms. Above to the northwest, you can see the saddle between the North Rim and Fishtail Mesa. Angle up the talus toward this saddle. A rock slide takes you through the buff-colored Coconino sandstone cliff, and you'll probably find traces of an old trail switchbacking upward. From the saddle, descend north down an easy talus slope into Indian Hollow, then turn left and follow the drainage downstream to the point where the canyon opens out onto the Esplanade, which is 4.7 miles from the Thunder River Trail. There are campsites here and seasonal water along Indian Hollow below this point.

Leave Indian Hollow and hike northwest and then north along the Esplanade. The object is to pass the heads of a tributary of Indian Hollow and Kwagunt Hollow. Right after crossing the main drainage of Indian Hollow you'll meet the Sowats Trail, 3.8 miles from Indian Hollow. (The approximate UTM coordinates are 12S 361340mE 4041010mN.) Turn left and follow the Sowats Trail 1.9 miles north across the Esplanade and down into Sowats Canyon. There is seasonal water along Sowats Canyon and at Mountain Sheep Spring downstream. Leave the Sowats Trail here and walk down Sowats Canyon 1.5 miles to Jumpup Canyon. There are limited campsites at this confluence. If you need water, you should be able to find it at Lower Jumpup Spring, 0.9 mile up Jumpup Canyon.

Continue the loop by turning left and descending into Jumpup Canyon. The going is easy along the gravel wash, which is normally dry. You'll pass the mouth of Kwagunt Hollow while Jumpup Canyon is still cutting through the Supai formation, and the mouth of Indian Hollow after the start of the Redwall limestone gorge. Both canyons are interesting side trips. Lower Jumpup Canyon cuts an impressive gorge through the Redwall limestone, and the confluence with Kanab Creek is sudden and dramatic, 4.5 miles from Sowats Canyon. You can sometimes find a pool of water in the last small side canyon on the right side of Jumpup Canyon before its end.

There are campsites on terraces at the confluence, and in fact, finding campsites is not difficult along the length of lower Kanab Creek. Continue the loop by turning left and following Kanab Canyon downstream. The creek is usually dry at this point—if it is flooding, abandon the trip because travel downstream will be difficult or impossible. Kanab Creek begins to flow about 2 miles downstream from the mouth of Jumpup Canyon, fed by permanent springs that flow out of the Redwall limestone. Travel down Kanab Canyon, while cross-country, is mostly a matter of boulder hopping and crossing the creek occasionally. There are several side canyons that are worth exploring, and you can't miss Showerbath Spring, which pours out of an overhanging mass of travertine like a giant showerhead. One sign that you're nearing the end of Kanab Canyon at the Colorado River is the appearance of a couple of long terraces of Muav limestone at creek level. These terraces make a welcome change from boulder hopping. Kanab Canyon ends 14.1 miles from the mouth of Jumpup Canyon, and campsites are plentiful on the broad river terrace next to Kanab Rapids.

Continue the loop by turning left and hiking upstream along the bank of

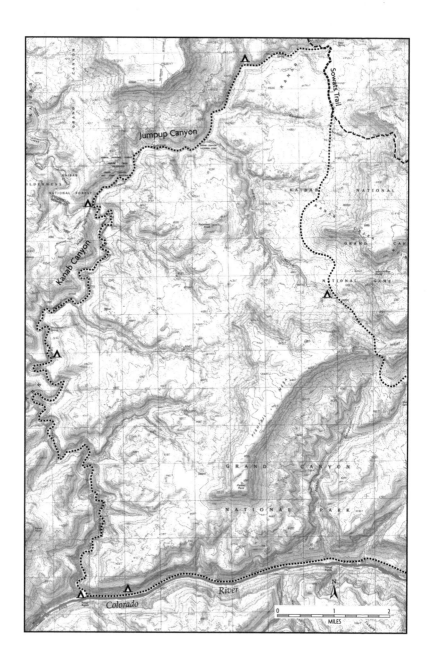

Jumpup Canyon

Sowats Trail

Kanab Canyon

Colorado   River

N

0   1   2

MILES

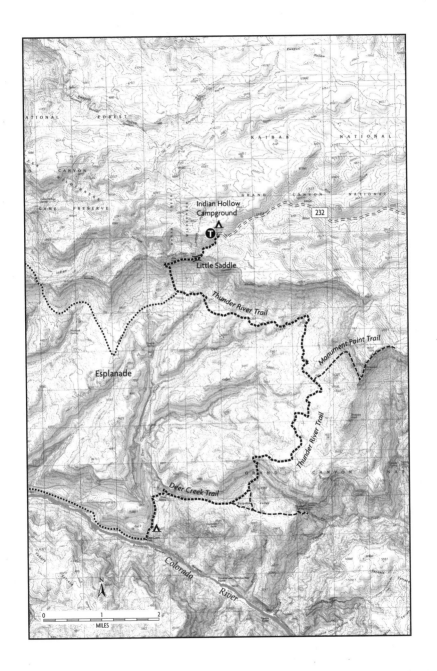

Backpacking along the Esplanade, Grand Canyon

the Colorado River. If the lagoon at the mouth of Kanab Creek is too deep to wade, you'll have to cross the creek farther upstream, then use a sketchy trail along the east bank to reach the Colorado River upstream from the mouth of the creek. Occasional sandy beaches offer a break from boulder hopping as well as campsites. Avoid camping too close to river level, as the river rises and falls as much as 5 feet a day due to fluctuating power production at Glen Canyon Dam, upstream of Grand Canyon National Park. There's little shade along the south-facing riverbank, so you may want to hike this stretch early in the morning. Pick up water at the mouth of Fishtail Canyon, because riverside cliffs force the route away from the river for a couple of miles. After crossing Fishtail Canyon, climb up several hundred feet and continue upstream along the terrace. After passing a nameless canyon about a mile east of Fishtail Canyon, the going becomes rougher. You can return to the river's edge south of the hill marked 3136 on the topo map, and the last mile to Deer Creek Falls is at river level. Deer Creek Falls is 7.8 miles from the mouth of Kanab Creek.

Famous Deer Creek Falls bursts out of a slot canyon and plunges about 200 feet to the river's edge. It's a popular spot for river runners and backpackers alike. Continue the loop by picking up the Deer Creek Trail on the west side of the falls. The trail ascends a slope, then contours into Deer Creek above the falls. The trail follows ledges through an impressive narrows well above the creek, then comes out into open Deer Creek Valley. After about a mile of easy walking up Deer Creek Valley, the trail leaves the creek and climbs the slope to the east. Passing Deer Spring, the source of Deer Creek, the trail climbs easily out of a ravine before meeting the Thunder River Trail at the edge of Surprise Valley just east of a saddle. This junction is 2.6 miles from Deer Creek Falls.

Surprise Valley is a giant slump block. The summit of Cogswell Butte, south of the trail junction, is Supai formation, but these rocks are well below the Supai formation to the north, which is above the Redwall limestone. Ap-

parently the entire valley slid down toward the Colorado River along a series of faults parallel to the Redwall cliff above you, rotating as it did so.

From this junction, you can take a 2.4-mile round-trip side-hike along the
Thunder River Trail across Surprise Valley to a point overlooking Thunder
River. Thunder River is the shortest river in the world, bursting suddenly
from Thunder Cave and cascading 0.5 mile to end at Tapeats Creek.

Continue the loop by turning left on the Thunder River Trail, which
climbs the Redwall limestone and then the Supai formation in a series of
short switchbacks. Once on the Esplanade, the well-used trail heads east
and then north to head the many tributaries of Deer Creek. West of Monument Point, you'll meet the Monument Point Trail, now the most popular
way to reach Thunder River and Deer Creek. This junction is 3.7 miles from
the end of the Deer Creek Trail.

Stay left on the Thunder River Trail and follow it around the head of the
main arm of Deer Creek, then west to the point where you left the trail to
start the cross-country portion of the loop, 4.2 miles from the Monument
Point Trail. Retrace your steps 1.8 miles over Little Saddle and back to the
trailhead at Indian Hollow Campground.

2 ┊ POWELL PLATEAU LOOP

Round trip ■	**54.7 miles**
Loop direction ■	Counterclockwise
Hiking time ■	9 days, or longer for exploration
Starting elevation ■	7470 feet
Lowest point ■	2250 feet
Elevation gain ■	10,000 feet
Seasonal water availability ■	Muav Saddle Spring, Key Spring, Hakatai Canyon, and White Creek. Tapeats Creek, the Colorado River, and Shinumo Creek are permanent.
Best hiking time ■	Mid-September through November
Maps ■	King Arthur Castle, Tapeats Amphitheater, Powell Plateau, Fossil Bay, Topocoba Hilltop, Explorers Monument, Havasupai Point USGS, Grand Canyon Trails Illustrated
Contact ■	Grand Canyon National Park. Permits required.

Driving directions: From Jacob Lake on US 89A, go 26.8 miles south
on Arizona 67. Turn right on Forest Road 22. After 2.1 miles, turn left

on Forest Road 270. After 2.2 miles, turn right on Forest Road 223. Continue 5.3 miles, then turn left on Forest Road 268. After 0.5 mile, turn left on Forest Road 268B. A maze of new logging roads confuses the next section. Try each left spur until you find the road that continues through the unmarked park gate to the Kanabonits Road junction. Turn right onto Swamp Point Road and drive 7.2 miles to Swamp Point. **This road is snowed in during the winter and spring, and major snowstorms are possible from November through April.**

This long loop starts from the Swamp Point Trailhead on the North Rim, then descends Saddle and Tapeats Canyons to the Colorado River. The hike then follows the Colorado River around the base of Powell Plateau to Shinumo Creek, where it ascends the long abandoned North Bass Trail to complete the loop.

Nearly all the hiking on this loop is strenuous cross-country, and this hike should be attempted only by those with previous experience hiking on Grand Canyon trails. The Horseshoe Mesa and Boucher-Hermit Loops are good preparation for this hike. At least one member of the group should have Grand Canyon cross-country hiking experience. While the Trails Illustrated map gives a good overview of the trip, you must have the USGS topographic maps to find critical portions of this route. The loop is best hiked counterclockwise because this gets the cross-country descent of Saddle Canyon out of the way at the beginning, as well as the flooded narrows in Tapeats Creek.

You'll start on the upper section of the North Bass Trail, which descends 0.6 mile to Muav Saddle. This short cherry-stem section will be used for the return also, and it is the easiest hiking of the entire trip. In Muav Saddle, you can turn sharply left on an unmarked spur trail to reach Muav Saddle Spring, which is at the base of the Coconino sandstone cliff east of the saddle. This spring is too close to the trailhead to be of much use on the loop. Just beyond the spur trail to the spring, the lower North Bass Trail also goes left—this will be your return 9 days from now. The main trail continues across the saddle and eventually climbs onto Powell Plateau, but just as it reaches the low point of the broad saddle, you'll spot Theodore Roosevelt Cabin below the trail on the right. Recently restored, this historic cabin was built by trail crews during the 1930s, and it is named in honor of the far-sighted president who established Grand Canyon National Monument, the predecessor to the present National Park.

From the cabin, strike off cross-country down the bed of Saddle Canyon

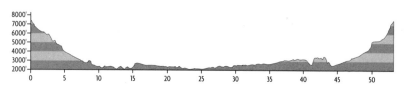

to the north. Ponderosa pine and Gambel oak forest soon gives way to brushy slopes as you descend through an old burn. By staying right in the bed of the normally dry drainage you can avoid the worst brush. At about the 5800-foot contour you'll encounter a dry fall in the red Supai formation. A cairned route bypasses this obstacle to the left (west), leading down a ridge just west of the bed. At about 5100 feet the route returns to the bed of Saddle Canyon and soon enters the Redwall limestone gorge. A narrow chute in the Redwall limestone known as the "Slicky Slide" is not a problem when it has the usual small trickle of water, but a cold pool at the bottom must be waded. The last obstacle in Saddle Canyon is a high, dry fall at the base of the Redwall, but it is easily bypassed on the left via a trail along a broad ledge. The route returns you to the canyon floor at the confluence with Stina Canyon, which comes in from the right. Crazy Jug Canyon comes in on the right 4.7 miles from Muav Saddle, and marks the beginning of Tapeats Creek. The creek normally flows, but if it is dry, you should be able to find water a short distance upstream in Crazy Jug and Stina Canyons. There are a few small campsites in the area.

Follow Tapeats Creek downstream, boulder-hopping down the bed. Campsites aren't hard to find along the relatively open canyon bottom, and the flow of water increases dramatically when you pass the mouth of the canyon containing Tapeats Spring. In fact, in spring the water can be too high to get through the short narrows in the brown Tapeats sandstone, which is downstream from this confluence. Even in the fall, the normal time for this hike, you'll be wading in about a foot of fast-moving water for about 100 yards and you'll find a walking stick or trekking poles handy. Below the narrows, Thunder River comes in from the right, 4.2 miles from Crazy Jug Canyon, and adds even more water to Tapeats Creek. Thunder River flows just 0.5 mile from its source at Thunder Spring.

An informal but well-used trail follows Thunder River to Tapeats Creek, and then continues down Tapeats Creek. Follow this trail 1.4 miles downstream, until Tapeats Creek starts to enter its lower gorge and the trail begins to contour on the west side of the canyon. Cross the creek and follow another informal trail along the east side of the canyon. This trail stays on the rim of the Tapeats sandstone and comes out above the Colorado River after about a mile. Follow the trail downstream past Hundred and Thirtythree Mile Canyon to Stone Creek, where you can follow the bed of this side canyon down to the river. The mouth of Stone Creek is 3.2 miles from the point where you left Tapeats Creek. You'll find campsites along the small beach. Stone Creek is interesting to explore, as is Galloway Canyon a short distance south. Both are popular destinations for river runners landing at Tapeats Creek, which is why the informal trail exists to this point.

Follow the Colorado River downstream to the mouth of Galloway Canyon, then climb the broken Vishnu schist slope to the south just high enough so that you can continue downriver. After 1.4 miles you'll reach

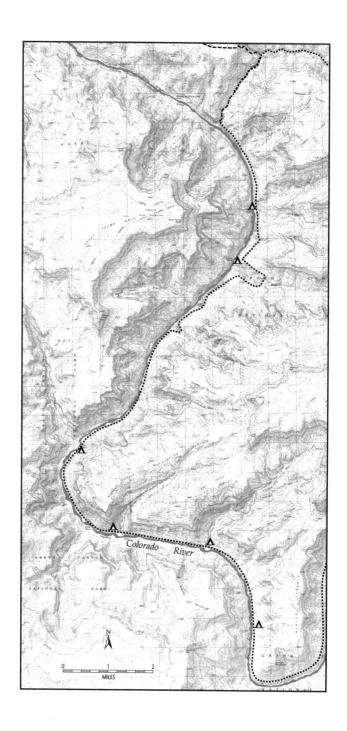

Colorado River

N

0   1   2
MILES

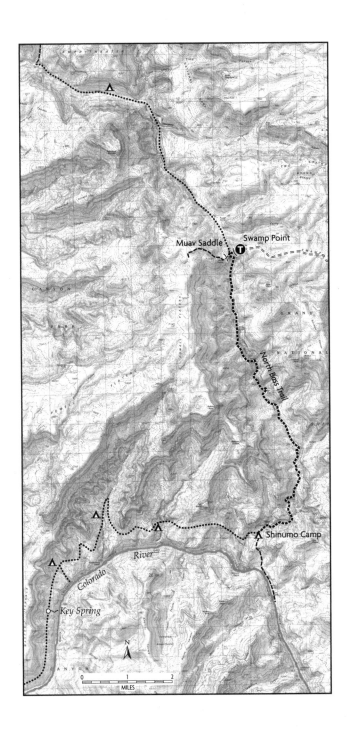

Muav Saddle · Swamp Point

North Bass Trail

Shinumo Camp

River

Colorado

Key Spring

N

0   1   2
MILES

the mouth of Bedrock Canyon at the river. Cliffs will make the river inaccessible for the next 7.3 miles, until Fossil Rapids, and there are no other permanent water sources along this section, so make certain you have enough water before continuing.

South of Bedrock Canyon you'll have to climb to the top of the Tapeats sandstone, which forms the rim of Middle Granite Gorge. The terrace formed in the soft Bright Angel shale on top of the Tapeats sandstone is called the Tonto Plateau, although here it hardly qualifies as a plateau. Hike cross-country south along the Tapeats rim. At Hundred and Twentyeight Mile Canyon you'll have to detour up the side canyon along the Tapeats rim to find a way across. Detours are much shorter at the numerous unnamed canyons and at Hundred and Twentyseven Mile Canyon. Middle Granite Gorge ends at Fossil Rapids, opposite the mouth of Fossil Creek, and the route reaches the river here. There are plenty of campsites along the broad terraces, especially upstream of the rapids.

Downstream, the cross-country hiking is slow and rough along the broken slope above the river as you are forced to skirt travertine cliffs that fall into the river. As the river gorge swings east into Conquistador Aisle, the going becomes easier and in several places you'll walk along flat slabs of Tapeats sandstone exposed at river level. You'll reach the mouth of Hundred and Twentytwo Mile Canyon 2.9 miles from Fossil Rapids, where campsites are near the river. East of this canyon mouth, the Tapeats sandstone forms a cliff above the river, forcing the route to follow the rim just above the river, but just 2 miles of this leads to Blacktail Canyon, where there is a route to the Colorado River and more possible campsites. Blacktail Canyon is interesting to explore.

River access is severely limited along the next section of the route, from Blacktail Canyon to Hakatai Canyon, so plan to carry enough water. When George Steck originally pioneered this route, the lack of water sources made this section dangerous, especially in hot weather. Since then, Steck and others have discovered a spring not shown on the maps, as well as new routes to the river that make this section more reasonable.

From Blacktail Canyon, continue east and then south along the rim of the Tapeats sandstone. The next access to the river is 2.2 miles from Blacktail Canyon, at a hard-to-find route through the Tapeats cliff discovered by Jim Haggart and Art Christiansen. It is located just south of the third unnamed rapids upriver of Blacktail Canyon, as shown on the USGS topo map. (UTM coordinates are 12S 369255mE 4009185mN.) Look for a large, nearly flat square ledge in the Tapeats sandstone, well below the rim you've been following. Scramble down to this ledge, then walk to its downriver end. You can work your way along ledges and down to the river from this point. The square ledge also makes a great fair-weather campsite.

As the river gorge turns east again and swings around Explorers Monument, there is another route to the river, 2.3 miles from the route described above. This route, first noticed by Steck while he was hiking the opposite

Middle Granite Gorge, Grand Canyon

side of the river, descends the first nameless ravine west of the longer nameless ravine that descends from the east side of Explorers Monument. (UTM coordinates are 12S 370455mE 4007090mN.) This descent is long enough that you'd only use it if short on water.

Continue hiking cross-country along the Tapeats sandstone rim as the gorge turns north and Granite Gorge begins. The next water source is Key Spring, discovered and named by Steck. Not shown on the maps, this somewhat alkaline but drinkable spring is in a nameless side canyon 2.3 miles north of the route below Explorers Monument, 0.4 mile northeast of the 4850 elevation point shown on the USGS topo. (UTM coordinates are 12S 371711mE 4009550mN.)

There is a route to the Colorado River in the nameless side canyon 1.5 miles north of Key Spring, which was discovered by Jim Haggart and myself. This descent begins 0.8 mile east-northeast of the 5140 elevation point shown on the USGS topo. (UTM coordinates are 12S 372278mE 4011158mN.) Follow the dry bed of the canyon downstream until it is blocked by a dry fall, then work your way down slopes south of the bed. Dramatic views of Granite Gorge make this a nice side hike even if you don't need water.

As the river turns northeast and the Tapeats rim slowly broadens into the Tonto Plateau, walking becomes a bit harder. There are more side canyons to contour around, and Walthenberg Canyon forces a big detour. There are a few small campsites and seasonal water pockets in the longest of the unnamed west-side tributaries of Walthenberg, but the next good camping and reliable water is at Hakatai Canyon, 8.2 miles from Key Spring. East of Walthenberg Canyon the going becomes easier as the Tonto slope is somewhat gentler. Descend into Hakatai Canyon on the west side of Hakatai just north of the Granite Gorge rim. (UTM coordinates for the start of this descent are 12S 375559mE 4012405mN.) Work your way north down talus slopes to the bed of Hakatai Canyon at the prospect shown on the USGS topo.

There's usually a trickle of water in Hakatai Canyon, and it's easy to do a side trip about 2 miles round trip to the Colorado River. Watch for a trail climbing a steep ravine on the east side of the lower canyon. This short trail climbs to a platform that was the terminus of a cable crossing spanning the river. Although the cable was cut in the 1970s, if you look carefully you can see the other terminus on the slope across the river, as well as traces of the trail leading to it. The cable crossing was built by William Bass, an early prospector. Bass built both the North and South Bass Trails to reach his mines and prospects in the Bass and Shinumo Canyon areas, and he built cable crossings here and at Bass Canyon to use when the river was in spring flood and too dangerous to cross by boat.

The route east of Hakatai Canyon ascends to the Tonto Plateau via the broken, nameless ravine directly east of the prospect shown on the USGS topo. Contour generally east across the slopes southwest of Fan Island, then start the descent into Burro Canyon at a point overlooking Granite Gorge before reaching the west rim of Burro Canyon. (UTM coordinates are 12S 377872mE 4012600mN.) This descent starts 0.5 mile south-southeast of Fan Island and descends a sloping ledge formed on the Grand Canyon Series of rock formations. Once you pass below the point between Granite Gorge and Burro Creek, you can descend east to the bed of Burro Creek. You'll likely find traces of the trail built by Bass from Shinumo Creek to Hakatai Creek. Cross Burro Creek above a high, dry fall, then climb south around a point and descend a sloping ramp east to Shinumo Creek. It's 2.6 miles from Hakatai Creek to Shinumo Creek. This is the junction of the trail down Shinumo Creek and the North Bass Trail, which comes down the slope to the south. Follow the Shinumo Creek Trail, which is little used and has been heavily damaged by floods, upstream along Shinumo Creek to the site of Shinumo Camp, which is shown on the USGS topo. There are numerous campsites along the broad terrace, and Shinumo Creek provides reliable water. A few artifacts remain from the days when Bass used this place as his main camp at the bottom of the canyon. Like many other early Grand Canyon prospectors, Bass soon found guiding tourists to be more profitable than mining, and Shinumo Camp made a handy base camp for excursions to the wild and remote North Rim.

Continue the loop by following Shinumo Creek upstream to White Creek. Although the maps show the North Bass Trail climbing a slope west of White Creek, this section has almost disappeared and it's much easier to follow Shinumo Creek. After 1.6 miles from the trail junction below Shinumo Camp, turn left (north) into White Creek. If you need water, fill up in Shinumo Creek, as White Creek has only seasonal flow. White Creek gradually narrows and soon enters a narrows in the Tapeats sandstone that is marked by a huge chock stone jammed between the walls high above. When you see this chock stone, you've gone too far, as the gorge ahead is blocked by a fall. Backtrack just a bit, and exit the gorge via a ravine on the east side. Walk the east rim of the narrows north to rejoin the bed of White Creek. There is little trace of the North Bass Trail, but it's easy to walk up the bed to the north. As the creek enters the Redwall limestone gorge, there is often seasonal water. Watch for the cairned beginning of the Redwall ascent (UTM 12S 379320mE 4018200mN, although your GPS may not work in this narrow canyon), where the North Bass Trail climbs the impressive cliffs west of the bed via a clever route. One short section of trail near the top of the Redwall is somewhat exposed, as the trail crosses a narrow ledge with a drop below. Above the Redwall, follow the North Bass Trail across several brushy ravines west of the bed before it drops back into the dry bed of White Creek. The trail stays near the bed to the benchmark shown on the USGS topo map (BM5692), where it starts a steep ascent up the terraces and cliffs of the Supai formation, finally emerging on Muav Saddle 7.1 miles from Shinumo Creek. Stay on the North Bass Trail to retrace your steps 0.6 mile to Swamp Point and the trailhead.

3: BOUCHER-HERMIT LOOP

Round trip ■	**19.1 miles**
Loop direction ■	Clockwise
Hiking time ■	3 to 5 days
Starting elevation ■	6600 feet
Lowest point ■	2910 feet
Elevation gain ■	7100 feet
Seasonal water availability ■	Boucher Creek, Hermit Creek
Best hiking time ■	October through November and March through April. Winter can be cold, but the trails are passable unless heavy snow has fallen recently.
Maps ■	Grand Canyon USGS, Grand Canyon National Park Trails Illustrated
Contact ■	Grand Canyon National Park. Permits and reservations required

Driving directions: To reach the trailhead from Grand Canyon Village, drive west 12 miles on the West Rim Drive to the road's end at Hermits Rest and park at the Hermit Trailhead. During the summer half of the year, the West Rim Drive is closed to private vehicles except for backpackers.

This is the classic Grand Canyon loop hike, easily reached via paved roads on the South Rim. While none of the trails are regularly maintained, the Hermit Trail is considered the easiest of the old Grand Canyon Trails. The Boucher Trail, while well-traveled, was not built to the same standards as the Hermit, and it is steeper and rougher. By doing this loop clockwise, you'll have the easier Hermit Trail for the long climb to the South Rim.

Three days is the minimum time for this loop, but if you'd like time to hike to the Colorado River and do other side trips, 5 days is a more reasonable time. Don't let the relatively short distances fool you—Grand Canyon hiking is rough and slow. Even trails that appear level on the map, such as the Tonto Trail, constantly climb and descend as they work their way around ridges, side canyons, and other obstacles. Experience on well-maintained trails in the mountains does not apply to Grand Canyon hiking.

The Hermit Trail immediately descends through the rim formation of Kaibab limestone and switchbacks to the north. Kaibab limestone is an off-white fossil-bearing sedimentary rock layer about 250 feet thick throughout most of the Grand Canyon. Limestone is deposited underwater, which indicates that the Grand Canyon region was underwater when the Kaibab was deposited. Being a hard rock that is resistant to erosion, the Kaibab tends to form a cliff. Grand Canyon trails and routes usually take advantage of faults

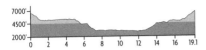

or rockslides to descend through cliff-forming rock layers such as the Kaibab limestone. The Hermit Trail turns back to the southwest as it breaks through the last of the Kaibab limestone and emerges onto slopes formed from the Toroweap formation. The Toroweap is a mixture of limestone and sandstone layers about 200 feet thick, and being softer than the Kaibab limestone, it usually erodes into a slope, or terrace. On the map, and from a distance, such terraces look level, but they are often quite steep. In

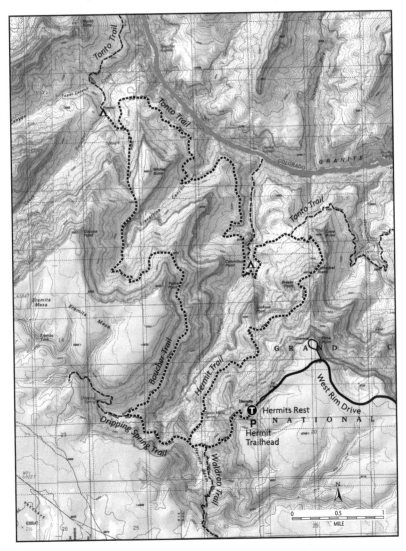

addition, Toroweap terraces are cut by numerous ravines and gullies, as well as small cliffs, so the Hermit Trail must work its way through these obstacles.

As the trail turns west and descends toward Hermit Basin, it passes through the Coconino sandstone. Usually the Coconino forms a persistent buff-colored cliff about 350 feet high, but the Hermit Trail takes advantage of a broken slope to switchback down through this formation. You can see fine examples of Coconino cliffs on the far side of Hermit Basin. Close up, you may notice that outcrops of Coconino are cross-bedded. Even though the entire layer of sandstone is horizontal, it is made up from layers that are tilted in various directions. If you had a microscope, you could see that the individual grains of sand are frosted, which indicates they were tumbled in the wind. The Coconino sandstone was deposited in a vast, Sahara-like desert of drifting sand dunes, and the cross-beds are the sloping surfaces of these ancient, petrified dunes. Fossil tracks are visible on a slab of Coconino along the Hermit Trail. These tracks are always going down, never up, because an animal climbing a sand dune wipes out its own tracks.

The Hermit Trail was once the major tourist trail in the Grand Canyon before that honor was transferred to the Bright Angel Trail. Serious trail construction was necessary to handle the heavy mule traffic to and from Hermit Camp at Hermit Creek. Evidence of this construction is still visible in the Coconino descent where sections of the trail were paved with slabs of sandstone set on edge.

As the Hermit Trail completes its descent into Hermit Basin, it comes out onto gentler slopes formed in the Hermit shale. A layer of soft rock about 500 to 1000 feet thick, the Hermit shale almost always erodes into a distinctive red terrace skirting the base of the Coconino sandstone. The Hermit shale was deposited in a tidal-flat environment along an ancient coast. Hermit Basin is relatively open and gentle because it is formed on the Hermit shale. One mile from the Hermit Trailhead, you'll pass the little-used Waldron Trail, which goes left. Continue straight ahead on the Hermit Trail. About 1.2 miles from Hermit Trailhead, you'll reach the dry wash that drains Hermit Basin and meet the Dripping Spring Trail. The Hermit Trail turns right, and will be your return route. For now, stay left on the Dripping Spring Trail to start the loop portion of the hike.

Taking advantage of the sloping terrace formed on the Hermit shale, the Dripping Spring Trail contours around the head of Hermit Canyon, swinging around ridges and crossing side canyons. Below you, steep cliffs and slopes of Supai formation rock layers fall away into the impressive depths of upper Hermit Canyon. A mile of this hiking brings you to a major side canyon coming in from the west, and the junction with the Boucher Trail.

An optional side hike of 0.8 mile round trip with an elevation gain of 300 feet on the Dripping Spring Trail takes you to Dripping Spring at the base of the Coconino sandstone. This is a popular destination for birders and others who want to see a relatively accessible Grand Canyon spring.

The main loop continues on the Boucher Trail, which heads north along

Backpacking on the Tonto Trail, Grand Canyon

the west side of Hermit Canyon, staying on the Hermit shale terrace. The upper gorge of Hermit Canyon gradually opens up as you proceed north, and it's easy to spot the Hermit Trail ascending the red cliffs and terraces of the Supai formation on the opposite side of the canyon. Finally, the Boucher Trail swings west below Yuma Point into the head of Travertine Canyon, where it at last finds a break in the Supai formation cliffs and abruptly descends. The start of this descent is 2.9 miles from the Dripping Spring Trail. The Boucher Trail makes up for its long, fairly level traverse by descending with a vengeance through the layers of reddish sandstone, shale, and limestone that make up the Supai formation. About 1000 feet thick, the Supai formation erodes into a series of 100- to 200-foot cliffs with intervening terraces. The alternating rock layers, as well as fossils, indicate that the Supai formation was created in a near-shore environment, where the ocean was shallow and sediment washed into it from nearby land. The reddish color of many of the Supai rock layers shows that the sea occasionally receded, exposing the sand and silt to the air. Iron present in the layers oxidized on contact with the atmosphere, forming red iron oxides. At the base of the Supai, the Boucher Trail reaches the top of the Redwall limestone and contours along the west rim of Travertine Canyon. Passing through a saddle south of Whites Butte, the trail plunges down a fault ravine through the Redwall limestone.

The Redwall limestone is consistently about 550 feet thick throughout the Grand Canyon, and it forms a distinct red cliff that is a serious barrier to travel within the Canyon. Hundreds of miles of Redwall cliff are exposed in the Grand Canyon, and there are only about 200 known routes through it that don't require technical climbing gear. Of these routes, only a few dozen are good enough for a trail. The location of the Boucher Trail is determined primarily by the Redwall break west of Whites Butte. The Redwall limestone is composed of trillions of microscopic fossil seashells, and was laid down in a deep ocean that once covered the region. Nearly pure limestone, the Redwall is actually gray but is usually stained red by minerals leaching down from the overlying Supai formation.

At the base of the Redwall, purplish Muav limestone makes its appearance. This shaly, sandy limestone isn't as resistant as the Redwall limestone, and it usually forms a series of alternating low cliffs and terraces. As the Boucher Trail continues its steep descent, it comes out onto slopes formed in the Bright Angel shale, a thick layer of slope-forming, greenish-purplish rock that erodes out into a broad terrace known as the Tonto Plateau. Watch for the junction with the Tonto Trail, 2.4 miles from the start of the Supai descent. The main loop continues on the Tonto Trail, but you'll probably want to stay left for now and follow the Tonto Trail 0.2 mile down to Boucher Creek for water and campsites. This descent takes you through the 200-foot cliff formed by Tapeats sandstone, a coarse-grained, brown to purplish rock layer. If Boucher Creek is dry, look either upstream or down and you should find a flow. There are several campsites on the streamside terraces.

Louis Boucher, the builder of the Boucher Trail, was a reclusive man who built his trail single-handedly to reach mineral deposits at Boucher Creek. The ruins of his stone cabin and the mine workings are still visible.

An optional side trip takes you 3.2 miles down Boucher Creek to the Colorado River and back. You'll descend 400 feet on this easy cross-country hike. Follow the Tonto Trail north down the bed of Boucher Creek to the point where Topaz Canyon joins from the left. Here the trail climbs out of Boucher Creek to the north, but to reach the river, stay in the bed of Boucher Creek all the way to the river. The entire walk down Boucher Creek descends through one of the most ancient rock formations exposed anywhere on earth, the Vishnu schist. A metamorphic rock, the Vishnu represents the roots of ancient mountains which were raised to great heights by movement of the earth's crust, then eroded away to a flat plain. The mountain-building process changed the Vishnu schist beyond recognition, as enormous pressure and heat twisted the original rock layers and chemically altered its minerals. At the mouth of Boucher Canyon, the Colorado River crashes through Boucher Rapids as it makes its way through the somber, gray cliffs of Granite Gorge. Boucher Rapids, formed by boulders and debris brought down Boucher Creek by floods, is actually a minor rapid as Grand Canyon rapids go. Granite Gorge is about 1200 feet deep and the resistant Vishnu schist forms cliffs and very steep slopes, making the gorge an impressive setting for the Colorado River.

Back at Boucher's old camp, retrace your steps on the Tonto Trail 0.2 mile to the junction with the Boucher Trail, then stay left to remain on the Tonto Trail as it heads north across the Tonto Plateau.

The Tonto Plateau is the most persistent and conspicuous terrace in the eastern Grand Canyon, and the Tonto Trail takes advantage of it to contour along above Granite Gorge for more than 70 miles. Up close, though, the Tonto Plateau is anything but level. Numerous ridges fan out from the base of the Muav and Redwall cliffs above, and side canyons cut deep into the terrace. This forces the Tonto Trail to constantly twist and turn, descend and climb. This means that you may hike 5 miles on the Tonto Trail to gain one straight line mile. As you hike along, though, don't be tempted to second-guess the trail designers. Every time I've felt that leaving the trail would be quicker, I've been wrong. It turns out that the Tonto Trail was laid out by an extremely experienced team that hardly ever made a mistake—wild burros!

Many of the early prospectors and explorers who invaded the Grand Canyon in search of mineral riches used burros for transport. The sure-footed animals proved to be adept at navigating the Canyon's steep, loose slopes. They were so much at home that a few inevitably escaped or got lost, and soon established a feral population in the eastern Grand Canyon—the section dominated by the Tonto Plateau. Natural-born trail makers, the burros always picked the most efficient route through difficult terrain. Though prospectors built trails in places, the majority of the Tonto Trail was burro engineered. Unfortunately for the wild burros, native plants and desert bighorn sheep suffered from burro competition. The National Park Service removed the burros from the national park by a combination of adoption and shooting during the 1970s. Bighorn sheep made an immediate comeback, and there's enough hiker traffic to maintain the Tonto Trail.

About 0.5 mile north of the Boucher Trail junction, the Tonto Trail crosses a low saddle and heads east. Often the trail is somewhat back from the rim of Granite Gorge, but occasionally it goes right to the edge of the Tapeats sandstone cliff to give you a great view. These places make excellent rest stops! The trail contours, more or less, around a number of minor drainages before rounding Hill 3303 and heading south into Travertine Canyon. The Tonto Trail crosses the normally dry bed of Travertine 2.2 miles from the Boucher Trail. This canyon is named for the travertine rock formations found here. Since travertine is formed by mineralized springs, there must have once been an active, large spring in Travertine Canyon.

Heading northeast, the Tonto Trail follows the east rim of Travertine Canyon around a point above the river and immediately heads south into Hermit Canyon. Hermit is a major South Rim side canyon, and it's 2.4 miles from Travertine Canyon to the bed of Hermit Canyon, and most of the distance is spent hiking south along Hermit's west rim. The Tonto Trail descends through the Tapeats to cross Hermit Creek, and the Hermit Creek Campground is located downstream from the crossing. Since the Hermit Creek area is so heavily used, backpackers are required to camp in the designated campground.

Here you have an option to hike down Hermit Creek to the Colorado River and Hermit Rapids. The Hermit Trail originally continued to the river, but little trace of the constructed trail remains today. Hikers keep a path beaten in, though, so the walk is easy. Hermit Rapids is one of the hardest ten rapids on the Colorado River in Grand Canyon. All Grand Canyon rapids have been formed in the same way, by flood debris brought down from side canyons. The capacity of moving water to carry silt, sand, pebbles, rocks, and boulders increases with the cube of its velocity. Since side canyons like Hermit have a steeper gradient than the river, they can carry boulders too large for the river to move. In addition, floods in side canyons often become debris flows, which are a thick slurry of mud that can carry even more debris than a typical flash flood. This debris forms a dam across the river, and as the water cascades over it, the waves, holes, and other features of a rapid are formed. The Colorado River carries a heavy load of sand and sediment and acts like a rasp on its bed and the debris fans. Eventually, if no more floods occur, the rapids will be worn away.

After you return to the campground, you may wish to spend some time poking around the remains of Hermit Camp. Located on the east rim of Hermit Canyon, on the Tonto Trail, Hermit Camp was a tourist resort until about 1930, when the present trans-canyon Kaibab Trail was built. Supplied by mules and an aerial tramway from Pima Point on the South Rim, the camp had tent cabins, roads, and even a Model T Ford. Since Hermit Creek has a small but permanent flow, the camp had a good supply of water.

Another possibility for a side trip is to explore upstream along Hermit Creek, above the Tonto Trail crossing. The cross-country walking becomes easier when you pass the source of Hermit Creek at the base of the Redwall limestone. The upper gorge becomes very steep, and it requires technical climbing skills to climb through the cliffs in the Supai formation.

To continue the loop, leave Hermit Canyon on the Tonto Trail, passing the site of Hermit Camp as you head generally northeast. Turn right on the Hermit Trail, 1.1 miles from Hermit Creek, and start the ascent toward the base of the Redwall limestone. A few switchbacks lead up the slope toward Cope Butte, then the trail swings south and heads for a north-facing ravine. Here the Hermit Trail ascends the Redwall limestone through a narrow fault ravine called the Cathedral Stairs. At the top of the Redwall, the Hermit Trail heads generally southwest around Breezy Point, then starts to climb along the Supai formation terraces. Long traverses are punctuated by sudden ascents where the trail finds a break in the cliff bands. Near the end of this section, you'll pass an old rest house at Santa Maria Spring. Don't rely on the spring—it's a small seep at best. The Hermit Trail doesn't break through the final Supai cliff until past Santa Maria Spring, where it drops into the bed of Hermit Creek, now dry, and meets the Dripping Spring Trail, 5.3 miles from the Tonto Trail, and closes the loop. Follow the Hermit Trail to the South Rim and the Hermit Trailhead to complete the trip.

4 HORSESHOE MESA LOOP

Round trip ■	**11.3 miles**
Loop direction ■	Counterclockwise
Hiking time ■	9 to 10 hours or 2 to 3 days, if time is allowed for exploration
Starting elevation ■	7330 feet
Lowest point ■	3640 feet
Elevation gain ■	6100 feet
Seasonal water availability ■	Miners Spring, Hance Creek, Cottonwood Creek
Best hiking time ■	October through April. The upper Grandview Trail may be difficult during a snowy winter.
Maps ■	Grandview Point, Cape Royal USGS; Grand Canyon National Park Trails Illustrated
Contact ■	Grand Canyon National Park. Permits and reservations required.

Driving directions: From Grand Canyon Village on the South Rim, drive 8.6 miles east on the East Rim Drive and then turn left and drive 0.8 mile to Grandview Point.

This loop with a cherry stem explores the Horseshoe Mesa area in eastern Grand Canyon, using the upper Grandview Trail for the descent to Horseshoe Mesa and Hance Creek, a section of the Tonto Trail, and the West Grandview Trail for the return. Highlights include the old copper mine and ruins on Horseshoe Mesa and two optional side trips to the Colorado River, one cross-country and one on trail.

The Grandview Trail starts from the north end of the parking lot and immediately starts its descent through the rim cliffs formed by the Kaibab limestone. (See the Boucher-Hermit Loop for details on Grand Canyon rock formations. If you have basic knowledge of rock layers in the canyon, you can determine your altitude in relation to the rim nearly as easily as with an altimeter, and knowing the rocks certainly adds to the pleasure of the trip.) Numerous switchbacks lead down to steep slopes in the Toroweap formation. Impressive sections of trail construction get the old trail through the Coconino sandstone cliffs. In some places log cribs filled with rocks enable the trail to get through cliff bands. Some of these places are somewhat exposed and can be exciting with snow on the trail. The trail reaches the base of the Coconino sandstone at a notch with a view down into Hance Canyon to the east. Now the trail heads east and north to descend the reddish Hermit shale and Supai formations at the head of Cottonwood Creek. Horseshoe Mesa, the immediate goal, is visible ahead. The top of Horseshoe Mesa is formed on the rim of the Redwall limestone, but when the Grandview Trail reaches the first outcrops of Redwall it is still well above Horseshoe Mesa. As you continue the last section of trail to the mesa, you're descending a sloping surface of Redwall limestone. This downslope in the normally horizontal sedimentary rock layers is caused by the Grandview Monocline, which cuts across the neck at the south end of Horseshoe Mesa. In a monocline, horizontal rock layers suddenly dip downward at an angle, then level out at a lower elevation. Monoclines are caused when rock layers on one side are raised or lowered with respect to the other side, and the rocks bend rather than break. The rock layers now exposed to view in this section of the Grand Canyon were probably deeply buried when the monocline was formed. Deeply buried rocks flow like toothpaste because of the immense heat and pressure at depth.

On Horseshoe Mesa, 2.2 miles from Grandview Point, you'll meet the junction with the East Grandview Trail, which is the start of the loop portion of the hike. Backpackers are required to camp in the designated campground, north of the trail junction. The nearest water is at Miners Spring, which is a long side trip, and backpackers who plan to camp here should carry water down from the trailhead. You may wish to spend some time exploring the remains of the Last Chance Mine, parts of which are located near the trail junction. The old stone cookhouse still stands, and there are artifacts and pieces of ore scattered around. The Grandview Trail was built to service the mine, but like many other Grand Canyon trails, the miners soon turned to tourism as a more profitable enterprise. Horseshoe Mesa is dry, and water for the miners had to be hauled from Cottonwood Creek on the west side of Horseshoe Mesa or Miners Spring on the east.

As you start the loop on the East Grandview Trail, you'll immediately descend below the rim of the Redwall limestone into a nameless tributary of Hance Canyon and pass one of the horizontal shafts of the mine workings. Lower down, you'll meet the junction with the short spur trail to Miners Spring, a small spring at the base of the Redwall on the south side of the canyon. Below the turnoff to the spring, the East Grandview Trail crosses the

drainage, then climbs around a low ridge to end at the Tonto Trail, 1.1 miles from the junction on Horseshoe Mesa.

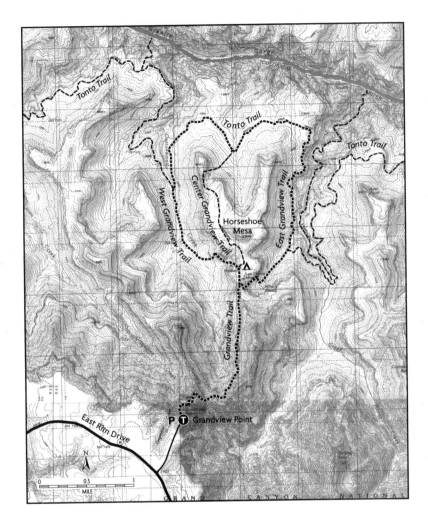

Hance Creek, about 0.4 mile southeast on the Tonto Trail, offers seasonal water and campsites. You can also do an interesting side trip down Hance Canyon to the Colorado River. From the end of the East Grandview Trail, this side trip is 6.8 miles round trip, with 1670 feet of elevation gain on the return. John Hance built a trail down Hance Canyon at the end of the nineteenth century, but today the route of the original Hance Trail is cross-country. Four waterfalls block the lower gorge, and you'll have to bypass them by climbing well above the bed of the creek along fault lines. Your reward for this effort is a look at wild Sockdolager Rapids.

Continue the main loop from the end of the East Grandview Trail by turning left and hiking north on the Tonto Trail. The trail soon crosses the nameless side canyon descended by the East Grandview Trail, then turns north again along the west side of lower Hance Canyon. After the Tonto Trail passes north of the east prong of Horseshoe Mesa, it turns west and then southwest, crosses the drainage coming from between the east and west prongs of Horseshoe Mesa, and passes the junction with the Center Grandview Trail, 2.9 miles from the end of the East Grandview Trail. After the drainage and junction, the Tonto Trail swings around the west prong of Horseshoe Mesa and heads into Cottonwood Creek to the junction with the West Grandview Trail. You've come 1.4 miles from the Center Grandview Trail. There is seasonal water in Cottonwood Creek and a few small campsites. There's another seasonal spring west in the next arm of Cottonwood Creek, and also up the present arm just off the West Grandview Trail.

You can take another side trip to the Colorado River, using the Tonto Trail and the original lower Grandview Trail. This trip is 4.6 miles round trip and you'll gain 1510 feet on the return. Hike west on the Tonto Trail around the unnamed west arm of Cottonwood and out onto the point above the Colorado River. This point is directly north of the Redwall spur with the spot elevation 4262 on the USGS topo. The old Grandview Trail descends west of the point to get below the upper Tapeats sandstone cliff, then contours below it to a notch, where it starts a steep, switchbacking descent that continues to the Colorado River. The spot is quiet and peaceful, with only the river gliding through the 1500-foot-deep Granite Gorge to break the silence.

Back at the main arm of Cottonwood Creek, continue the loop by following the West Grandview Trail south up Cottonwood Creek. After passing the spring shown on the topo map, the trail climbs the Redwall limestone through a break on the west side of Horseshoe Mesa and meets the Center Grandview Trail 1.5 miles from the Tonto Trail. Turn right (south) and walk 0.1 mile to the old Last Chance Mine and the end of the loop at the Grandview Trail.

Stay right and follow the Grandview Trail south out of the canyon to *Grandview Trail, Grand Canyon* Grandview Point and your vehicle.

WILLIAMS

5 : DOGTOWN RESERVOIR TRAIL

Round trip ■	**2.3 miles**
Loop direction ■	Counterclockwise
Hiking time ■	1 hour
Starting elevation ■	7060 feet
High point ■	7060 feet
Elevation gain ■	None
Seasonal water availability ■	None
Best hiking time ■	April through November
Maps ■	Williams South, Davenport Hill USGS
Contact ■	Kaibab National Forest, Williams Ranger District

Driving directions: To get there from Williams, drive south on Fourth Street, which becomes County 73. After 3.9 miles, turn left on Forest Road 140. Stay on this maintained dirt road for 3 miles, and then turn left onto Forest Road 132. Go 1 mile to Dogtown Campground. The trailhead parking is near the boat ramp.

This easy, nearly level trail loops around Dogtown Reservoir, a lake set in the ponderosa pines southwest of the town of Williams. It's a pleasant hike on a summer morning, or during the fall.

To start, cross the dam and then turn left on the trail along the north side of the lake. This portion of the trail follows an old logging railroad grade. One of several reservoirs in the forest south of Williams, Dogtown Reservoir is fed by Dogtown Wash and several unnamed dry washes. You'll cross Dogtown Wash at the southwest corner of the lake. Dry most of the year, Dogtown Wash runs during snowmelt in late winter and early spring, and sometimes after a heavy summer thunderstorm. The reservoir is dependent on these sporadic flows and may become very low after several dry years. The trail continues around the south side of the lake, past the picnic area, and returns to the boat launch and trailhead.

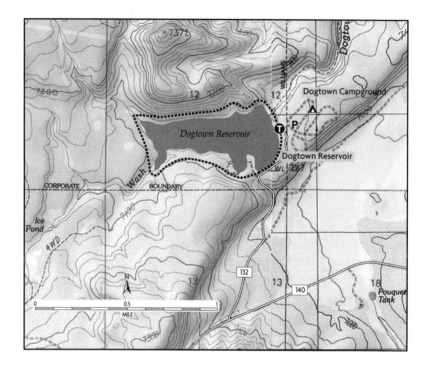

6 : SYCAMORE RIM TRAIL

Round trip ■	**10.9 miles**
Loop direction ■	Counterclockwise
Hiking time ■	4 hours
Starting elevation ■	6730 feet
High point ■	7290 feet
Elevation gain ■	1130 feet
Seasonal water availability ■	None
Best hiking time ■	May through November
Maps ■	Garland Prairie, Davenport Hill USGS
Contact ■	Kaibab National Forest, Williams Ranger District

Driving directions: To get there from Williams, go east on I-40 past the junction with Arizona 64. Exit at Garland Prairie Road, less than 2 miles east of Arizona 64 and about 4 miles from Williams. Turn right and go south on Garland Prairie Road (Forest Road 141) 8.5 miles, where

Forest Road 141 turns left. Continue straight on Forest Road 131 and continue 1.5 miles to the Dow Trailhead.

This easy and very scenic loop trail traverses ponderosa pine country on the edge of the far western Mogollon Rim, offering views into the head of Sycamore and Big Spring Canyons. Hiking counterclockwise saves the dramatic canyon rims for last.

From the Dow Trailhead, walk a few yards west to a T junction with the Sycamore Rim Trail and then turn right to start the loop. (You'll also cross the marked route of the Overland Road Historic Trail, a pioneer route from Flagstaff to Prescott.) The Sycamore Rim Trail follows along the rim of Sycamore Canyon, which is just a shallow drainage here, near the canyon's headwaters. Sycamore Canyon is about 40 miles long, flowing generally south from Garland Prairie to empty into the Verde River upstream from Clarkdale. Less than a mile from the Dow Trailhead, you'll pass the ruins of an old lumber mill,

Old logging railroad near Sycamore Rim Trail

pointed out by a Forest Service sign. Logging on the plateau was carried out by railroad until about 1960, and temporary mills such as this one were set up to saw the freshly cut logs.

When Sycamore Canyon opens out into a meadow, the trail crosses it and Forest Road 56, at a point 1.1 miles from the trailhead. A trailhead here is for both the Sycamore Rim Trail and the Overland Road Historic Trail. On the west side of the road, the Sycamore Rim Trail starts to climb the southeast slopes of KA Hill, a small cinder cone. The trail follows the summit ridge over the 7287-foot peak, then descends the west and southwest slopes through open ponderosa pine forest. As the descent levels out, the trail turns west and crosses Forest Road 13, which is 2.9 miles from Forest

Road 56. After crossing the road, the trail drops into the bed of Big Spring Canyon and follows it south past Pomeroy Tanks, a series of

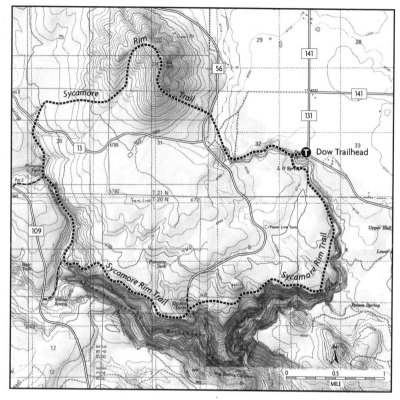

natural stone basins in the drainage that sometimes hold water. Here you again cross the Overland Road Historic Trail, which runs southwest to the Pomeroy Tanks Trailhead on Forest Road 109.

The Sycamore Rim Trail continues south along the shallow canyon, then meets another side trail 1.6 miles from Forest Road 13; this one goes to the Sycamore Falls Trailhead on Forest Road 109. A series of falls mark a sudden deepening of Big Spring Canyon, and these basalt cliffs are a popular rock climbing area. The Sycamore Rim Trail climbs to the east rim of the canyon and follows it southeast as the canyon below rapidly becomes wider and deeper. West of the point between Big Spring and Sycamore Canyons, you'll pass a fine viewpoint and then reach the short spur trail to Sycamore Vista Trailhead, 1.7 miles beyond the Sycamore Falls Trailhead side trail.

From this junction, the Sycamore Rim Trail heads east to meet the rim of Sycamore Canyon, which it follows as the canyon becomes shallower. Sycamore Canyon turns abruptly north and the trail follows suit, staying on the west rim. Not too long after the canyon makes a turn northwest, you'll pass LO Spring, which is in the bed of the canyon, and the trail crosses the now-shallow canyon and closes the loop at the short side trail to Dow Trailhead.

FLAGSTAFF

7 | PUMPKIN LOOP

Round trip	■	**10.4 miles**
Loop direction	■	Clockwise
Hiking time	■	7 hours
Starting elevation	■	7280 feet
High point	■	10,418 feet
Elevation gain	■	3380 feet
Seasonal water availability	■	None
Best hiking time	■	May through October
Maps	■	Kendrick Peak, Moritz Ridge USGS
Contact	■	Kaibab National Forest, Williams Ranger District

Driving directions: Starting from Flagstaff, drive north on US 180 for 17 miles and then turn left on Forest Road 193. After 3.2 miles, turn right on Forest Road 171. It's another 7.8 miles to the Pumpkin Trailhead on the right side of the road.

Starting from the Pumpkin Trailhead on the west side of Kendrick Peak, this loop with a short cherry stem uses the lesser-used Pumpkin Trail, the Connector Trail, the Bull Basin Trail, and the Pumpkin Trail to complete a loop over the top of 10,418-foot Kendrick Peak, one of many volcanic peaks on the Coconino Plateau. Highlights include cool pine-fir-aspen forests and 100-mile views. A few years ago, most of Kendrick Peak burned in a lightning-caused wildfire. In some areas, all the trees were burned, while in others, the fire burned on the ground and spared the treetops. You'll be hiking through this mosaic of burned and unburned forest throughout this hike. The elevation gain is somewhat more gradual when you hike clockwise, and you'll also be facing the views as you descend the upper Pumpkin Trail.

From the Pumpkin Trailhead, hike east on the Pumpkin Trail through open ponderosa pine forest. The trail climbs up a ridge and meets the Connector Trail after 1.4 miles. Turn left here and follow the Connector Trail as it contours along the base of Kendrick Peak, heading generally east. In 1.1 miles, turn right on the Bull Basin Trail, which soon starts to climb

steadily up the head of Bull Basin. After passing through a meadow and a saddle on the north ridge of Kendrick Peak, the trail heads south and climbs toward the summit through what's left of a thick fir and aspen forest. After 3 miles of hiking from the Connector Trail, the Bull Basin Trail ends at the junction with the Kendrick Trail in a meadow on the east shoulder of the mountain. A log cabin here was built as a base for the Kendrick fire lookout staff. Now the lookout is a live-in tower, and the cabin is no longer used.

Turn right to continue the loop and follow the Kendrick Trail 0.3 mile to the summit and Kendrick Lookout. Not actually a tower, the lookout cab is built on a single-story cinder-block base, but it doesn't need height to command an incredible view. (Ask permission of the lookout before climbing the stairs—the lookout is their home as well as place of work. Most lookouts welcome visitors unless they are busy.) The San Francisco Peaks, the state's highest mountains, dominate the view eastward. Old maps refer to the area as the San Francisco Mountains, and the name lingers as the official name for the San Francisco Peaks. Grand Canyon can be seen to the north and the Mogollon Rim to the south. Closer at hand, hundreds of old volcanoes, large and small, dot the Coconino Plateau. Kendrick Peak is one of the larger of the old volcanoes that make up the San Francisco Volcanic Field.

From the lookout, continue the loop by descending west on the Pumpkin Trail, which switchbacks through several open meadows with fine views to the southwest, generally following the west ridge of the mountain. As the angle of descent moderates, the forest changes from a fir and aspen mix to

Camp on Kendrick Mountain

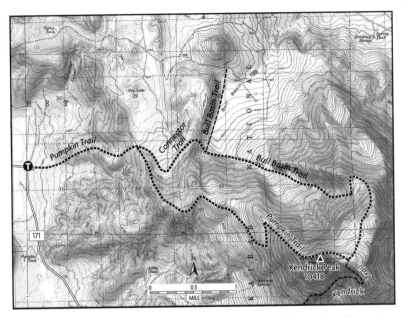

ponderosa pine, and 3.1 miles from the summit, you'll meet the Connector Trail. Stay left on the Pumpkin Trail to return to the trailhead.

8 : ABINEAU-BEAR JAW LOOP

Round trip ■	**7.1 miles**
Loop direction ■	Counterclockwise
Hiking time ■	4 to 5 hours
Starting elevation ■	8430 feet
High point ■	10,400 feet
Elevation gain ■	1980 feet
Seasonal water availability ■	None
Best hiking time ■	June through October. Early October is the best time for fall color.
Maps ■	White Horse Hills, Humphreys Peak USGS
Contact: ■	Coconino National Forest, Peaks Ranger District

Driving directions: Starting from Flagstaff, drive north 18 miles on US Highway 180 and then turn right on Hart Prairie Road, Forest Road 151.

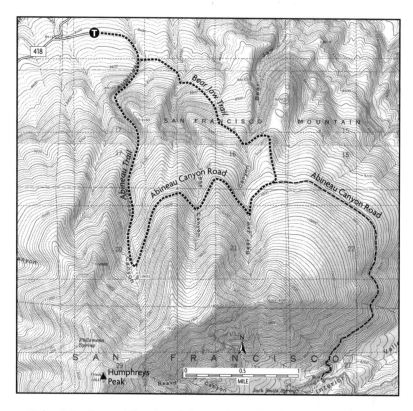

Drive 1.6 miles and then turn left onto Forest Road 418. It's another 3.1 miles to the Abineau Trailhead turnoff. Turn right and drive 0.3 mile to the trailhead.

A great hike for a hot summer day, this loop on the north side of the San Francisco Peaks uses the Abineau Canyon Trail to reach scenic views of the north side of 12,633-foot Humphreys Peak, and then follows the old Abineau Canyon Road through fine aspen stands to return via the Bear Jaw Trail and its historic aspen carvings. Hiking counterclockwise gets all of the climbing over with pretty quickly, and the Abineau Canyon opens up as you reach the avalanche runout zone.

Follow the Abineau Trail 0.4 mile through open ponderosa pine forest into Abineau Canyon, where the trail meets the Bear Jaw Trail, the return route. Start the loop by staying right on the Abineau Trail and following it

as it climbs the cool shady depths of Abineau Canyon, which is densely forested with ponderosa pine, Douglas fir, and quaking aspen. About

2.5 miles from the trailhead, the trail ends at the old Abineau Canyon Road. The views from the alpine meadows are stunning. Above you towers the 12,633-foot summit of Humphreys Peak, Arizona's highest, and its slopes are often graced with snow into August. Several large avalanche paths descend the northeast slopes of the mountain from timberline and meet where you're standing. Some of the avalanches are large enough to descend Abineau Canyon, where the masses of snow have swept away the trees, leaving only grass, low brush, and shattered wood. Conditions are favorable for avalanches most winters.

Note that cross-country hiking is prohibited above 11,400 feet (the approximate elevation of timberline) on the San Francisco Peaks in order to protect the San Francisco Peaks groundsel, a low-growing plant with yellow flowers that grows only in loose cinders above timberline. It is found nowhere else in the world.

Continue the loop by hiking along the Abineau Canyon Road to the northeast. This old road was built in the 1950s as part of the city of Flagstaff's attempt to tap springs on the San Francisco Peaks for the city's water supply. Apparently, in an effort to improve on a spring in Abineau Canyon, they destroyed it. As you walk the road, you'll find remnants of the pipeline that was built to carry the water down the mountain. The Abineau Canyon Road, like the rest of the roads that service the watershed project, is closed to public vehicle access, and it makes a pleasant and easy walk along the north side of the mountain. The road descends gradually through fine aspen groves, mixed with Douglas fir and Arizona cork bark fir. The road turns southeast and crosses Reese Canyon, swings around a ridge, and then contours into Bear Jaw Canyon. After the Abineau Road crosses Bear Jaw Canyon, it starts around the broad ridge to the east. Here, 2.3 miles from Abineau Canyon, you'll turn left on the Bear Jaw Trail.

The trail descends the gentle slope

Abineau Canyon, San Francisco Peaks

through a great stand of aspens, then turns west and crosses Bear Jaw Canyon, 0.6 mile from the Abineau Canyon Road. Watch for aspen carvings left by the Basque sheepherders who once grazed their sheep high on the mountain. Some of the carvings are elaborate, depicting cabins and other complicated subjects. The Bear Jaw Trail continues to descend steadily to the northwest, and the forest changes gradually from the closed-in fir forest to open ponderosa pine forest. It crosses lower Reese Canyon 0.8 mile from Bear Jaw Canyon, then continues to angle northwest down the slope to reach Abineau Canyon and the Abineau Trail in another 0.5 mile. Turn right on the Abineau Trail and retrace your steps to the trailhead.

9 ┊ INNER BASIN LOOP

Round trip ■	**4.3 miles**
Loop direction ■	Counterclockwise
Hiking time ■	2 to 3 hours
Starting elevation ■	8560 feet
High point ■	9410 feet
Elevation gain ■	920 feet
Seasonal water availability ■	Untreated spring water is available from a tap at the Watershed Cabins during the summer.
Best hiking time ■	June through October. The first half of October is the best time for fall color.
Maps ■	Sunset Crater West, Humphreys Peak USGS
Contact: ■	Coconino National Forest, Peaks Ranger District

Driving directions: Starting from Flagstaff, drive north on US Highway 89 about 18 miles to the Lockett Meadow/Schultz Pass Road located across the divided highway from the Sunset Crater National Monument turnoff. Go 0.5 mile and then turn right on the Lockett Meadow Road (Forest Road 522). Stay on this road 4.6 miles to the trailhead parking on the Lockett Meadow Campground Loop Road.

Another good choice for a hot day, this loop uses the Inner Basin Trail and the Waterline Road (closed to public vehicle use) to traverse a classic glacial valley high on the San Francisco Peaks.

This easy loop is best done counterclockwise, as the route is easier to find. From the trailhead, hike up the Inner Basin Trail through the Interior

Valley. Notice that the valley is wide and the canyon walls are steep—a classic U-shaped glacial valley. The floor of the Interior Valley is a layer of till, which is an unsorted mixture of pebbles, rocks, and boulders of all sizes—the load carried by the glacier and dropped when it melted. In contrast, in valleys formed by rivers the silt, sand, pebbles, rocks, and boulders are sorted by size. At one time, glaciers filled the entire Interior Valley and Inner Basin of the San Francisco Peaks, which is the southernmost glaciated mountain in the United States. The Inner Basin Trail wanders through a beautiful mixed forest of ponderosa pine, quaking aspen, Douglas fir, and limber pine. Limber pines are easily distinguished from ponderosa pines; the needles are shorter and grow in bunches of five, unlike the long three-needled bunches of the ponderosa. The limber pine are well-named—they have long, flexible branches, which help shed heavy winter snow loads. After 1.6 miles, the Inner Basin Trail reaches the Watershed Cabins, and the junction of several roads. The Interior Valley has a number of springs and drilled wells, and water is collected via pipelines

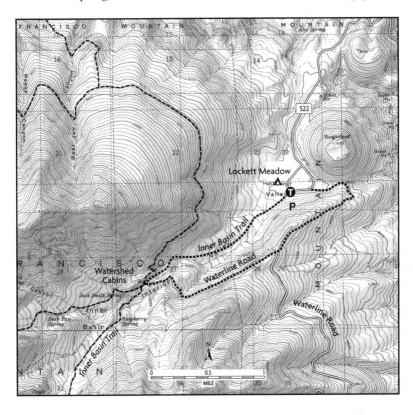

Fremont Peak from the Interior Valley, San Francisco Peaks

and brought to this point. The two smaller buildings are the junctions of the various pipelines. A single pipeline leaves via the Waterline Road, on the left, and takes water to Flagstaff. This road is the continuation of the loop.

The springs in the Interior Valley were first tapped in the 1930s, hoping that piping their water to Flagstaff would solve the city's recurring water shortages once and for all. Of course, it didn't, so the watershed project was greatly expanded in the 1950s. A series of wells were drilled throughout the Interior Valley, and several of these proved productive enough to install pumps. All of the springs shown on the topographic maps are capped and locked to protect the water supply, so the only public water source in the valley is a tap provided by the Watershed Cabins. Also, camping is not allowed. On the plus side, the watershed roads are closed to the public and most of them are pleasant hiking routes.

If you want to get a better view of the Interior Valley and its glacial features, you can do an optional side hike by staying on the Inner Basin Trail, which continues up the valley from the Watershed Cabins. This side hike is 2 miles out and back and climbs 590 feet. Just 0.1 mile above the cabins, turn left at a fork. This takes you past one of the city's wells, which is usually running during the summer. After about 0.5 mile, the valley starts to open up into a broad alpine meadow, and you are treated to a great view of the surrounding peaks. A good stopping point is the city well at the 10,000-foot level, where you'll find a small rest house.

To continue the loop, leave the Watershed Cabins on the Waterline Road and follow it as it contours along the south side of the valley through cool, shady fir-and-aspen forest. After 1.4 miles of this easy walking, the road passes through a gate and swings sharply south as it crosses the ridge coming down from Doyle Peak. Turn left here onto an old, closed road, which more or less follows the ridge to the northeast. The ridge is the boundary between dense fir forest on the north slopes to your left and open ponderosa pine forest on the drier slopes to your right. You'll have good views to the east and southeast as you descend. About 0.9 mile after leaving the Waterline Road, the old road turns north and then west, passing through a saddle at the base of Sugarloaf Mountain. Old logging roads may be confusing here—just stay left and make sure you go through the saddle headed west. In a few hundred yards more the trail comes out into the southeast corner of Lockett Meadow. Stay left on the one-way loop road and walk 0.2 mile to the day-use parking area and your vehicle.

10 ▐ KACHINA LOOP

Round trip ▪	**16.9 miles**
Loop direction ▪	Clockwise
Hiking time ▪	10 to 11 hours, or 2 days
Starting elevation ▪	9400 feet
High point ▪	12,060 feet
Elevation gain ▪	4350 feet
Seasonal water availability ▪	None
Best hiking time ▪	July through October; after heavy winters, snow may linger through July on the highest portions of this loop. Thunderstorms are common during July through mid-September afternoons; plan to be off the ridges and below timberline before noon during lightning season.
Map ▪	Humphreys Peak USGS
Contact ▪	Coconino National Forest, Peaks Ranger District

Driving directions: Starting from Flagstaff, drive north on US 180 about 7 miles and then turn right on Snow Bowl Road. Continue 6.5 miles to the ski area lodge, then turn right into the upper parking lot. The trailhead for the Kachina Trail, the return route, is at the south end of the parking lot. Walk across the main road, past the lodge, to the north end of the parking lot below the lodge to reach the Humphreys Peak Trailhead, where the loop starts.

This loop takes you across timberline country on Arizona's highest mountain and through beautiful alpine forests and meadows. It can be done as either a very long day hike or an overnight. Since there is no water along the

way, backpackers may want to do the hike in July when snowdrifts can usually be melted for water.

Follow the Humphreys Peak Trail under the ski lift and across the meadow, where the route enters dense fir-aspen forest. The trail climbs steadily up the west slopes of the mountain in a series of broad switchbacks. As you climb, the forest gradually changes to spruce and the aspen zone is left behind. Finally, the trail swings southeast into the canyon above the ski area. A series of short switchbacks lead through sparse bristlecone pine forest to the Humphrey-Agassiz Saddle at 11,800 feet and the junction with the Weatherford Trail.

Here you can do an optional side trip on the Humphreys Peak Trail to the summit of Humphreys Peak, which at 12,633 feet is Arizona's highest point. This side trip is 2 miles round trip with an elevation gain of 800 feet. Note that cross-country hiking is prohibited above 11,400 feet (the approximate elevation of timberline) on the San Francisco Peaks in order to protect the San Francisco Peaks groundsel, a low-growing plant with yellow flowers that grows only in loose cinders above timberline. It is found nowhere else in the world.

Continue the main loop on the Weatherford Trail, which climbs 0.2 mile southeast to the high point of the hike at 12,060 feet. This point overlooking the Humphrey-Agassiz Saddle was the end of the old Weatherford Road, built in the 1920s as a scenic toll road. The turnaround loop is still visible on this exposed ridge above timberline.

Follow the Weatherford Trail as it descends across the east face of Agassiz Peak in a broad switchback. Views of the glacially carved Interior

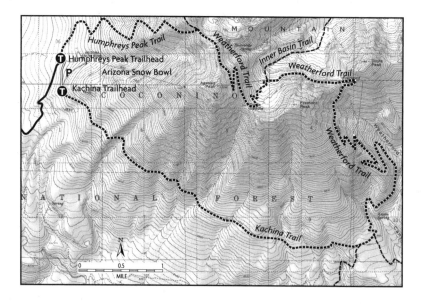

Early snowfall and fall colors, San Francisco Peaks

Valley are stunning, and the view extends more than 100 miles to the northeast, taking in a vast swath of the Painted Desert. After the switchback, the trail descends below timberline and passes through Fremont Saddle (misnamed Doyle Saddle on the USGS topographic map). A series of switchbacks lead down the gentle slope to the north, passing the junction with the Inner Basin Trail. From the junction, the trail heads east across the north face of Fremont Peak. Numerous large avalanche paths interrupt the forest, and evidence of frequent large slides is plain in the form of bent and damaged trees. The old road climbs slightly to reach Doyle Saddle (misnamed Fremont Saddle on the topo map), then descends south of the saddle. The Weatherford Trail crosses two more avalanche paths on the east face of Fremont Peak, then descends through the thick forest in a series of broad switchbacks.

After crossing a tributary of Weatherford Canyon, the trail comes out into a broad meadow and meets the Kachina Trail. Turn right and follow the Kachina Trail west across the south slopes of Fremont Peak through a delightful series of aspen groves and alpine meadows. The Kachina Trail climbs gradually and crosses Freidlein Prairie, a broad meadow on the southwest ridge of Fremont Peak, before crossing a dry gully and heading across the south and west slopes of Agassiz Peak. After wandering through a delightful forest of fir, aspen, and large boulders, the Kachina Trail ends at the Kachina Trailhead.

11 ┆ SCHULTZ PEAK

Round trip ■	**6.2 miles (11.1 miles with the optional traverse of Doyle Peak)**
Loop direction ■	Clockwise
Hiking time ■	4 hours (8 hours with the optional traverse of Doyle Peak)
Starting elevation ■	8020 feet
High point ■	10,083 feet
Elevation gain ■	2120 feet (4520 with the optional traverse of Doyle Peak)
Seasonal water availability ■	None
Best hiking time ■	May through October
Map ■	Humphreys Peak USGS
Contact ■	Coconino National Forest, Peaks Ranger District

Driving directions: To reach the trailhead from Flagstaff, drive north 3 miles on US 180 (Humphreys Street), then turn right on Schultz Pass

Road. After passing through a
gate, the road, now Forest Road
420, becomes dirt. Continue 5.3
miles from US 180 to Schultz Pass
and park in the Schultz Pass
Trailhead on the right.

Partly on trail and partly cross-
country, this loop takes you to the
summit of 10,083-foot Schultz Peak,
the lowest peak of the San Francisco
Peaks' five major peaks, via the historic Weatherford Trail and returns
via a cross-country descent with expansive views of the pine-forested
Coconino Plateau and the Mogollon
Rim. Optionally, you can loop over
a higher summit, Doyle Peak. This
loop is best hiked clockwise because
the climb is more gradual and it
simplifies routefinding on the cross-
country portion of the loop.

Cross Schultz Pass Road and
walk up the Weatherford Trail, an
old, closed road. Schultz Peak, your
destination, really the south ridge of
Doyle Peak, towers 2000 feet above
you to the northeast. Just 0.8 mile

*Aspens, Schultz Peak, San
Francisco Peaks*

from the trailhead, take note of an unmarked junction where a trail forks
right and heads into Weatherford Canyon. This trail will be the return route;
for now, stay left on the Weatherford Trail. The old road climbs gradually
northwest, coming out onto a gently sloping meadow dotted with large ponderosa pines. At the top of the meadow, 1.8 miles from the trailhead, the old
road cuts into the steep slopes at the base of Fremont Peak and heads northeast into Weatherford Canyon. Stay on the Weatherford Trail another mile,
to a point almost directly west of Schultz Peak. Here it is easy to leave the
trail and descend east to the bottom of Weatherford Canyon, which is visible
a short distance below the trail. (If it isn't, you haven't come far enough on
the Weatherford Trail. On the other hand, if you've reached the first
switchback on the trail, you've gone 0.3 mile too far.)

Climb cross-country up the forested slope directly toward the shallow
saddle between Schultz Peak and
the south ridge of Doyle Peak.
Though steep, the climb is short,
and soon you're on the beautiful

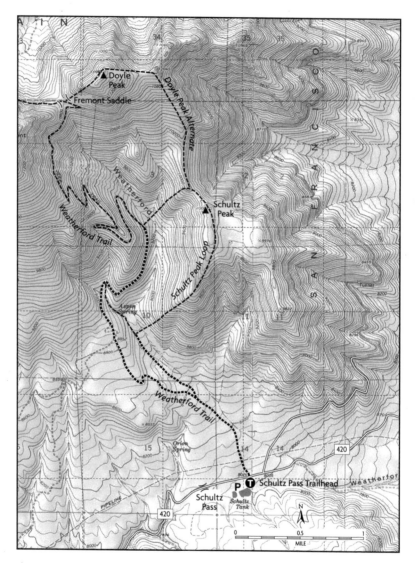

ridge. Turn right and walk south along the ridge, which is a delightful mix of alpine meadows, aspen, limber pine, and Douglas fir. The summit of Schultz Peak itself is a nondescript bump on the ridge. Beyond the high point, stay right, along the edge of the ridge, as it opens into a small plateau. As the west edge of the plateau veers southwest, it becomes a narrow ridge and starts to descend more steeply. Heading generally southwest, drop straight down the ridge until you reach the floor of

Weatherford Canyon, where you'll meet the unnamed trail descending from Aspen Spring, 1.9 miles from the point where you left the Weatherford Trail. Turn left and follow the trail down the forested canyon 0.7 mile to the end of the loop at the junction with the Weatherford Trail. Stay left and walk 0.8 mile south on the Weatherford Trail to the Schultz Pass Trailhead.

To do the optional, extended loop over Doyle Peak, stay on the Weatherford Trail all the way to Doyle Saddle (which is misnamed as Fremont Saddle on the USGS topographic map). Doyle Saddle is the pass between Doyle and Fremont Peaks and is 5.9 miles from the trailhead. You'll have great views as the old road switchbacks up through alpine meadows and avalanche paths, alternating with stretches of dense forest. Doyle Saddle, at 10,800 feet, is open and windswept and offers expansive views of the Interior Valley and the surrounding peaks.

Leave the Weatherford Trail and hike cross-country northeast directly up the slopes of Doyle Peak. A steep but short climb takes you to the gentle summit ridge, where you can walk past the ruins of Doyle's old camp (he was an early guide who built several structures on Doyle Peak and in Fremont Saddle) to the summit of Doyle Peak itself. From the top, continue the loop by walking cross-country down the east ridge 0.4 mile to Peak 11045. Here the ridge splits—turn right and descend southeast and then south to the shallow saddle between the ridge and Schultz Peak, rejoining the main loop 1 mile from Peak 11045.

12 ┆ LITTLE BEAR-HEART LOOP

Round trip ■	6.3 miles
Loop direction ■	Counterclockwise
Hiking time ■	4 to 5 hours
Starting elevation ■	7160 feet
High point ■	8790 feet
Elevation gain ■	1820 feet
Seasonal water availability ■	None
Best hiking time ■	April through October
Map ■	Flagstaff East USGS
Contact ■	Coconino National Forest, Peaks Ranger District

Driving directions: From Flagstaff, drive north on US 89. Continue 2.8 miles past the traffic light at Fort Townsend-Winona Road and turn left onto the Little Elden Road (Forest Road 556). Drive 2.1 miles to the Little Elden Horse Campground and park.

Using two of the newest trails in the Mount Elden trail system, this loop takes you up the canyon between Mount Elden and the Dry Lake Hills on the Little Bear Trail, then along the scenic ridge south of Little Elden Mountain. Return is via the Heart Trail, where you'll have scenic views of the Cinder Hills and distant Painted Desert.

Hike west on the Little Elden Trail, which runs through open ponderosa pine forest at the north base of Little Elden Mountain. After 1.3 miles, turn left

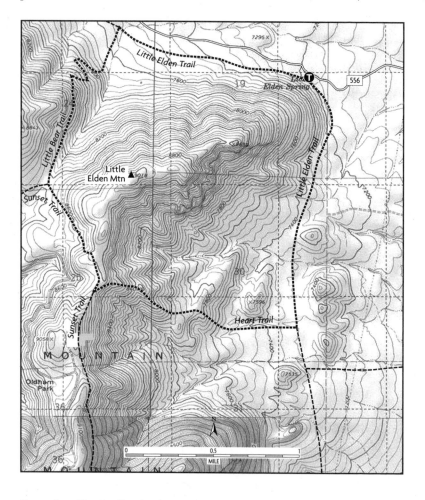

Opposite: *The Radio Fire burned the south and east sides of Mount Elden in 1977.*

on the Little Bear Trail. You'll catch glimpses of a forested canyon splitting the mountainside to the southwest of the trail. The Little Bear Trail climbs the east side of this "Little Bear Canyon" to the saddle between Little Elden Mountain and the Dry Lake Hills. At first, the Little Bear Trail climbs directly up the gentle slope at the base of the mountain, but as the slope abruptly gets steeper, the trail begins to switchback. At the unnamed saddle between Little Elden Mountain and the Dry Lake Hills, which I'll call Little Bear Saddle, turn left on the Sunset Trail. This junction is 1.2 miles from the Little Elden Trail.

From the saddle, the Sunset Trail climbs south up a gradual slope and onto the ridge south of Little Elden Mountain. After 0.7 mile, you'll reach the junction with the Heart Trail.

Turn left and follow the Heart Trail as it descends the open slopes on the east side of Little Elden Mountain. Until June 1977, this area was densely forested but on a hot, windy day a careless person started a wildfire which quickly climbed the south side of Mount Elden, then roared across the east side of the mountain. After 1.6 miles, the Heart Trail ends at the junction with the Little Elden Trail.

Turn left and follow the Little Elden Trail 1.4 miles north along the base of Little Elden Mountain to the Little Elden Horse Camp and the trailhead.

13 ┊ SUNSET-BROOKBANK LOOP

Round trip ■	5.5 miles
Loop direction ■	Clockwise
Hiking time ■	4 hours
Starting elevation ■	8070 feet
High point ■	8750 feet
Elevation gain ■	1100 feet
Seasonal water availability ■	None
Best hiking time ■	April through November
Maps ■	Sunset Crater West, Humphreys Peak USGS
Contact ■	Coconino National Forest, Peaks Ranger District

Driving directions: To reach the trailhead from Flagstaff, drive north 3 miles on US 180 (Humphreys Street), then turn right on Schultz Pass Road. After passing through a gate, the road, now Forest Road 420, becomes dirt. Continue 5.2 miles from US 180 to Schultz Pass and park at the Sunset Trailhead on the right.

This excellent loop on the Dry Lake Hills uses the Sunset Trail to ascend to

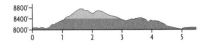

a ridge overlooking Mount Elden and the Brookbank Trail to return through alpine meadows featuring a seasonal lake.

Follow the Sunset Trail as it contours east above Schultz Tank for 0.4 mile, passing the junction with the Little Elden Trail. Stay right; the Sunset Trail drops into a drainage and follows it uphill through a fine mixed forest of ponderosa pine, Douglas fir, quaking aspen, and limber pine. The mix of forest colors is especially pleasing during October when the aspens are golden. After crossing an old road, the trail veers left out of the gully, then climbs up an open ponderosa pine slope to the crest of the Dry Lake Hills. On the far side of the ridge, the trail descends slightly to meet the Brookbank Trail, 1.4 miles from the Little Elden Trail junction.

Stay right on the Brookbank Trail, which contours southwest across the heavily forested slopes of the Dry Lake Hills, then turns northwest and passes through an unnamed saddle on the crest of the Dry Lake Hills. A gentle descent through alpine meadows and forest leads through another broad saddle, where the trail contours around the

Brookbank Trail, Dry Lake Hills

north side of a hill and into a third saddle. Just south of this saddle, the Brookbank Trail meets an unnamed trail at a junction, 2.1 miles from the Sunset Trail. Turn right on the unnamed trail and follow it 0.1 mile to a large meadow, where it becomes an old two-track road. A foot trail goes right just as you emerge into the meadow; go right here, through the trees at the edge of the meadow. This spot has some great views of the San Francisco Peaks. After a snowy winter, part of the meadow becomes a shallow, temporary lake, which is where the Dry Lake Hills got their name. About 0.3 mile from the Brookbank Trail, you'll pass a stock tank and the foot trail joins an old road. Follow this old road north down the canyon below the stock tank for 0.8 mile to the junction with the Schultz Loop Trail, one branch of which continues down the canyon and the other goes right. Follow the right branch of the Schultz Loop Trail 0.5 mile to the trailhead.

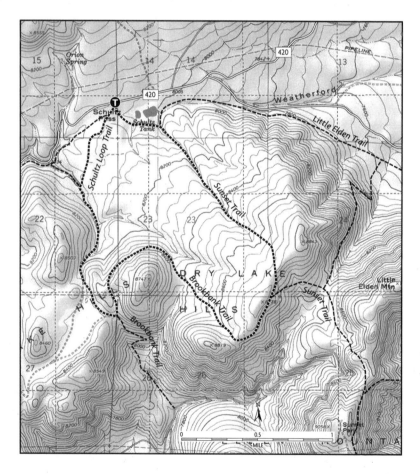

14 FATMANS LOOP

Round trip ■	2.2 miles
Loop direction ■	Clockwise
Hiking time ■	1.5 hours
Starting elevation ■	6880 feet
High point ■	7370 feet
Elevation gain ■	500 feet
Seasonal water availability ■	None
Best hiking time ■	March through November. Since the trail is on a southeast slope, it is one of the first Flagstaff area trails to dry out.
Map ■	Flagstaff East USGS
Contact ■	Coconino National Forest, Peaks Ranger District

Driving directions: From Flagstaff, drive northeast on US 89 (Route 66, the main street through town) past Flagstaff Mall and just past the Peaks Ranger Station to Elden Trailhead on the left.

Thin hikers as well as fat ones can enjoy this interesting loop through complex volcanic rock formations on the east slopes of Mount Elden.

From the trailhead, walk up the trail to the northwest 0.1 mile to the first trail junction. Fatmans Loop starts here, and the trail on the right will be the return route. Stay left as the trail continues to climb up the gentle slope through open ponderosa pine forest. Another 0.3 mile brings you to the Pipeline Trail junction, reached just as the grade starts to steepen. Stay right to remain on Fatmans Loop. The trail now veers more to the north as it climbs the base of Mount Elden through a rugged landscape of volcanic rocks.

Scenic view of Cinder Hills from Fatmans Loop

You'll reach the high point of the loop at the junction with the Elden Lookout Trail, 0.8 mile from the trailhead; stay right on Fatmans Loop. The trail contours for a short distance, then begins to descend. At a switchback, the trail turns sharply southeast and works its way down through huge boulders. About 1.5 miles from the trailhead, the Christmas Tree Trail joins from the left and Fatmans Loop continues to the south. The trail wanders south to meet the other end of the loop 2.1 miles from the trailhead. Turn left and walk 0.1 mile to return to the Elden Trailhead.

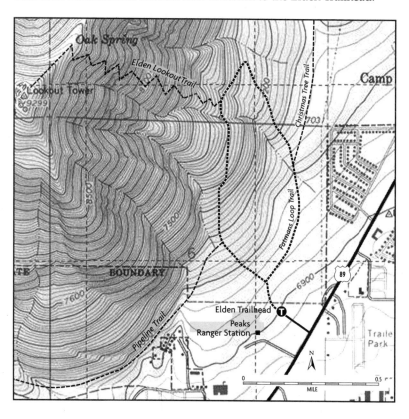

SYCAMORE CANYON

15 KELSEY-DORSEY LOOP

Round trip ■	**6.5 miles**
Loop direction ■	Counterclockwise
Hiking time ■	4 hours
Starting elevation ■	6650 feet
High point ■	7000 feet
Lowest point ■	5880 feet
Elevation gain ■	1370 feet
Seasonal water availability ■	Kelsey, Babes Hole and Dorsey Springs
Best hiking time ■	April through November; the dirt roads may not be passable until May some years
Maps ■	Sycamore Point USGS, Coconino National Forest
Contact ■	Coconino National Forest, Peaks Ranger District

Driving directions: From Flagstaff, drive west on West Route 66 and turn left on Woody Mountain Road, Forest Road 231. The road is paved at first and then turns to dirt. After 13.7 miles, turn right onto Forest Road 538. Continue 5.3 miles, then turn right onto Forest Road 538G. Drive 0.6 mile, then stay right at a junction to remain on Forest Road 538G another 1.3 miles to the Kelsey Trailhead.

This loop on and below the east rim of Sycamore Canyon uses the Kelsey Trail to start and the Dorsey Trail to finish the loop. Highlights include cool hiking through tall ponderosa pines and views of rugged Sycamore Canyon.

From the Kelsey Trailhead, follow the Kelsey Trail down a short but steep descent below the rim of Sycamore Canyon. After this descent, the trail heads generally west through mixed ponderosa pine and juniper forest, passing Kelsey Spring. Continuing to descend gradually, the trail heads south around an unnamed canyon, then turns northwest to reach Babes Hole Spring and the junction with the Dorsey Trail, 1 mile from the trailhead.

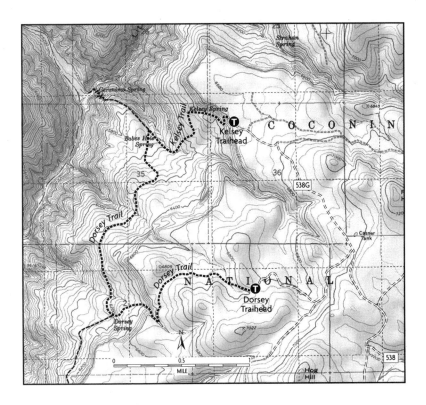

Turn left on the Dorsey Trail, which heads generally southwest and stays on a broad bench between the upper and lower rims of Sycamore Canyon. As the trail swings around minor drainages and ridges, it alternates between pine forest on the northwest-facing slopes and chaparral brush on the southwest slopes. These southwest slopes offer some great views of rugged Sycamore Canyon. You'll reach Dorsey Spring and the junction with the trail to Winter Cabin 1.6 miles from the Kelsey Trail; turn left here to stay on the Dorsey Trail. The trail climbs a ravine to the upper rim of Sycamore Canyon and ends at the Dorsey Trailhead, 1.4 miles from Dorsey Spring. Follow the two-track road 0.6 mile to a junction, then stay left. Another 0.5 mile brings you to the junction with Forest Road 538G, where you'll bear left again (parts of Forest Road 538G are not shown on the USGS topo map). Another 1.3 miles of pleasant walking through ponderosa pine forest returns you to the Kelsey Trailhead.

Opposite: *Sycamore Canyon near the end of the Kelsey Trail*

16 WINTER CABIN LOOP

Round trip ■	**14.5 miles**
Loop direction ■	Counterclockwise
Hiking time ■	9 to 10 hours or 2 days
Starting elevation ■	6650 feet
Lowest point ■	4640 feet
Elevation gain ■	3730 feet
Seasonal water availability ■	Kelsey, Babes Hole, Geronimo, Winter Cabin, and Dorsey Springs, and during early spring in Sycamore Creek
Best hiking time ■	April through November
Maps ■	Sycamore Point USGS, Coconino National Forest
Contact ■	Coconino National Forest, Peaks Ranger District

Driving directions: From Flagstaff, drive west on West Route 66 and turn left on Woody Mountain Road, Forest Road 231. The road is paved at first, then turns to dirt. After 13.7 miles, turn right onto Forest Road 538. Continue 5.3 miles, then turn right onto Forest Road 538G. Drive 0.6 mile, then stay right at a junction to remain on Forest Road 538G another 1.3 miles to the Kelsey Trailhead.

This is a longer loop, involving cross-country hiking, through upper Sycamore Canyon. This route uses the Kelsey Trail, the bed of Sycamore Canyon, and the Winter Cabin and Dorsey Trails to complete a loop from the east rim to the bottom of Sycamore Canyon and return. Highlights include ponderosa pine rim forests and the classic riparian corridor along Sycamore Canyon. Hiking counterclockwise lets you confirm that Sycamore Canyon is passable early in the loop. During the spring, runoff from snowmelt may make the canyon bed impassable.

From the Kelsey Trailhead, descend into Sycamore Canyon on the Kelsey Trail. Just below the rim, you'll pass Kelsey Spring, and after 1 mile, you'll reach Babes Hole Spring and the junction with the Dorsey Trail. The Dorsey Trail will be the return route; for now, stay right on the Kelsey Trail. The trail continues its descent northwest toward the inner gorge of Sycamore Canyon, and the descent soon becomes much steeper. The trail ends at Geronimo Spring near the mouth of Little LO Canyon, 0.6 mile from

Babes Hole Spring. Fill up your water bottles at Geronimo Spring, as the next seasonal water is at Winter Cabin Spring, 7.9 miles ahead.

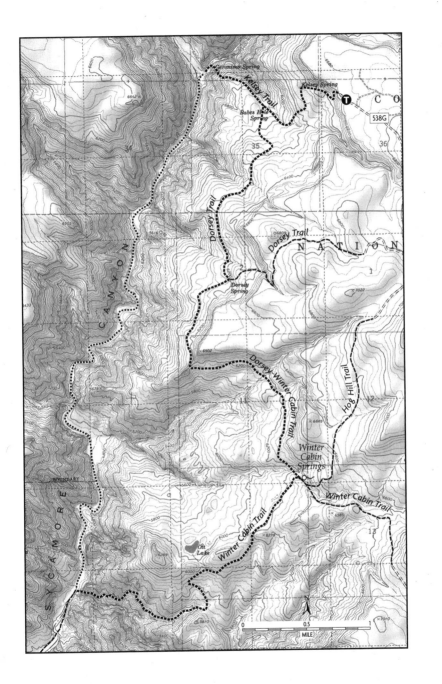

Continue the loop by turning left and hiking cross-country down Little LO Canyon 0.1 mile to Sycamore Canyon. Head south down Sycamore Canyon. Although cross-country, the walking is straightforward boulder hopping down the bed, which is easy unless the canyon is in flood from the spring runoff. Even after the creek has stopped running, deep pools may impede your progress. The ideal time to do this hike is just before the pools dry up, so that there's plenty of water to drink but not enough to stop you. About 1 mile downstream from Geronimo Spring, you'll pass through a short narrows in the buff-colored Coconino sandstone. Continue down Sycamore Canyon to the Winter Cabin Trail, which exits the canyon on the left (east) at the mouth of an unnamed side canyon, 5.1 miles downstream from Geronimo Spring. The start of Winter Cabin Trail can be hard to find—watch for a large cairn. (UTM coordinates are 12S 411770mE 3875749mN.)

Coconino sandstone narrows, Sycamore Canyon

Exit the canyon on the Winter Cabin Trail, which climbs up the brushy, open slope north of the nameless side canyon to the junction with the spur trail to Ott Lake, 1.9 miles from Sycamore Canyon. Ott Lake is a small flat just north of a saddle which occasionally holds water after a wet winter. After this junction the Winter Cabin Trail heads generally northeast and passes through a saddle into pinyon-juniper woodland. You'll reach Winter Cabin Spring and the junction with the Dorsey-Winter Cabin Trail 1 mile from the Ott Lake junction. The cabin itself is a ruin.

Turn left on the Dorsey-Winter Cabin Trail and follow it north. The trail stays below the upper rim of Sycamore Canyon on an intermediate bench and gradually turns west to swing around a point. Sheltered north slopes have ponderosa pine–Gambel oak forest, while the south-facing slopes are mostly covered with chaparral brush. You'll reach Dorsey Spring and the junction with the Dorsey Trail 2.4 miles north of Winter Cabin Spring.

Stay left on the Dorsey Trail,

which continues along the bench 1.6 miles to Babes Hole Spring and the Kelsey Trail. Turn right on the Kelsey Trail and hike 1 mile to the trailhead.

17 TAYLOR CABIN LOOP

Round trip ■	19 miles
Loop direction ■	Clockwise
Hiking time ■	11 hours or 2 days
Starting elevation ■	4770 feet
High point ■	6800 feet
Elevation gain: ■	4450 feet
Seasonal water availability ■	Seasonally in Sycamore Creek and Cedar Creek
Best hiking time ■	April through November. April, right after snowmelt, is the best time to find seasonal water in Sycamore Creek. During the summer and fall there are no water sources on this loop.
Maps ■	Sycamore Basin, Loy Butte, Sycamore Point USGS
Contact ■	Coconino National Forest, Red Rock Ranger District

Driving directions: Starting in Sedona, drive about 8 miles south on Arizona Highway 89A and turn right on Forest Road 525. Follow this road 2.2 miles, and then turn left onto Forest Road 525C, which you'll follow 8.8 miles to the Dogie Trailhead. The last mile may be impassable to low-clearance cars.

Starting from the Dogie Trailhead, this loop through the central portion of Sycamore Canyon uses the Dogie, Taylor Cabin, and Casner Mountain Trails to take you through the red rock country of Sycamore Canyon, past a historic rancher's line cabin, and over the top of Casner Mountain, where you'll find views of much of the western Mogollon Rim and the Verde Valley. You'll definitely want to do this loop clockwise to avoid the steep climb up the south slopes of Casner Mountain. A Red Rock Pass, obtainable at the Red Rock Ranger Station in Sedona, is required for parking at the trailhead.

Follow the Dogie Trail northwest over Sycamore Pass, where a broad vista of Sycamore Canyon Wilderness immediately spreads before you. The

Taylor Cabin, Sycamore Canyon

Dogie Trail continues northwest across the sloping bench west of Casner Mountain, winding through red rock formations and pinyon-juniper woodland. Gradually, the bench narrows and the trail closes in on the rim of Sycamore Canyon's inner gorge. When the inner gorge shallows and comes to an end, the Dogie Trail crosses Sycamore Creek and ends at the junction with the Taylor Cabin and Parson Trails, 4.3 miles from the trailhead.

During spring you should be able to find water in pools along Sycamore Creek near the crossing, except in dry years. Another seasonal water source is Cedar Creek, reached by hiking south on the Parsons Trail 0.5 mile. Walk upstream in Cedar Creek and look for pools. During summer and fall there are no water sources on this loop.

To continue the loop, turn right on the Taylor Cabin Trail, which stays on a low bench just west of Sycamore Creek and heads northeast. Watch for Taylor Cabin, an old rancher's line cabin, 3.1 miles from the Dogie Trail junction on the west side of the creek. Ranchers used line cabins during roundups and other range work. Continue up Sycamore Canyon on the Taylor Cabin Trail. The trail crosses the dry creek several times and is faint in places. If you lose the trail, it's easy enough to boulder hop up the bed of the creek. Watch carefully for the junction with the Winter Cabin Trail, which is the point where the Taylor Cabin Trail leaves the canyon bottom. This junction is 2.7 miles from Taylor Cabin. (The UTM coordinates are 12S 411510mE 3873780mN.)

Turn right to stay on the Taylor Cabin Trail, which goes right up the bed of the nameless side canyon south of Buck Ridge. Near the head of the canyon the trail veers south and climbs steeply through a fine stand of ponderosa pine and Douglas fir to reach a rocky ridge crest with stunning views of Sycamore Canyon. The trail follows the ridge south to a saddle and the junction with the Casner Mountain and Mooney Trails, 2.5 miles from Sycamore Creek.

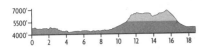

Turn right (southwest) on the Casner Mountain Trail, which is an old road built to construct a powerline along the ridge. Now closed to vehicles, the trail stays on or near the ridge crest and has fine views of much of the western Mogollon Rim and the red rock country. Follow the Casner Mountain Trail southwest over the top of its namesake mountain, a broad mesa. Right after crossing the top of Casner Mountain, which is the high point of the trip, the trail abruptly drops off the south rim of the mesa and descends rapidly in a series of short switchbacks. The trail ends at Forest Road 525C, 6.5 miles from the Taylor Cabin Trail. Turn right and walk up Forest Road 525C 0.8 mile to the Dogie Trailhead.

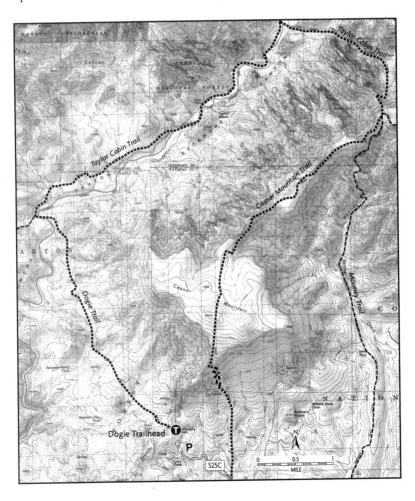

18 SYCAMORE CANYON LOOP

Round trip ■	**22.3 miles**
Loop direction ■	Counterclockwise
Hiking time ■	12 hours or 2 days
Starting elevation ■	3740 feet
High point ■	4930 feet
Elevation gain ■	3540 feet
Seasonal water availability ■	Sycamore Creek flows from Parsons Spring downstream, Summer Spring. Above Parsons Spring there may be seasonal water, especially in the spring. During summer and fall backpackers will have to carry all their water.
Best hiking time ■	April and May, October through mid-December
Maps ■	Clarkdale, Sycamore Basin USGS
Contact ■	Coconino National Forest, Red Rock Ranger District; Prescott National Forest, Verde Ranger District

Driving directions: Starting from Cottonwood on Arizona 89A, drive north toward Clarkdale and turn right on the Tuzigoot National Monument road. Cross the Verde River bridge, then turn left on County Road 139. Drive 10 miles to the Sycamore Canyon Trailhead at road's end.

This classic loop takes you up Sycamore Canyon through the gorgeous riparian lower gorge made possible by two permanent springs, Summers and Parsons Springs. Above Parsons Spring the loop continues cross-country through a rarely visited portion of the wilderness, then returns on the Sycamore Basin and Parsons Trails.

From the trailhead overlooking the confluence of Sycamore Creek and the Verde River, hike down the Parsons Trail to the north. Just 0.2 mile brings you to the creek's edge and the junction with the Packard Mesa Trail, which will be the return trail. Continue upstream on the Parsons Trail along the east bank of the creek, which is shaded by massive cottonwood trees and other riparian trees. Another 1 mile brings you to Summers Spring, one of two large springs

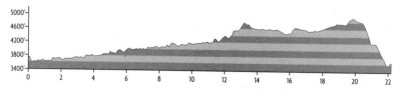

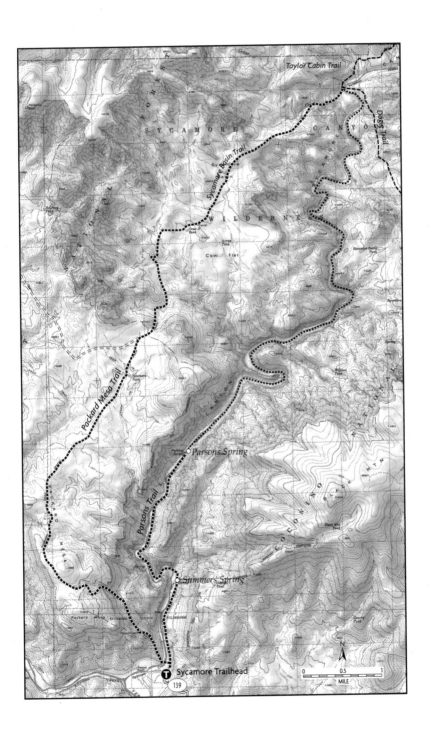

Taylor Cabin Trail

SYCAMORE CANYON

Sycamore Basin Trail

WILDERNE

Cow Flat

Packard Mesa Trail

Parsons Spring

Parsons Trail

Summers Spring

Sycamore Trailhead

139

N

0   0.5   1

MILE

that feed the year-round flow of lower Sycamore Creek. Upstream, the canyon swings through a couple of large bends, where the trail crosses the creek several times. Large pools are a delight during the warmer months. Parsons Spring is 2.4 miles from Summers Spring, and above this point Sycamore Creek is dry, except during spring runoff or summer flash floods. Continue up the dry wash cross-country. Periodic floods keep the canyon bottom mostly free of brush, so the going is relatively easy. The red layers of sandstone and other sedimentary rocks are the Supai formation, named after the Grand Canyon location where these rocks were first studied. After 8.1 miles of boulder hopping, the rims of the canyon become much lower and the inner gorge comes to an end. Watch for the Dogie Trail crossing Sycamore Creek at this point. Turn left and follow the Dogie Trail 0.1 mile to the junction with the Taylor Cabin and Sycamore Basin Trails on the west bank of Sycamore Creek. (The UTM coordinates of the junction are 12S 406130mE 3869930mN.)

Turn left on the Sycamore Basin Trail, which heads generally southwest through pinyon-juniper woodland on a bench between Sycamore Canyon's inner gorge, which you've just hiked, and the upper rim high to the west. There are plenty of possible campsites along the trail. The trail crosses Cedar

Creek 0.9 mile from the junction, and you may find seasonal water by walking up the creek. After this creek crossing, the Sycamore Basin Trail climbs over a low ridge into Sycamore Basin, which is flanked with spectacular red rock formations formed in the Schnebly Hill formation. Watch for Arizona cypress trees as you cross the drainages—these trees are found only in central and southeast Arizona. They resemble junipers except for their distinctive reddish, curly bark and straight trunks. At the south side of Sycamore Basin, the trail climbs through a low saddle and meets a two-track dirt road and the Packard Mesa Trail, 4.3 miles from Cedar Creek.

Continue on the Packard Mesa Trail, which wanders south along the crest of Packard Mesa for 5.5 miles before dropping off the east rim and meeting the Parsons Trail next to Sycamore Creek. Turn right and retrace your steps 0.2 mile to the Sycamore Trailhead.

Sycamore Creek, Sycamore Canyon Wilderness

SEDONA

19 ■ BEAR SIGN-SECRET CANYON LOOP

Round trip ■	**5.1 miles**
Loop direction ■	Counterclockwise
Hiking time ■	3 to 4 hours
Starting elevation ■	4790 feet
High point ■	4930 feet
Elevation gain ■	1170 feet
Seasonal water availability ■	None
Best hiking time ■	April though November
Map ■	Wilson Mountain USGS
Contact ■	Coconino National Forest, Red Rock Ranger District

Driving directions: Starting in Sedona, drive west on Arizona Highway 89A and turn right on Dry Creek Road. Go 2 miles and then turn right on Forest Road 152. Continue 4 miles to Dry Creek Trailhead at road's end.

This is an easy loop through the Red Rock–Secret Mountain country, using the Bear Sign Canyon Trail to ascend Bear Sign Canyon to a saddle and then following Secret Canyon Trail for the return. Attractions include rare Arizona cypress stands in the cool depths of Bear Sign Canyon and an optional side trip to the hidden recesses of Secret Canyon. A Red Rock Pass, obtainable at the Red Rock Ranger Station in Sedona, is required for parking at the trailhead.

Start off on the Dry Creek Trail, which follows the normally dry creek north through fine stands of Arizona cypress, mixed with pinyon pine and juniper trees. After 0.7 mile, turn left on the Bear Sign Canyon Trail, which heads generally northwest as it follows the twists and turns of the canyon. The high, forested cliffs of the Mogollon Rim form the backdrop, and red rock buttes, fins, and pinnacles create a dramatic foreground. After 1.4 miles, watch for an informal, unsigned trail that leaves Bear Sign Canyon on the left. (UTM coordinates are 12S 425770mE 3868280mN.)

Turn left on this trail and follow it over a low saddle. On the west side

of the saddle the trail works its way southwest though chaparral brush and small cliff bands, heading for Secret Canyon. After 0.5

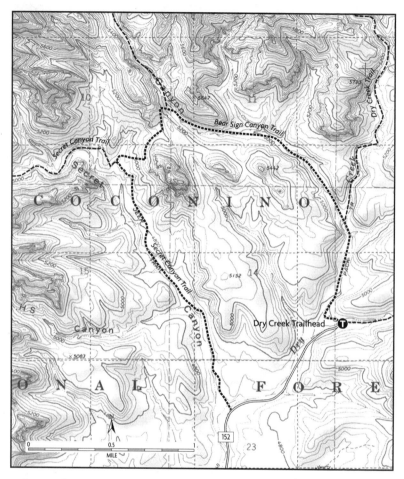

mile you'll meet the Secret Canyon Trail at a small clearing just above the bed of Secret Canyon.

Optionally, you can turn right on the Secret Canyon Trail and hike into the narrow, upper canyon. This hike is especially delightful in the fall when the Arizona maples and other deciduous trees are changing. Expect to see seasonal pools along the canyon bottom, and watch for poison ivy. The trail eventually peters out, so this side hike can be anything up to 5 miles round trip.

To continue on the main loop, turn left on the Secret Canyon Trail and follow it down the canyon to the southeast. Just 1.7 miles of easy walking on the broad trail brings you to the Dry Creek Road. Turn left and follow the road 0.8 mile to the trailhead.

Opposite: *Bear Sign Trail, Mogollon Rim*

20 EAGLES NEST–APACHE FIRE LOOP

Round trip ■	**2.4 miles**
Loop direction ■	Counterclockwise
Hiking time ■	1 hour
Starting elevation ■	3880 feet
High point ■	4090 feet
Elevation gain ■	370 feet
Seasonal water availability ■	Visitor Center
Best hiking time ■	All year
Map ■	Red Rock State Park map
Contact ■	Red Rock State Park

Driving directions: Starting from Sedona, drive west on Arizona 89A to the lower Red Rock Loop Road. Turn left, drive 2.9 miles, and then turn right into Red Rock State Park. Park at the Visitor Center.

Streamside meadow, Red Rock State Park

This is a very easy loop in Red Rock State Park along and above a beautiful section of lower Oak Creek. Numerous intersecting trails can be used to create several different loops, or to return early.

From the west side of the Visitor Center parking lot, start the loop on the Cottonwood Trail, which descends toward Oak Creek. At the creek bank, turn right on the Smoke Trail and cross the creek at Black Hawk Crossing. At the next junction, stay right on the Eagles Nest Trail, which climbs away from the creek, then turns south along a red rock ridge. Viewpoints along the ridge offer panoramic views of Oak Creek and the red rocks. After about a mile, the Eagles Nest Trail swings east, then north. Turn right on the Coyote Ridge Trail, which heads east. Next, turn right on the Apache Fire Trail. Stay right until you meet the Javalina Trail, then turn

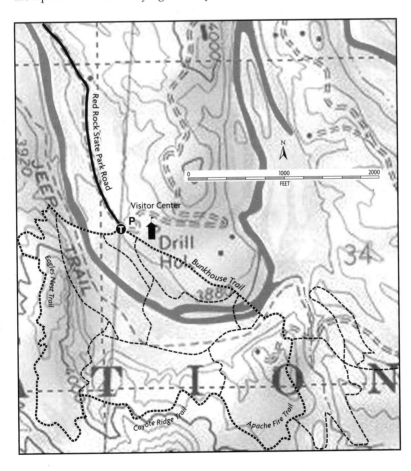

left to stay on the Apache Fire Trail. Follow the trail north to Oak Creek, and then cross the creek on the Kingfisher Bridge. Follow the Bunkhouse Trail back to the Visitor Center.

21 COURTHOUSE BUTTE

Round trip ■	**3.9 miles**
Loop direction ■	Clockwise
Hiking time ■	2 hours
Starting elevation ■	4200 feet
High point ■	4450 feet
Elevation gain ■	400 feet
Seasonal water availability ■	None
Best hiking time ■	All year
Maps ■	Sedona, Munds Mountain USGS
Contact ■	Coconino National Forest, Red Rock Ranger District

Driving directions: Starting from Sedona at the junction of Arizona 89A and Arizona 179, drive south 6 miles and then turn left into the South Bell Rock Pathway Trailhead.

Courthouse Butte

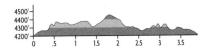

Using the Bell Rock Pathway and informal trails, this loop encompasses both Bell Rock and its towering neighbor, Courthouse Butte, and offers dramatic views of the red rock formations.

Walk north on the Bell Rock Pathway. Bell Rock is the obvious bell-shaped butte next to the highway, and Courthouse Butte is the massive butte to the east of Bell Rock. This loop passes around both buttes. The broad trail passes between Bell Rock and the highway. Turn right on an unmarked, informal trail, 0.7 mile from the trailhead. The old jeep trail works its way along the north side of Bell Rock and Courthouse Butte, then follows a drainage southeast toward the saddle northeast of Courthouse Butte. The trail descends southeast along a drainage, then meets

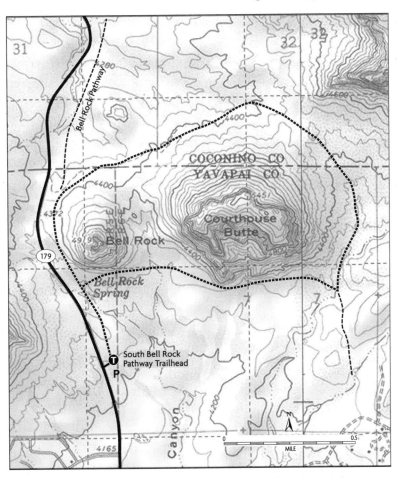

an unsigned junction 1.9 miles from the Bell Rock Pathway. Turn right on this informal trail, which heads west along the base of Courthouse Butte. As the trail nears the highway, you'll see a few cottonwoods marking Bell Rock Spring, 0.9 mile from the last junction. Turn left on the Bell Rock Pathway and walk 0.4 mile south to the trailhead.

22 HOT LOOP

Round trip ■	**16.9 miles**
Loop direction ■	Counterclockwise
Hiking time ■	10 hours
Starting elevation ■	4270 feet
High point ■	6510 feet
Elevation gain ■	2610 feet
Seasonal water availability ■	None
Best hiking time ■	April through November
Map ■	Munds Mountain USGS
Contact ■	Coconino National Forest, Red Rock Ranger District

Driving directions: Starting from Sedona at the junction of US 89A and Arizona 179, drive south on Arizona 179 for 7.3 miles to Jacks Canyon Road (traffic light). Turn left and drive 3 miles to the trailhead, which is on the right.

This loop follows the Hot Loop Trail up the length of Horse Mesa, then returns on the Jacks Canyon Trail. It offers you sweeping views of the red rock country, Oak Creek Canyon, and the Mogollon Rim country.

From the Jacks Canyon Trailhead, go south on the Hot Loop Trail, which climbs the slopes of Horse Mesa. After passing through a saddle, the trail turns east and meets the main Hot Loop Trail in a drainage, 1.2 miles from the trailhead. Turn left and finish the climb onto Horse Mesa. The trail heads northeast and north as it steadily ascends the gently sloping mesa through mixed chaparral brush and pinyon-juniper woodland. About 5.9 miles from the junction, the Hot Loop Trail makes a steep climb onto the Mogollon Rim via a series of switchbacks, then climbs gradually up the south slopes of Schnebly Hill. The trail ends at the Munds Mountain Trail, 2.9 miles farther. The optional side hike to Munds Mountain adds 1.6 miles round trip and 500 feet of elevation gain.

Turn left on the Munds Mountain Trail. This trail goes southwest 0.4 mile and drops into the saddle

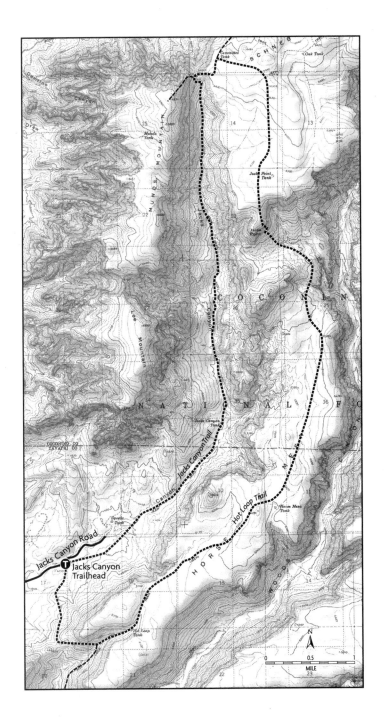

Cathedral Rock

between Schnebly Hill and Munds Mountain. The views are spectacular—you're looking across Bear Wallow Canyon into Oak Creek Canyon. The San Francisco Peaks tower in the distance to the north.

At the saddle, turn left on the Jacks Canyon Trail. An initial steep descent down the head of Jacks Canyon moderates shortly, and the trail follows the normally dry wash south below the high cliffs of Munds and Lee Mountains. It is 6.4 miles of pleasant and easy walking from the saddle to the trailhead.

PRESCOTT

23 LITTLE GRANITE MOUNTAIN LOOP

Round trip ▪	**6.1 miles**
Loop direction ▪	Clockwise
Hiking time ▪	4 hours
Starting elevation ▪	5660 feet
High point ▪	6520 feet
Elevation gain ▪	1220 feet
Seasonal water availability ▪	None
Best hiking time ▪	April through November
Maps ▪	Iron Springs, Jerome Canyon USGS
Contact ▪	Prescott National Forest, Bradshaw Ranger District

Driving directions: Starting from Prescott, drive about 4.5 miles northwest on Iron Springs Road, turn right on Granite Basin Road, and drive to the end of the road at Matate Trailhead. A fee is required for parking.

Looping around Little Granite Mountain, this trail traverses pinyon-juniper woodland interspersed with granite boulders and rock formations, and occasional ponderosa pines. You'll have great views of Granite Mountain and the world-class climbing wall, as well as an optional side hike to a viewpoint near the top of Granite Mountain. From this viewpoint you can see much of the well-named Sierra Prieta (pretty mountains).

From the trailhead, follow the Granite Mountain Trail west 0.2 mile and then turn left on the Little Granite Mountain Trail (the Granite Mountain Trail will be the return trail). The Little Granite Mountain Trail heads southwest, climbing steadily through mixed chaparral brush, juniper trees, and ponderosa pines. After 1.6 miles the trail reaches the saddle between Little Granite Mountain and Two Rock Mountain and the junction with the spur trail to Iron Springs Road. Turn right, and follow the Little Granite Mountain Trail around the south ridge of Little Granite Mountain. A gradual descent leads to gentler terrain along the west base of the mountain, as the trail heads generally north. After passing through an unnamed saddle,

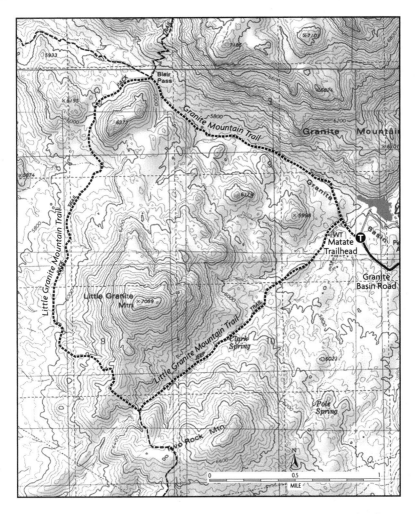

the trail ends at Blair Pass and a four-way trail junction, 2.2 miles from the spur trail junction.

From Blair Pass, you can do an optional side hike to Granite Mountain, which adds 3.6 miles out and back, and 1130 feet of elevation gain. To do this, go north on the Granite Mountain Trail, which soon starts switchbacking up the brushy slopes below Granite Mountain Wall. This imposing cliff above and east of the trail attracts rock climbers from all over the world. The trail, however, takes an easier route to the top, climbing to a saddle and then working its way through delightful granite slabs

Opposite: *Along the Little Granite Mountain Trail, Sierra Prieta*

and pines to a viewpoint on the top of the wall. From this vantage point, you can see much of the Sierra Prieta Mountains.

Continue the main loop at Blair Pass by taking the Granite Mountain Trail 1.7 miles southeast down the headwaters of Granite Wash to the junction with the Little Granite Mountain Trail. Another 0.2 mile leads back to the Matate Trailhead.

24 ┆ MINGUS RIM LOOP

Round trip ■	**3.8 miles**
Loop direction ■	Clockwise
Hiking time ■	3 hours
Starting elevation ■	7640 feet
High point ■	7830 feet
Elevation gain ■	1470 feet
Seasonal water availability ■	None
Best hiking time ■	April through November
Map ■	Hickey Mountain USGS
Contact ■	Prescott National Forest, Chino Valley Ranger District

Driving directions: Starting from the town of Jerome, drive approximately 7 miles west on Arizona 89A to the pass over Mingus Mountain. Turn left on Mingus Mountain Road (Forest Road 104) and drive 2.4 miles to the viewpoint at Mingus Mountain Campground.

This loop uses trails and a short section of dirt road to loop over the 7815-foot summit of Mingus Mountain. Highlights include sweeping views of the Verde Valley, the Verde Rim, and the Mogollon Rim.

From the viewpoint, hike 0.6 mile north on the Mingus Mountain Road, past the Forest Service work center, to the start of Trail 105. The trail heads northeast through the pine forest to the east rim of Mingus Mountain, where the entire sweep of the Verde Valley lies before you, backdropped by the Mogollon Rim. After following the rim for a short distance, the trail heads directly north and soon reaches a point on the north rim of Mingus Mountain. Here the trail drops off the west side of the point in a series of short switchbacks, then reaches a saddle and trail junction, 1.2 miles from the work center.

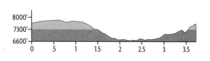

Opposite: *Verde Valley from Trail 106, Mingus Mountain*

Turn right on Trail 105A, which contours south along the east slopes of the mountain to meet Trail 106 in 0.5 mile. Turn right on Trail 106, which continues across the east side of Mingus Mountain, climbing toward the rim through chaparral brush. Views from this section are outstanding. Switchbacks lead to the east rim viewpoint and your vehicle, 1.5 miles from Trail 105A.

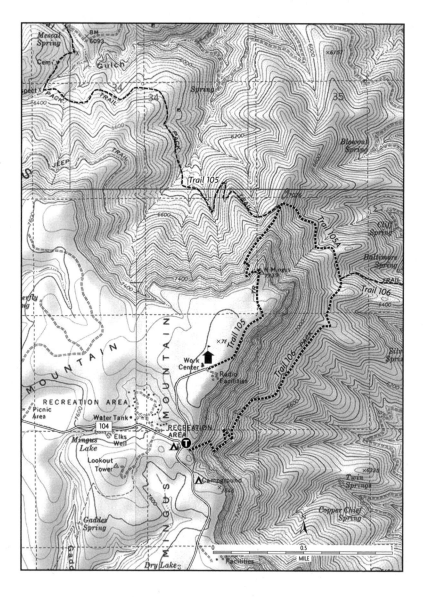

25 ┊ YAEGER CANYON LOOP

Round trip	■	**5.6 miles**
Loop direction	■	Counterclockwise
Hiking time	■	4 hours
Starting elevation	■	5990 feet
High point	■	7270 feet
Elevation gain	■	1560 feet
Seasonal water availability	■	None
Best hiking time	■	April through November
Map	■	Hickey Mountain USGS
Contact	■	Coconino National Forest, Chino Valley Ranger District

Driving directions: Starting from Prescott, drive 10 miles east on Arizona 89A, then turn right into the Little Yaeger Canyon Trailhead.

This loop ascends to the west rim of pine-forested Mingus Mountain via the Little Yaeger Canyon Trail, then returns to Yaeger Canyon and the trailhead via the Yaeger Canyon Trail.

Yaeger Canyon Loop, Mingus Mountain

Follow the Little Yaeger Canyon Trail up the pinyon-juniper slopes south of the trailhead. Switchbacks lead onto the rim of Mingus Mountain, where ponderosa pine forest takes over from the pygmy pinyon-juniper woodland. The Little Yaeger Canyon Trail ends at the Allen Spring Road, 1.8 miles from the trailhead.

Turn left and walk 0.2 mile along the road to the Yaeger Cabin Trail. Follow this trail north through pine and oak forest as it descends gradually along a tributary of Little Yaeger Canyon, then climbs the headwaters of the canyon. About 1.5 miles from the Allen Spring Road, turn left at a junction (the right branch goes to the Allen Spring Road). Just 0.1 mile farther, the Yaeger Cabin Trail arrives at a four-way trail junction. Turn left on the Yaeger Canyon Trail, which heads west to the rim of Mingus Mountain. A steep descent down chaparral-covered slopes leads to the bottom of Yaeger Canyon, where the trail follows the old highway roadbed along the east side of the creek and back to the trailhead.

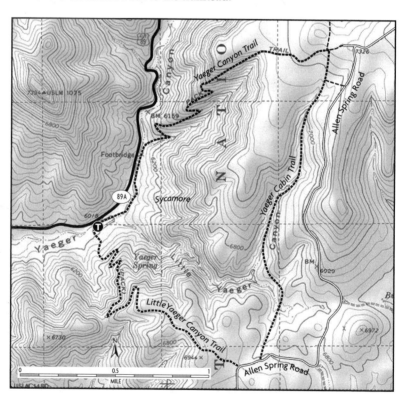

PINE MOUNTAIN AND MOGOLLON RIM

26 PINE MOUNTAIN LOOP

Round trip ■	13.4 miles
Loop direction ■	Counterclockwise
Hiking time ■	8 to 9 hours
Starting elevation ■	5100 feet
High point ■	6814 feet
Elevation gain ■	3270 feet
Seasonal water availability ■	Nelson Place, Beehouse, Bishop, Pine and Willow Springs
Best hiking time ■	April through November
Maps ■	Tule Mesa USGS, Prescott National Forest
Contact ■	Prescott National Forest, Verde Ranger District

Driving directions: Starting from Phoenix, drive about 75 miles north on I-17 to exit at the Dugas Interchange. Turn right and drive east on County Road 171, which becomes Forest Road 68 at the forest boundary. Watch for Forest Road 68G at 10.9 miles; turn right to remain on Forest Road 68. Drive 6.6 miles to the trailhead at the end of the road.

This is a great loop over the pine-forested summit of Pine Mountain using the Beehouse Canyon Trail, Verde Rim Trail, and Pine Mountain Trail. Attractions include the ruins of a historic ranch along Sycamore Creek and views of the remote Verde River canyon and Mazatzal Mountains.

Walk up Sycamore Canyon on the Pine Mountain Trail, which soon passes the site of the Nelson Place ranch, marked by an old orchard, the ruins of several buildings, and Nelson Place Spring. After 0.8 mile, turn right on the Beehouse Canyon Trail and follow this trail southwest up Beehouse Canyon. Pinyon-juniper woodland and chaparral brush dominate the south-facing slopes, while canyon bottoms and north-facing slopes tend to favor ponderosa pines.

Turn left on the Pine Flat Trail at a junction at the head of Beehouse Canyon, 0.9 mile from the Pine

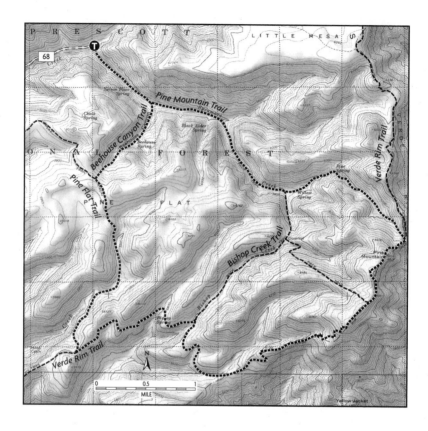

Mountain Trail. This trail heads generally south across Pine Flat, then drops into the head of the South Prong of Sycamore Creek. Just after the Pine Flat Trail turns southwest, it climbs out of the canyon on its east slopes and meets the Verde Rim Trail, 2 miles from the Beehouse Trail.

Turn left on the Verde Rim Trail to continue the loop. Staying generally on the contour, the trail crosses several drainages as it continues east past Bishop Spring and then meets the Bishop Creek Trail after 1.8 miles. Stay right on the Verde Rim Trail and follow it southeast to the Verde Rim. Now the trail turns northeast to follow the Verde Rim toward Pine Mountain. You'll pass another junction with the Bishop Creek Trail after 2.9 miles.

Stay right and continue northeast on the Verde Rim Trail, which soon passes just below the summit of Pine Mountain on the west. Walk a few yards to the top of the mountain for an incredible, panoramic view of the Wild and Scenic Verde River and Mazatzal Mountains to the east. North of Pine Mountain, the Verde Rim Trail drops down a steep ridge to a saddle, where it meets the Pine Mountain Trail.

Turn left and descend northwest into the head of Sycamore Canyon, which is graced with its namesake Arizona sycamores as well as ponderosa pines. For those who want to do the loop as an overnight, there are plenty of possible campsites along the canyon floor beyond Pine and Willow Springs. A third fork of the Bishop Creek Trail comes in from the left; continue down Sycamore Canyon on the Pine Mountain Trail. At Beehouse Canyon, you'll

Hiker on the Pine Mountain Trail

have closed the loop—return to the trailhead by staying right on the Pine Mountain Trail. The trailhead is 4.4 miles from Pine Mountain.

27 ■ WEST CLEAR CREEK LOOP

Round trip ■	**12.8 miles**
Loop direction ■	Clockwise
Hiking time ■	8 hours
Starting elevation ■	5330 feet
Lowest point ■	3600 feet
Elevation gain ■	3470 feet
Seasonal water availability ■	West Clear Creek has a permanent flow
Best hiking time ■	April through November
Maps ■	Walker Mountain, Buckhorn Mountain USGS
Contact ■	Coconino National Forest, Red Rock Ranger District

Driving directions: Starting from I-17 in the Verde Valley, exit on Arizona 260 and drive east through Camp Verde. After about 10 miles, turn left onto Forest Road 214. Continue 4.3 miles to the Blodgett Trailhead.

This loop uses the Bald Hill, West Clear Creek, and Blodgett Basin Trails to make an enjoyable loop from the rim of West Clear Creek's imposing canyon. Highlights include great views and a walk along the permanent stream.

From the Blodgett Trailhead, walk east on Forest Road 214 for 1.2 miles, around a sharp left bend. Turn right on a two-track road and walk 1.5 miles to the Bald Hill Trailhead. The Bald Hill Trail drops into a nameless tributary of West Clear Creek and descends steeply to the bottom of the canyon where it meets the West Clear Creek Trail, 1.4 miles from the trailhead.

Turn right and follow the trail along West Clear Creek. You'll have to cross the creek several times as you proceed. The stark canyon walls, covered with chaparral brush and pinyon-juniper woodland, stand in sharp contrast to the lush riparian trees and undergrowth along the creek. After 4.4 miles of this delightful walking, you'll come to the Bull Pen Trailhead.

Turn right on the Blodgett Basin Trail to start the climb out of the canyon. The trail heads generally

Opposite: *West Clear Creek, Mogollon Rim*

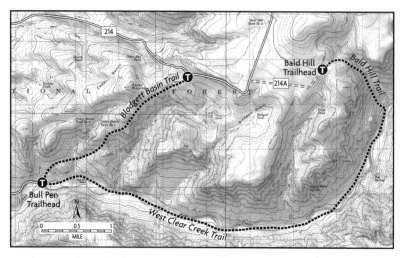

northeast as it works its way across small side canyons and minor ridges 2.8 miles to the trailhead.

28 CABIN LOOP

Round trip	■	**21.6 miles**
Loop direction	■	Counterclockwise
Hiking time	■	12 hours or 2 days
Starting elevation	■	7280 feet
High point	■	7820 feet
Elevation gain	■	2940 feet
Seasonal water availability	■	Seasonal at Barbershop, Buck, Dane, McClintock, Pinchot, Quien Sabe, Fred Haught, and General Springs, and Dane and Barbershop Canyons
Best hiking time	■	May through November
Maps	■	Dane Canyon, Blue Ridge Reservoir USGS
Contact	■	Coconino National Forest, Mogollon Rim District

Driving directions: From Flagstaff, drive south about 50 miles on County 3 and then turn right on Arizona 87. About 1 mile south of Clints Well, turn left on Forest Road 143. Continue 12 miles and then turn right on Forest Road 300. Drive 4.5 miles to General Springs Cabin and the trailhead.

This loop on the pine-, fir-, and aspen-forested ridges and through deep canyons north of the Mogollon Rim, uses the recently rediscovered historic General Crook, Houston Brothers, Barbershop, U Bar, Fred Haught, and Arizona Trails to wind past three historic cabins. Camping is plentiful on the broad ridges between canyons on this loop, as well as in some of the canyons.

General Springs Cabin at the trailhead is the first of the three historic cabins on the loop. These cabins were built as fire guard stations in the days when access to the forested backcountry was by pack animal and trail. An extensive road system has eliminated the need for local fire guards. All three cabins have been restored as historic sites.

Start the loop by walking south to Forest Road 300, then turning left on the General Crook Trail. This wagon road was built during the Apache Indian Wars late in the nineteenth century by General George Crook and connected Fort Whipple near Prescott to Fort Apache in eastern Arizona. Forest Road 300, the Rim Road, loosely follows the route of the General Crook Trail and you'll be crossing it several times. In places, the General Crook Trail is visible as a hand-built wagon road, while other stretches have disappeared. The trail is marked with white chevrons nailed to trees and occasional wooden mileage posts. Views from the rim are spectacular, looking across the rugged mountains of central Arizona. The Dude Fire burned up to the rim in 1989, and the effects of this devastating fire are obvious. Follow the trail southeast along the Mogollon Rim 3.9 miles to the junction with the Houston Brothers Trail.

Turn left and follow the Houston Brothers Trail south across the Rim

Backpacking the Houston Brothers Trail, Mogollon Rim

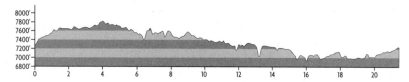

Road. The trail was built by early ranchers as a means of moving stock across the rugged Rim country. The old trails, like the modern road system, tend to follow ridges and take advantage of breaks to cross the deep canyons that drain north from the Mogollon Rim. Fresh tree blazes mark the Houston Brothers Trail—along with the occasional old blaze from the original trail. The trail heads north along Telephone Ridge, staying just west of the forest road on the ridge crest.

After 1.8 miles, turn right on the Barbershop Trail, which immediately crosses the road and then descends east past Barbershop Spring. After crossing Barbershop Canyon, the trail crosses McClintock Ridge and a road, then works its way across Dane Canyon and a couple of tributaries to

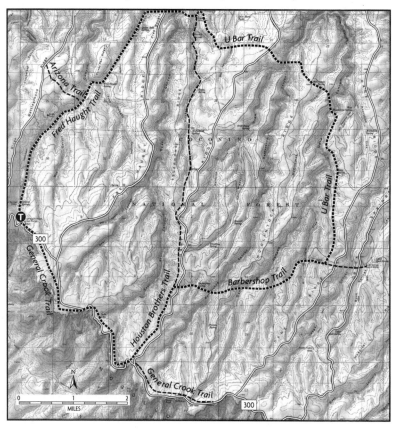

Bill McClintock Draw. The trail climbs an unnamed tributary to meet the U Bar Trail, 3.2 miles from the Houston Brothers Trail.

Here you can optionally take a short side hike (1.2 miles round trip) east to visit Buck Springs Cabin, the second historic cabin.

Continue the main loop by turning left on the U Bar Trail, which heads north into an unnamed drainage through beautiful ponderosa pine and Douglas fir forest. You'll pass Dane Spring and the ruins of a log cabin as the trail follows a bench on the east side of the deepening canyon. The U Bar Trail crosses Dane Canyon, which has a seasonal creek, then climbs west out of the canyon and then follows a road briefly, past McClintock Spring. Follow the tree blazes carefully so you don't miss the trail when it leaves the road. After crossing McClintock Ridge with its inevitable ridge-top forest road, the trail crosses Barbershop Canyon. Old trail construction is visible at both canyon crossings. The trail crosses Dick Hart Ridge, then works its way west across shallow Dick Hart Draw and turns northwest. Following roads in places, the U Bar Trail finally reaches Pinchot Cabin, 6.7 miles from the Barbershop Trail.

This restored cabin marks the junction of the Houston Brothers, U Bar, and Fred Haught Trails. Continue the loop on the Fred Haught Trail, which leaves the cabin area to the west. The trail works its way across Bear Canyon and Fred Haught Ridge into Quien Sabe Draw, where it turns south and follows the draw past Quien Sabe Spring. Near the head of the draw, the trail passes over a gentle saddle and descends into Fred Haught Canyon, then follows the canyon downstream to General Springs Canyon. Here the trail turns left up General Springs Canyon, passing the junction with the Arizona Trail 3.8 miles from Pinchot Cabin. Follow the Fred Haught Trail south another 2.6 miles to General Springs Cabin and the starting point.

29 HORTON CREEK LOOP

Round trip ■	**7.1 miles**
Loop direction ■	Counterclockwise
Hiking time ■	4 to 5 hours
Starting elevation ■	5460 feet
High point ■	6850 feet
Elevation gain ■	1600 feet
Seasonal water availability ■	Horton Creek
Best hiking time ■	April through November
Map ■	Promontory Butte USGS
Contact ■	Tonto National Forest, Payson Ranger District

Driving directions: Starting from Payson, drive about 15 miles east on Arizona 260 to Tonto Creek Road (Forest Road 289) and then turn left and drive 1 mile to Horton Trailhead, which is on the left opposite Upper Tonto Creek Campground.

Lying under the steep ramparts of the Mogollon Rim, this loop ascends the Derrick Trail to reach the Highline National Recreation Trail, which it follows to Horton Creek, using the excellent Horton Creek Trail to return to the trailhead. Highlights include views of the Mogollon Rim and the beautiful walk down Horton Creek through fine ponderosa pine glades.

Walk into the campground and look for an unsigned trail heading uphill to the east. Follow this trail, which is an old road, 0.7 mile up the ridge to the junction with the Derrick Trail. Turn left on the Derrick Trail and continue the gentle climb east through mixed ponderosa pine and juniper forest. Another 1.4 miles brings you to the junction with the Highline Trail, on the steep slopes below the Mogollon Rim.

Turn left and follow the Highline Trail north along the west side of Promontory Butte, a large peninsula projecting from the rim. Now a National Recreation Trail, the Highline Trail harks back to the pioneer days of Arizona, when trails were a means of point-to-point travel rather than recreational

Horton Creek, below the Mogollon Rim

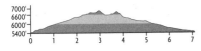

routes. Although the Highline Trail generally contours, it has an inordinate amount of short climbs and descents, a giveaway that it was laid out 'on the fly' by horsemen rather than planned and built by the Forest Service.

Two miles of the Highline Trail end with a steep descent into the pine- and fir-forested headwaters of Horton Creek. Here the trail turns right and climbs to Horton Spring. Instead of doing this, turn left and walk cross-country down Horton Creek. After just 0.4 mile of easy walking the Horton Creek Trail comes in from the right. This good trail follows the right bank of Horton Creek 2.7 miles to Upper Tonto Creek Campground and the trailhead.

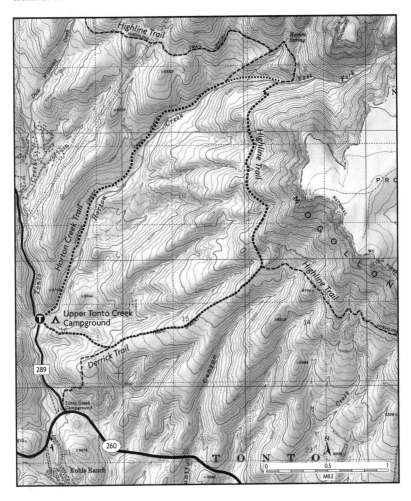

30 RIM LAKES VISTA LOOP

Round trip ■	**4.2 miles**
Loop direction ■	Clockwise
Hiking time ■	2 hours
Starting elevation ■	7550 feet
Elevation gain ■	None
Seasonal water availability ■	None
Best hiking time ■	May through November
Map ■	Woods Canyon USGS
Contact ■	Apache-Sitgreaves National Forest, Heber Ranger District

Driving directions: From Payson, drive about 30 miles east on Arizona 260. Just after the highway tops out on the Mogollon Rim, turn left on the Rim Road, Forest Road 300, then immediately turn right into the large trailhead parking area.

This easy loop with spectacular, 100-mile views from the Mogollon Rim uses the Rim Lakes Trail, Military Sinkhole Trail, and historic General Crook Trail to traverse cool ponderosa pine and quaking aspen forest.

From the trailhead, follow the Rim Lakes Vista Trail west out of the

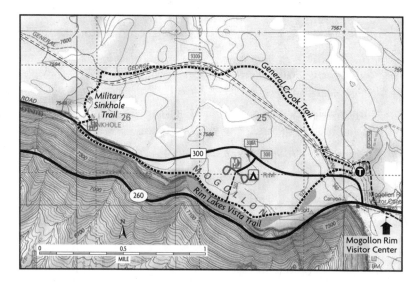

Opposite: *Chevrons nailed on trees mark the General Crook Trail.*

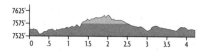

parking area. It parallels the Rim Road for a hundred yards or so, then crosses the road at a signed crossing. Now the trail heads generally southwest through the level ponderosa pine forest, eventually reaching the edge of the Mogollon Rim and turning west. Sweeping views are almost continuous, but one of the best is from a slight promontory 1.3 miles from the trailhead. At 1.9 miles, the Rim Lakes Vista Trail meets the Military Sinkhole Trail at a viewpoint next to the Rim Road.

Turn right on the Military Sinkhole Trail and cross the Rim Road. The trail wanders north across a shallow sinkhole before ending at the General Crook Trail, 0.4 mile from the rim. Turn right on the General Crook Trail. This historic wagon road is vague in places but is clearly marked with white chevrons nailed to the trees. It stays north of the Rim Road for 1.8 miles to reach the trailhead.

31 | BLUE RIDGE MOUNTAIN LOOP

Round trip ■	**7.8 miles**
Loop direction ■	Clockwise
Hiking time ■	4 to 5 hours
Starting elevation ■	7070 feet
High point ■	7610 feet
Elevation gain ■	780 feet
Seasonal water availability ■	None
Best hiking time ■	May through November
Map ■	Lakeside USGS
Contact ■	Apache-Sitgreaves National Forest, Lakeside Ranger District

Driving directions: From Pinetop-Lakeside on Arizona 260 (White Mountain Boulevard), just east of Blue Ridge High School, turn north on Moonridge, right on Mountain, left on Festival, right on Meadow, right on Pine Shadow, and continue across a cattle guard onto Forest Road 187. Drive 0.8 mile east to Trailhead 1 on the right side of the road.

This loop, part of the extensive White Mountain Trail System in the forest surrounding the towns of Show Low and Pinetop-Lakeside, takes you over the broad summit of Blue Ridge Mountain and back along Thompson and Billy Creeks.

Go north, across the road, on the Blue Ridge Mountain Trail, which turns northeast and ascends the gentle slopes of Blue Ridge Mountain through mixed pinyon-juniper and ponderosa pine. Marked by blue diamonds nailed to the trees, the trail is easy to follow as it wanders up the hill for 0.6 mile to the junction with the Ice Cave Trail. Stay right on the Blue Ridge Mountain Trail, which reaches the broad summit area in another 1.5 miles. On the east slopes of the mountain, the trail follows an old road and eventually turns southeast to reach Trailhead 2.

Cross Forest Road 187 and hike southwest through nearly flat forest on the Springs Trail. When the trail reaches Thompson Creek, it turns west and follows the creek to Billy Creek. After crossing under a powerline, the trail follows the creek a bit farther, then turns north to return to Trailhead 1, 3.8 miles from Trailhead 2.

Flowers, Blue Ridge Mountain Loop

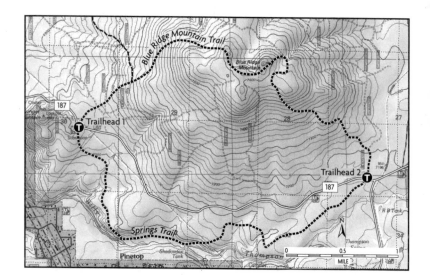

WHITE MOUNTAINS

32 MOUNT BALDY

Round trip ■	**15.6 miles**
Loop direction ■	Clockwise
Hiking time ■	10 hours or 2 days
Starting elevation ■	9260 feet
High point ■	11,350 feet
Elevation gain ■	3180 feet
Seasonal water availability ■	East Fork and West Fork Little Colorado River flow all year
Best hiking time ■	June through October
Maps ■	Mount Baldy, Big Lake North USGS
Contact ■	Apache-Sitgreaves National Forest, Springerville Ranger District

Driving directions: Starting from Springerville, drive 3 miles south on US 180 to Eagar and turn right on Arizona 260. Drive 16 miles west and then turn left on Arizona 273. Continue 8.7 miles to Sheep Crossing Trailhead.

Ascending Arizona's second highest mountain, this classic loop uses the Connector Trail and East Baldy and West Baldy Trails. Features include a cool aspen, fir, and spruce forest, alpine meadows, and the headwaters of the Little Colorado River.

From the trailhead, follow the West Baldy Trail southwest through the pine-fir forest. After about a mile the trail descends to the old trailhead near the West Fork Little Colorado River, which is a mountain creek. You'll meet the Connector Trail 1.6 miles from the trailhead.

Cross the creek on a log bridge, then follow the Connector Trail southeast up a densely forested slope and over a saddle. The trail wanders for 2.7 miles through alpine meadows and over three more saddles before descending to end at the East Baldy Trailhead.

Turn right here on the East Baldy Trail. The trail stays close to the creek for 1 mile, passing numerous possible campsites, then climbs north through interesting volcanic rock formations to reach the crest of the ridge to the north of the East Fork Little Colorado River. The next section of trail

Morning dew, White Mountains

follows the ridge through more rock formations and gives you great views of the White Mountains. After passing through a saddle, the trail moves onto north-facing slopes where the spruce-fir forest is denser and the views limited. Steady climbing brings you to the summit ridge of Mount Baldy and the start of the West Baldy Trail.

To reach the high point of the mountain, turn left and walk less than 0.2 mile up an informal trail along the crest of Mount Baldy. The high point is near the "o" in "Mount" and is likely a few feet higher than Baldy Peak to the south. Warning! Baldy Peak is on the Fort Apache Indian Reservation and is closed to all access. Indian rangers patrol the

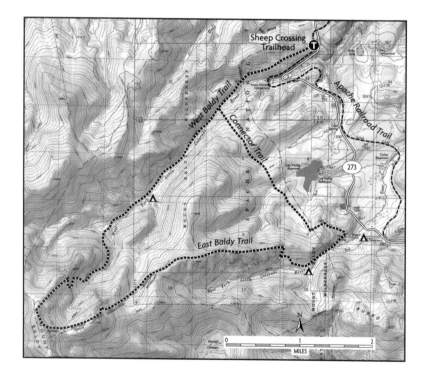

summit area from logging roads high on the west slopes. Hikers have been arrested and their gear confiscated for hiking to Baldy Peak. Content yourself with the high point of Mount Baldy and you'll be safely within the national forest. As shown on the topo map, the reservation boundary runs just west of the crest of the Mount Baldy ridge. It's marked with small survey marks on the ground.

The windblown summit ridge, though not true alpine tundra, certainly has an alpine feel because of the stunted timberline trees and the short, high-altitude plants that form the meadow.

To continue the loop, follow the West Baldy Trail down the northeast ridge of the mountain. Switchbacks lead down into the headwaters of the West Fork, and the trail follows this delightful mountain stream 4.6 miles back to the junction with the Connector Trail, closing the loop. There are plenty of campsites all along the West Fork. Follow the West Baldy Trail 1.6 miles back to Sheep Crossing Trailhead.

33 KP CREEK

Round trip ■	**21.4 miles**
Loop direction ■	Counterclockwise
Hiking time ■	13 to 14 hours or 2 days
Starting elevation ■	9080 feet
Lowest point ■	6560 feet
Elevation gain ■	4750 feet
Seasonal water availability ■	KP Creek and seasonally at Mud Spring and Grants Creek
Best hiking time ■	June through October
Maps ■	Strayhorse, Bear Mountain, Hannagan Meadow USGS, Blue Range Primitive Area USFS
Contact ■	Apache-Sitgreaves National Forest, Alpine Ranger District

Driving directions: Starting from Alpine, drive about 24 miles south on US 191 to the KP Rim Trailhead.

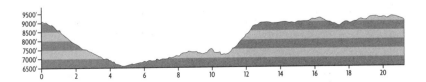

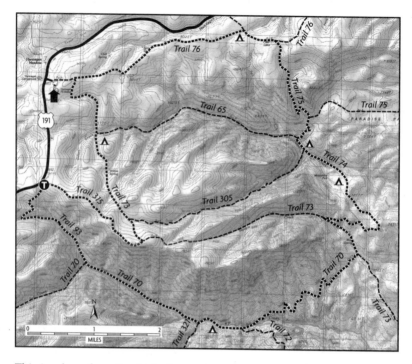

This is a loop from the high, forested eastern Mogollon Rim into the rugged Blue Range country, using the KP Creek and KP Rim Trails to loop around the headwaters of KP and Grant Creeks. Attractions include alpine meadows and a waterfall.

Portions of the KP Creek and Grants Creek headwaters burned during the Grants Creek fire in 2003 and again in 2004 in the KP Fire. Expect sections of the trails to be eroded and blocked with deadfall, especially early in the season.

From the trailhead, hike south on Trail 93, which descends into the head of KP Creek through spruce-fir forest. After 2.2 miles, you'll meet Trail 70 where you'll turn left. Look for a small but pretty waterfall on KP Creek at this trail junction, just below the confluence of the two arms of the creek. Trail 70 follows KP Creek downstream, and there are several small campsites along the creek. After 2.7 miles, Trail 72 branches right; stay left on Trail 70, which leaves KP Creek and traverses the north slopes of the canyon, heading generally northeast. Notice how pinyon-juniper woodland dominates this drier, south-facing slope. You'll meet the junction with Trail 73 after 3.1 miles.

Turn left on Trail 73, which heads northwest past Mud Spring just 0.7 mile to Steeple Creek and another trail junction. Turn sharply right onto Trail 74, which runs east around the end of a ridge before heading north

KP Falls, Blue Range

past Moonshine Park. The USGS topo shows the trail passing the west side of Moonshine Park, but it actually passes east of the park and a short spur trail leads to the park. There's plenty of camping but no water. After 2.7 miles, Trail 305 comes in from the left; stay right here and also 0.2 mile farther on, where Trail 65 also joins on the left in Grant Creek. There's water here but campsites are limited.

Follow Trail 74 north 0.4 mile out of Grant Creek to yet another junction, this time with Trail 75. Turn left and follow this trail up a steep unnamed canyon. It's 1.5 miles of steady climbing to P Bar Lake and the end of Trail 75. Turn left on Trail 76 and head west along the nearly flat ridge. There's plenty of camping, but P Bar Lake is too shallow to be a reliable water source. After 3.2 miles, you'll reach the junction with Trail 73, just east of US 191 and the Hannagan Trailhead.

Turn left and hike south on Trail 73 down into the headwaters of Grant Creek. You'll cross Grant Creek at the junction with Trail 65; there's water here as well as campsites. Continue on Trail 73 over a low saddle into another fork of Grants Creek, where you'll pass Willow Spring. After two more saddles, you'll drop into a fine alpine meadow at the west end of Trail 305. Continue southeast on Trail 73 to the junction with Trail 315. This junction is 3 miles from Trail 76. Turn right onto Trail 315 and hike 1.9 miles west along the rim of KP Creek to the KP Rim Trailhead.

34 BEAR MOUNTAIN

Round trip ■	**23.4 miles**
Loop direction ■	Clockwise
Hiking time ■	15 hours or 2 days
Starting elevation ■	5620 feet
High point ■	8460 feet
Elevation gain ■	5360 feet
Seasonal water availability ■	Lanphier Canyon, Largo Creek, and Cashier, Franz, Tige, Maple, and Dutch Oven Springs
Best hiking time ■	May through November
Maps ■	Bear Mountain, Blue USGS; Blue Range Primitive Area USFS
Contact ■	Apache-Sitgreaves National Forest, Alpine Ranger District

Driving directions: Starting from Alpine, drive east 3.2 miles on US 180 and turn right onto Forest Road 281. Continue 22 miles to the Blue Trailhead.

This hike loops through a remote section of the Blue Range over the eastern-most portion of the Mogollon Rim via the Lanphier Canyon, WS Mountain, and Largo Creek Trails, with an optional shorter loop, as well as a short side hike to the top of Bear Mountain. Attractions include views of much of the eastern Blue Range. Campsites are plentiful but water is scarce, especially during late summer and fall.

Starting from the Blue Trailhead, cross the Blue River and follow Trail 52 along the east side of Lanphier Creek. After 0.6 mile, Trail 51 comes in from

Wildfire on WS Mountain, Blue Range

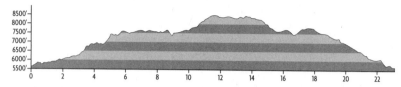

the right; this will be the return trail. For now, stay left on Trail 52 and follow it southeast as the canyon gradually ascends through ponderosa pine forest. The trail stays near the creek with its seasonal flow until you have gone 2.5 miles, then it climbs away on the left and traverses a bench high above the creek. The trail doesn't descend back to the creek until nearly to Cashier Spring, 1.7 miles after leaving the creek. Beyond the spring, the trail climbs up the south slopes above the creek, then heads 0.5 mile east to the junction with Trail 55.

Stay left here and hike another 0.2 mile to another trail junction. Turn left on Trail 55, which climbs 0.5 mile north over a saddle, past Cow Flat, to yet another junction, this time with Trail 53. Stay right on Trail 55, which heads northeast 0.7 mile along the gentle, pine-forested slopes below Bonanza Bill Point. Just as the trail reaches Bonanza Bill Flat, turn right at a junction onto Trail 23.

Trail 23 works its way southeast across the heads of several canyons and passes Tige Spring, finally reaching a saddle on the Mogollon Rim.

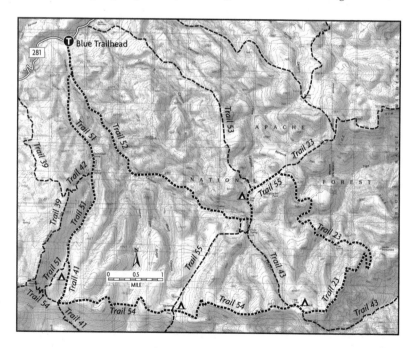

Now the trail turns abruptly west and climbs onto the east end of WS Mountain, then follows the rim southwest. This section of trail offers views of much of the eastern Blue Range country. Trail 43 joins from the right on the broad summit of WS Mountain; this junction is 6.1 miles from Trail 55. Continue west, now on Trail 43, just 0.3 mile to another junction. Stay left on Trail 54, which continues west along the Mogollon Rim.

A descent leads to Campbell Flat, where Trail 55 crosses, 2.7 miles from Trail 43. Continue straight ahead 2.5 miles on Trail 54 along the Mogollon Rim to another trail crossing, Trail 41.

If you wish to climb the loop's namesake mountain, continue west on Trail 54, which switchbacks up the east side of the mountain to its summit. A fire lookout stands on the top of Bear Mountain, overlooking much of the Blue Range area. This side trip is 2.7 miles round trip, with an elevation gain of 880 feet.

Continue the main loop by heading north on Trail 41, which descends the headwaters of Largo Creek. After 0.8 mile, Trail 41 ends when Trail 51 comes in from the right; continue north down Largo Creek on Trail 51. You'll reach Maple Spring in another 1.7 miles; Trail 42 merges from the left. Again, continue north on Trail 51, passing Dutch Oven Spring. A hike of 2.1 miles closes the loop at the junction with Trail 52 in Lanphier Canyon; turn left and hike 0.6 mile to the Blue Trailhead.

35 STRAYHORSE-SQUAW CREEK LOOP

Round trip ■	**36.6 miles**
Loop direction ■	Clockwise
Hiking time ■	3 days
Starting elevation ■	7090 feet
High point ■	8300 feet
Lowest Point ■	4660 feet
Elevation gain ■	6840 feet
Seasonal water availability ■	Bear Pen Spring, Strayhorse Spring, Strayhorse Creek, Blue River, Rousensock Creek, and Squaw Creek
Best hiking time ■	April through November
Maps ■	Rose Peak, Dutch Blue Creek USGS; Blue Range Primitive Area USFS
Contact ■	Apache-Sitgreaves National Forest, Alpine Ranger District

Driving directions: Starting from Alpine, drive south 50.3 miles on US 191 to Forest Trail 32 at Hogtrail Saddle, the trailhead. Since the exit trailhead is 2.3 miles south along the highway at the AD Bar Trail, you might want to stash your packs at Hogtrail Saddle, move your vehicle to the AD Bar Trailhead (Forest Trail 14), and then walk back to Hogtrail Saddle on the highway.

This is a rugged and demanding loop through one of the most remote portions of the Blue Range. Starting from the historic Coronado Trail highway, the loop starts on the Bear Pen Trail and traverses the east slopes of Rose Peak, offering views of much of the portion of the country traversed by this loop. A descent of rugged Strayhorse Canyon, much of which is cross-country, leads to the Blue River, which you follow through a dramatic box canyon. The return is via the little-used but good AD Bar Trail past several historic homestead sites. A short section of highway connects the two trailheads. Hike this loop clockwise to get the cross-country in Strayhorse Creek and along the Blue River out of the way first.

Starting from Hogtrail Saddle, hike north on the Bear Pen Trail, which follows an old road around the east side of Rose Peak. After 3.5 miles, the Red Mountain Trail goes right; stay left and continue 1 mile to a saddle on US 191 and the unmarked trailhead of the Strayhorse Trail. (The UTM coordinates are 12S 651500mE 3701970mN.)

The trail, unmaintained and little used, switchbacks east into the head of Strayhorse Creek, reaching an old cabin and Strayhorse Spring after 1.1 miles. There is camping and water here. Below the spring, the trail has nearly disappeared. Usually it's easier to walk down the creek bed. You won't pick up a trail again for 6.3 miles of rugged walking, when you approach the junction with the Lengthy Canyon Trail.

For a while you'll have easy walking along pine flats in the bottom of the canyon, with water in the creek and plenty of camping sites. Watch carefully for the point where the trail leaves the canyon bottom and climbs out to the north (UTM coordinates are 12S 661600mE 3706900mN) to bypass a difficult section of canyon bottom. The faint trail drops back into Strayhorse Creek and disappears for good, but the cross-country is easy along the broad gravel wash, which is usually dry. After 4.9 miles, you'll reach the Blue River.

Turn right and follow the river downstream. Although the maps show a trail along the Blue River, floods have destroyed it, and you'll be walking cross-country. You'll also have to cross the river several times. After snowmelt ends, the Blue River is just creek sized, but the broad flood plain and piled debris attest to the river's power when flooding. There are plenty of

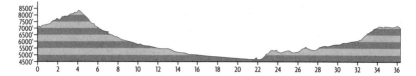

Abandoned ranch on Squaw Creek Trail, Blue Range

campsites under the cottonwood trees along the river. The river canyon is broad except at HU Bar Box, where a short narrows closes in. You'll reach the ruins of HU Bar Ranch after 5.8 miles along the Blue River.

Leave the river and hike west on the AD Bar Trail, which climbs the rocky ridge west of the ranch building. (The UTM location is 12S 668310mE 3698830mN.) Though the start is vague, once on it you'll find the trail to be distinct, though little used. The trail climbs west through open pinyon-juniper woodland, crosses Benton Creek, and reaches another old ranch site at Thomas Creek. Still heading west, the trail climbs over a saddle and drops into Rousensock Creek, where you'll find the first reliable water since leaving the Blue River. Here the trail turns abruptly southeast, follows Rousensock Creek downstream for a while, then turns southwest up a tributary. Passing over a low saddle, the trail drops into Squaw Creek. There are plenty of campsites here and west along the creek. There is a nameless spring 0.5 mile downstream of the

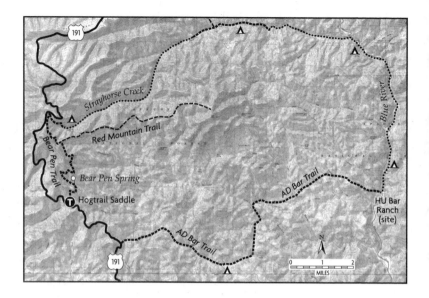

point where the trail first meets Squaw Creek, and you should find seasonal water along Squaw Creek.

The trail follows Squaw Creek to the west through pine flats, passing a third old ranch site, the AD Bar. As the trail enters the headwaters of Squaw Creek, it abruptly leaves the creek bed (at UTM 12S 657100mE 3696760mN) and climbs a steep ridge to the west. The AD Bar Trail ends at the highway, US 191, 14.1 miles from the Blue River.

MAZATZAL MOUNTAINS

36 WET BOTTOM LOOP

Round trip ■	**43 miles**
Loop direction ■	Clockwise
Hiking time ■	5 to 7 days
Starting elevation ■	2100 feet
High point ■	6140 feet
Elevation gain ■	9950 feet
Seasonal water availability ■	Bull Spring, Fuller Seep, Wet Bottom Creek, and Dutchman Grave Spring; the Verde River flows all year
Best hiking time ■	March through May, and October through November
Maps ■	Cane Springs Mountain, Verde Hot Springs, Wet Bottom Mesa, and Chalk Mountain USGS, Mazatzal Wilderness USFS
Contact ■	Tonto National Forest, Cave Creek Ranger District

Driving directions: The Sheep Bridge Trailhead may be reached two ways, both of which involve long, poorly maintained dirt roads which may be impassable during wet weather. From the Phoenix area, drive north through Carefree on Scottsdale Road. After passing through town, the pavement ends and it becomes Forest Road 24. Drive 35 miles north and then turn right on Forest Road 269. Continue 10 miles to Sheep Bridge Trailhead.

The second route leaves I-17 just south of Cordes Junction at the Bloody Basin exit. To reach the junction of Forest Roads 269 and 24, drive east 25 miles on the Bloody Basin Road, which becomes Forest Road 269 at the Tonto National Forest Boundary. A low-water crossing at the Agua

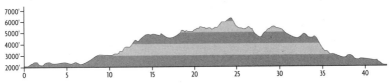

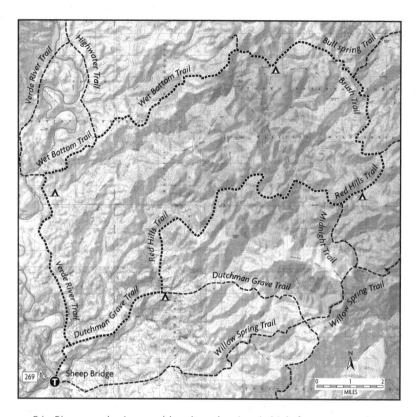

Fria River may be impassable when the river is high from snowmelt or after a storm.

One of several classic loops into the remote Mazatzal Mountains starting from Sheep Bridge on the Verde River, this loop uses the little-used Verde River Trail, Wet Bottom Mesa Trail, Red Hills Trail, and Dutchman Grave Trail to loop from Sonoran Desert to the pine-covered crest and back. The Willow Fire burned much of the Mazatzal Mountains in June 2004. Expect eroded trails and deadfall at higher elevations.

Cross the Verde River on Sheep Bridge and turn left on the Verde River Trail at the junction with the Willow Spring Trail. The Verde River Trail crosses Sycamore Creek, then climbs into the Sonoran Desert hills east of the Verde River. Just 1.2 miles from the trailhead, stay left at the junction with the Dutchman Grave Trail, which will be the return trail.

The Verde River Trail was built to move sheep between their desert winter pastures to the south and summer pastures on the Mogollon Rim far to the north. Staying east of the river, the trail heads north through classic desert, marked by widely spaced saguaro cactus and paloverde trees. After 6.2 miles, the trail crosses Wet Bottom Creek (it is easy to camp in the open desert here, and the river is easy to reach if the creek is dry) and climbs onto Wet Bottom Mesa to meet the Wet Bottom Trail.

The Verde River Trail turns west to cross the river, but the loop goes right, on the Wet Bottom Trail. Another 2.3 miles brings you to the junction with the Highwater Trail, which is an alternate trail for use when the Verde River is too high to cross. Stay right on the Wet Bottom Trail as it continues northeast along the hilly mesa. At the end of the mesa the trail starts its long climb to the Mazatzal high country, working its way northeast up the broad ridge system between Wet Bottom Creek and Canyon Creek. After 7.2 miles, the trail drops into Bull Basin, marked by an old rancher's line cabin and Bull Basin Spring. If the spring is dry, walk south down the drainage, where you should find water. Campsites are plentiful in the pinyon-juniper woodland.

The trail, now called the Bull Spring Trail, climbs northeast onto chaparral brush hills reaching the east Verde Rim at a saddle at the head of Bullfrog Canyon. Turning southeast, the trail meets the Brush Trail at a junction that is 4.1 miles from Bull Spring. Turn right on the Brush Trail, which is the route followed by the Arizona Trail, and follow it south 3.5 miles onto Knob Mountain and the high point of the loop at the junction with the Red Hills Trail (UTM 12S 450840mE 3780880mN).

The Red Hills Trail is little used and takes an indirect route through the complex country around Cypress Butte. Use care to follow the rock cairns that mark the trail, and watch for sudden changes in direction. Though the Red Hills Trail is not shown on the USGS maps, it is on the USFS wilderness map.

Turn right on the Red Hills Trail, which plunges down a steep ridge into a basin marked by a small spring, Fuller Seep, and several campsites. The trail climbs a bit as it heads west out of the basin, then turns northwest and descends to Wet Bottom Creek. Sections of the trail are faint, but it is marked with rock cairns. There's water in Wet Bottom Creek but no campsites at the crossing. The Red Hills Trail climbs steeply up a ridge through

Verde River, Mazatzal Wilderness

a beautiful grove of red-barked Arizona cypress trees, then wanders west and north along a ridge system to a saddle west of Wet Bottom Creek (UTM 12S 445020mE 3780520mN). At the saddle, the trail abruptly turns west and descends a nameless drainage. Another abrupt turn, this time south (at UTM 12S 442750mE 3779670mN) takes the trail up a side drainage to a broad saddle about a mile northwest of Cypress Butte. The Red Hills Trail now descends to the southwest onto a broad ridge, then turns northwest to reach another saddle at UTM 12S 449960 3778510mN. Turning sharply southwest, the trail descends a nameless canyon past an old mine site, then turns south to reach the Dutchman Grave Trail, 13.1 miles from the Brush Trail (UTM 12S 440100mE 3775070mN). There is water and camping at Dutchman Grave Spring, 0.4 mile east on the Dutchman Grave Trail.

To continue the loop, turn right on the Dutchman Grave Trail. This trail is not shown on the USGS topo, but it is on the USFS wilderness map. The trail heads west through the desert basin and climbs over a saddle, then turns south and descends onto HK Mesa. Staying on top of the mesa, the Dutchman Grave Trail follows it southwest to its end and the junction with the Verde River Trail, 4.3 miles from the Red Hills Trail, closing the loop. Turn left and follow the Verde River Trail 1.2 miles back to Sheep Bridge and the trailhead.

37 MIDNIGHT MESA LOOP

Round trip ■	40.8 miles
Loop direction ■	Counterclockwise
Hiking time ■	6 to 7 days
Starting elevation ■	2100 feet
High point ■	6290 feet
Elevation gain ■	10,080 feet
Seasonal water availability ■	Horse Creek, Willow Spring, Mountain Spring, Lost Spring, Fuller Seep, Wet Bottom Creek, and Dutchman Grave Spring
Best hiking time ■	March through May and October through November
Maps ■	Chalk Mountain, Table Mountain, Cypress Butte, Wet Bottom Mesa USGS; Mazatzal Wilderness USFS
Contact ■	Tonto National Forest, Cave Creek Ranger District

Driving directions: The Sheep Bridge Trailhead may be reached two ways, both of which involve long, poorly maintained dirt roads which may be impassable during wet weather. From the Phoenix area, drive north through Carefree on Scottsdale Road. After passing through town, the pavement ends and it becomes Forest Road 24. Drive 35 miles north and then turn right on Forest Road 269. Continue 10 miles to Sheep Bridge Trailhead.

The second route leaves I-17 just south of Cordes Junction at the Bloody Basin exit. To reach the junction of Forest Roads 269 and 24, drive east 25 miles on the Bloody Basin Road, which becomes Forest Road 269 at the Tonto National Forest Boundary. A low-water crossing at the Agua Fria River may be impassable when the river is high from snowmelt or after a storm.

This big Mazatzal Mountain loop starting from Sheep Bridge uses the Willow Spring Trail, Mazatzal Divide Trail, Red Hills Trail, and Dutchman Grave Trail to traverse both saguaro cactus-studded desert and ponderosa pine-covered mountains. The Willow Fire burned much of the Mazatzal Mountains in June 2004. Expect eroded trails and deadfall at higher elevations.

From the trailhead, cross Sheep Bridge and the Verde River. Just 0.3 mile from the trailhead, the Verde River Trail comes in from the left; this will be the return route. Continue east on the Willow Spring Trail, which climbs very gradually through open Sonoran Desert. As it nears the foothills, the trail climbs onto a low ridge north of Horse Creek, then suddenly turns north and climbs steeply to a saddle overlooking Willow Spring Basin. Above the saddle, the trail climbs east up a steep ridge, finally leaving the desert behind as it descends slightly into the Mountain Spring basin. A junction here, 9.9 miles from the trailhead, marks the Deadman Trail coming in from the right, and the Dutchman Grave Trail on the left. Mountain Spring itself is on a short spur trail (not on the Deadman Trail as shown on the USGS topo). Several campsites are in the area.

The loop continues east on the Willow Spring Trail, which climbs up a ridge in a series of short switchbacks, then passes through two saddles before descending to Lost Spring. Climbing north through another saddle, the trail skirts the east side of Midnight Mesa, then crosses an unnamed tributary of Wet Bottom Creek before starting another steep climb. The Willow Spring Trail finally levels out along a ridge west of Maverick Basin, then contours north to meet the Mazatzal Divide Trail, 7.3 miles from Mountain Spring. A ponderosa pine-filled basin here, at the headwaters of Wet Bottom Creek, is called The Park. There's plenty of camping but no water.

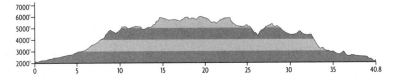

Turn left on the Mazatzal Divide Trail and follow this well-graded trail north 3.3 miles across the east end of Knob Mountain to the junction with the Red Hills Trail (UTM 125 450840mE 3780880mN).

Turn left on the Red Hills Trail, which crosses the north side of Knob Mountain (not the top as shown on the USGS topo) and passes the Brush Trail junction after 2.1 miles.

Stay left on the Red Hills Trail, which plunges down a steep ridge into the Fuller Seep basin, where there are several campsites. The trail climbs a bit as it heads west out of the basin, then turns northwest and descends to Wet Bottom Creek. Sections of the trail are faint, but it is marked with rock cairns. There's water in Wet Bottom Creek but no campsites at the crossing. The Red Hills Trail climbs steeply up a ridge through a beautiful grove of red-barked Arizona cypress trees, then wanders west and north along a ridge system to a saddle west of Wet Bottom Creek (UTM 12S 445020mE 3780520mN). At the saddle, the trail abruptly turns west and descends a nameless drainage. Another abrupt turn, this time south (at UTM 12S 442750mE 3779670mN) takes the trail up a side drainage to a broad saddle about a mile northwest of Cypress Butte. The Red Hills Trail now descends to the southwest onto a broad ridge, then turns northwest to reach another saddle at UTM 12S 449960mE 3778510mN. Turning sharply southwest, the trail descends a nameless canyon past an old mine site, then turns south to reach the Dutchman Grave Trail, 13.1 miles from the Brush Trail (UTM 12S 440100mE 3775070mN).

There is water and camping at Dutchman Grave Spring, 0.4 mile east on the Dutchman Grave Trail.

To continue the loop, turn right on the Dutchman Grave Trail. This trail is not shown on the USGS topo, but is on the USFS wilderness map. The

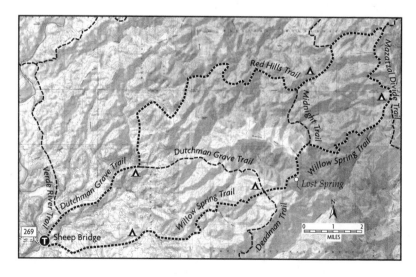

Camp, Willow Spring Trail, Mazatzal Mountains

trail heads west through the desert basin and climbs over a saddle, then turns south and descends onto HK Mesa. Staying on top of the mesa, the Dutchman Grave Trail follows it southwest to its end and the junction with the Verde River Trail, 4.3 miles from the Red Hills Trail, closing the loop. Turn left and follow the Verde River Trail 1.2 miles back to Sheep Bridge and the trailhead.

38 DEADMAN CREEK LOOP

Round trip ■	**43.1 miles**
Loop direction ■	Counterclockwise
Hiking time ■	6 to 7 days
Starting elevation ■	2100 feet
High point ■	6800 feet
Elevation gain: ■	10,040 feet
Seasonal water availability ■	Andrea Spring, Midway Spring, Club Ranch Spring, South Fork Deadman Creek, Horse Camp Seep, Hopi Spring, Lost Spring, Mountain Spring, and Horse Creek
Best hiking time ■	March through May and October through November
Maps ■	Chalk Mountain, Table Mountain, Mazatzal Peak, North Peak, Cypress Butte USGS; Mazatzal Wilderness USFS
Contact ■	Tonto National Forest, Cave Creek Ranger District

Driving directions: The Sheep Bridge Trailhead may be reached two ways, both of which involve long, poorly maintained dirt roads which may be impassable during wet weather. From the Phoenix area, drive north through Carefree on Scottsdale Road. After passing through town, the pavement ends and it becomes Forest Road 24. Drive 35 miles north and then turn right on Forest Road 269. Continue 10 miles to Sheep Bridge Trailhead.

The second route leaves I-17 just south of Cordes Junction at the Bloody Basin exit. To reach the junction of Forest Roads 269 and 24, drive east 25 miles on the Bloody Basin Road, which becomes Forest Road 269 at the Tonto National Forest Boundary. A low-water crossing at the Agua Fria River may be impassable when the river is high from snowmelt or after a storm.

Yet another long loop starting from historic Sheep Bridge, this rugged hike uses a section of easy cross-country hiking through the Sonoran Desert foot-

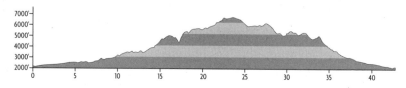

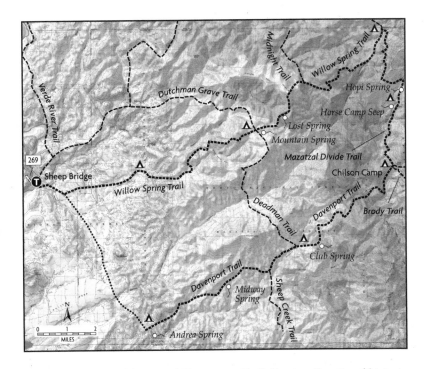

hills to reach the seldom-used Davenport Trail. Passing the site of historic Club Cabin, an old cowboy line cabin which burned in 2004, the trail climbs to another old cowboy camp on the Mazatzal Mountain crest, then follows an especially scenic portion of the Mazatzal Divide Trail also used for the route of the Arizona Trail. At The Park, a ponderosa pine-filled glade, the loop uses the rugged Willow Spring Trail for the return. This loop should be done counterclockwise so that the most difficult routefinding is at the start, on the cross-country and Davenport Trail portions. The Willow Fire burned much of the Mazatzal Mountains in June 2004. Expect eroded trails and deadfall at higher elevations.

Cross the Verde River on Sheep Bridge and head east on the Willow Spring Trail for 1.4 miles to the approximate point where the trail reaches its southernmost point (UTM 12S 436460mE 3770410mN). Leave the trail and head southeast cross-country across the open Sonoran Desert 5.5 miles to the Davenport Trail at a point just north of Andrea Spring. (This spring is shown on the USFS Mazatzal Wilderness map but not on the USGS topo. UTM coordinates where you should reach the Davenport Trail are 12S 440850mE 3763230mN.) Keep the low ridge that's west of you on your right and pass just west of Horse Mountain. After you cross Deadman Creek, the terrain will become hillier, but you should be able to reach the Davenport Trail on a sort of bench, avoiding the steeper terrain to the east.

Andrea Spring is in Davenport Wash, about 0.6 mile farther, at UTM 12S441400mE 3762550mN.

Continue the loop by turning left on the little-used Davenport Trail, which is shown on the USFS Mazatzal Wilderness map but not on the USGS topo. The trail stays north of Davenport Wash and climbs steadily to the northeast, passing through a series of low saddles. About 5.3 miles from where you picked up the Davenport Trail, the Sheep Creek Trail comes in from the right. Continue on the Davenport Trail another 1.2 miles, where the Deadman Trail goes left and the Davenport Trail crosses Davenport Wash for the first time. Stay on the Davenport Trail, which now climbs directly east 0.7 mile to the site of Club Cabin. Club Spring is up the drainage behind the cabin site. Beyond the site, the trail heads north, climbing across grassy slopes, and then turns northeast to climb over a broad pass overlooking the impressive canyon of the South Fork Deadman Creek. The trail descends steeply through pinyon-juniper woodland to cross the creek, with

Horse Camp Seep, Mazatzal Mountains

an equally steep climb up the far side. After rounding a spur ridge, the trail climbs more gradually to its end at Chilson Camp, 5.3 miles from Club Spring.

The site of another cowboy line cabin, now torn down, Chilson Camp used to have a reliable spring, but it is now dry most of the time. There are plenty of campsites, though, and a great view of Mazatzal Peak and the crest of the range.

The Davenport Trail ends at Chilson Camp, meeting the Brody Trail. To continue the loop, turn left on the Brody Trail and hike north just 0.1 mile to the Mazatzal Divide Trail. Turn left on this well-used trail and head north. After 2.1 miles, you'll pass the Sandy Saddle Trail on the right, and another 0.3 mile on the Mazatzal Divide Trail brings you to the Horse Camp Seep Trail on the left. Horse Camp Seep is 0.2 mile down this trail and offers good campsites under ponderosa pines, seasonal water, and a scenic expanse of open rock ledges. About 0.9 mile farther north on the Mazatzal Divide Trail, you'll pass the Rock Creek Trail and Hopi Spring. Continue on the Mazatzal Divide Trail, which climbs a little farther north before swinging west across the gentle, headwaters of the North Fork Deadman Creek. The trail turns north at the ridge on the west side of the basin, which as the high point of the loop offers appropriately fine views. Follow the Mazatzal Divide Trail north to The Park, which is 3.2 miles from Hopi Spring. There's plenty of camping at The Park but no water.

Turn left on the Willow Spring Trail, which heads southwest through mixed ponderosa pine and pinyon-juniper woodland, eventually coming out on the west rim of Maverick Basin. A steep descent leads across a tributary of Wet Bottom Creek, then the trail turns west and runs along a ridge to the junction with the Midnight Trail, 4.5 miles from The Park. Stay left on the Willow Spring Trail, which now turns south along the east side of Midnight Mesa. Passing Lost Spring, the trail soon starts another steep descent, reaching Mountain Spring and the junction with the Deadman and Dutchman Grave Trails after 3 miles. Continue on the Willow Spring Trail, which climbs a bit to get out of the Mountain Spring basin, then plunges down a ridge into high desert grassland, leaving the pinyon-juniper country behind. The descent continues until the trail comes out in saguaro cactus country again, near Horse Creek. Now the trail heads generally west, descending the gently sloping desert plains and reaching Sheep Bridge, which is 9.9 miles from Mountain Spring

39 ▮ BARNHARDT-ROCK CREEK LOOP

Round trip ■	**17.3 miles**
Loop direction ■	Clockwise
Hiking time ■	11 to 12 hours, or 2 days
Starting elevation ■	4170 feet
High point ■	7080 feet
Elevation gain ■	4970 feet
Seasonal water availability ■	Horse Camp Seep, Hopi Spring
Best hiking time ■	April through November
Maps ■	Mazatzal Peak, North Peak USGS; Mazatzal Wilderness USFS
Contact ■	Tonto National Forest, Payson Ranger District

Driving directions: Starting from Mesa, drive north approximately 67 miles on Arizona 87. Turn left on Barnhardt Road, Forest Road 419, and drive 5 miles to the Barnhardt Trailhead at road's end.

Starting from the easily accessed Barnhardt Trailhead on the east side of the Mazatzal Mountains, this scenic loop climbs spectacular Barnhardt

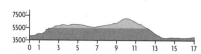

Canyon via one of the best trails in the range, passes the historic Chilson Camp, heads north on the Mazatzal Divide Trail, then returns via the Rock Creek and Half Moon Trails. Expect to see waterfalls in Barnhardt and Rock Creeks if you do this hike in early spring, just after snowmelt. At any season, you'll have panoramic views of the Mogollon Rim country.

The Willow Fire burned much of the Mazatzal Mountains in June 2004. Expect eroded trails and deadfall at higher elevations.

Walk west up the well-graded and popular Barnhardt Trail into Barnhardt Canyon. Just when you wonder how the trail is going to deal with the rugged, cliff-bound canyon, it suddenly turns south and climbs away from the canyon bottom via a series of switchbacks, then uses ledges to work its way west again. The Barnhardt Trail then rounds a ridge into the gentler terrain of Barnhardt Creek's headwaters, passing the junction with the Sandy Saddle Trail 3.5 miles from the trailhead. The Barnhardt Trail ends when it meets the Mazatzal Divide Trail, 1.8 miles farther.

Turn right on the Mazatzal Divide Trail, which heads west out of Barnhardt Saddle. Watch for water in the drainage below the trail 0.4 mile west of the saddle. The trail soon turns more to the northwest as it contours above Chilson Camp, a meadow below the trail. An old cowboy line camp, Chilson Camp has plenty of campsites and a great view of Mazatzal Peak.

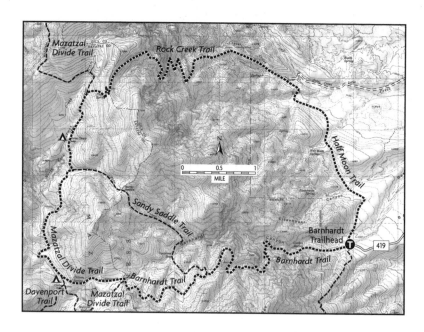

Hiking the Barnhardt Trail, Mazatzal Mountains

The spring shown on the maps is no longer reliable. The Davenport Trail, the route to the camp, meets the Mazatzal Divide Trail 1 mile from Barnhardt Saddle, after you've passed above the camp.

Continuing the loop north on the Mazatzal Divide Trail, you'll pass the west end of the Sandy Saddle Trail after 2.1 miles. After this junction, watch for the spur trail to Horse Camp Seep, which is 0.3 mile farther. Horse Camp Seep is 0.2 mile left on the spur trail and has the best campsites on the loop, as well as seasonal water. Back on the Mazatzal Divide Trail, it's 0.9 mile to the junction with the Rock Creek Trail. There's limited camping near the junction, and Hopi Spring is a few yards east.

Turn right on the Rock Creek Trail, which climbs east to the crest of the Mazatzal Mountains and the high point of the loop. The trail crosses the crest through a broad saddle, and the views of the Mazatzal Mountains are outstanding. East of the crest, the trail descends into the headwaters of Rock Creek, working its way through cliff bands to cross the creek. In the spring, this section has running water, pools, and small waterfalls. After crossing Rock Creek a second time, the trail stays north of the creek and switchbacks down a final series of cliff bands. The Rock Creek Trail then descends a steep, brushy ridge to end at the Rock Creek Trailhead, 4.8 miles from the Mazatzal Divide Trail. Turn right on the Half Moon Trail, which wanders 3.1 miles south along the base of the mountains to connect the Rock Creek Trail to the Barnhardt Trailhead.

40 Y BAR-BARNHARDT LOOP

Round trip ■	**13.8 miles**
Loop direction ■	Clockwise
Hiking time ■	9 to 10 hours or 2 days
Starting elevation ■	4170 feet
High point ■	6560 feet
Elevation gain ■	4110 feet
Seasonal water availability ■	Y Bar Tanks, Windsor Spring, Brody Seep
Best hiking time ■	April through November
Maps ■	Mazatzal Peak USGS; Mazatzal Wilderness USFS
Contact ■	Tonto National Forest, Payson Ranger District

Driving directions: Starting from Mesa, drive north approximately 67 miles on Arizona 87. Turn left on Barnhardt Road, Forest Road 419, and drive 5 miles to the Barnhardt Trailhead at road's end.

Also starting from the easily accessed Barnhardt Trailhead on the east side of the Mazatzal Mountains, this classic loop uses the Y Bar, Mazatzal

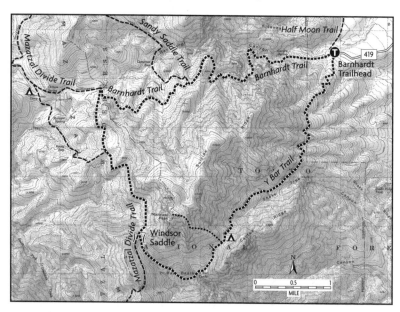

Divide, and Barnhardt Canyon Trails to loop around Mazatzal Peak, the highest summit in the range. The loop can be done in either direction. If you plan to spend the night, hike clockwise as described here so that you have a chance to pick up water at Y Bar Tanks, the most reliable water source on the loop. The Willow Fire burned much of the Mazatzal Mountains in June 2004. Expect eroded trails and deadfall at higher elevations.

From the Barnhardt Trailhead, hike southwest on the Y Bar Trail, which climbs a broad ridge through the pinyon-juniper woodland in a series of wide switchbacks. When the ridge narrows, the trail turns south and climbs along the steep slopes below Suicide Ridge, swinging around ridges and across side canyons. You'll have some great views of Tonto Basin and the Mogollon Rim to the east and northeast as you climb. As the Y Bar Trail enters Shake Tree Canyon, it climbs more steeply and passes through a few stands of ponderosa pines in this cooler, northeast-facing canyon. The climb ends at the nameless saddle between Cactus Ridge and Mazatzal Peak. There are campsites here, but the nearest water is at Y Bar Tanks.

The Y Bar Trail drops steeply into Y Bar Basin, and when it levels out, you should find a small spring in the drainage above Y Bar Tanks. If there's no water here, you can almost certainly find some at Y Bar Tanks themselves, which are 100 yards or so down the drainage.

After passing the spring, the Y Bar Trail turns northwest and climbs to Windsor Saddle, where it meets the Mazatzal Divide Trail, 5.6 miles from the trailhead. Windsor Spring, about 100 yards south of the saddle, has water only during wet periods. Camping is very limited on Windsor Saddle, but there are plenty of campsites in a broad, nameless saddle 0.8 mile south on the Mazatzal Divide Trail.

Backpacking the Mazatzal Divide Trail, Mazatzal Mountains

Continue the loop by turning right on the Mazatzal Divide Trail. This well-built trail, part of the Utah to Mexico route of the Arizona Trail, contours below the cliff-bound west face of Mazatzal Peak, crossing the headwaters of South Fork Deadman Creek. After 1.6 miles, the Brody Trail descends to the left. Brody Seep is 0.5 mile down this trail, but it's a marginal spring.

The Mazatzal Divide Trail now contours north 1.7 miles through alternating ponderosa pine and chaparral brush and meets the Barnhardt Trail at Barnhardt Saddle. Another possible water source is the drainage just south of the Mazatzal Divide Trail, 0.4 mile to the west.

Turn right on the Barnhardt Trail to continue the loop. The trail descends gradually into the broad basin at the head of Barnhardt Canyon, passing the Sandy Saddle Trail after 1.8 miles. Stay right on the Barnhardt Trail, which soon swings around the end of a ridge right above the upper end of Barnhardt Canyon's deep, narrow gorge. The trail works its way along ledges south of the gorge, finally descending nearly to the canyon bottom via a series of switchbacks. A gentle descent along the slopes above the canyon bottom leads back to the Barnhardt Trailhead, 3.5 miles from the Sandy Saddle Trail junction.

41 ░ GOLD RIDGE LOOP

Round trip ■	**15.8 miles**
Loop direction ■	Counterclockwise
Hiking time ■	9 to 10 hours or 2 days
Starting elevation ■	3320 feet
High point ■	6130 feet
Elevation gain ■	3810 feet
Seasonal water availability ■	Deer Creek flows all year; Pigeon Spring is seasonal
Best hiking time ■	April through November
Maps ■	Gisela, Mazatzal Peak USGS; Mazatzal Wilderness USFS
Contact ■	Tonto National Forest, Payson Ranger District

Driving directions: Starting from Payson, drive south on Arizona 87 to the junction with Arizona 188. The Deer Creek Trailhead is on the right (west) side of the highway, just south of the junction.

This loop starts from the only Mazatzal trailhead accessible from a paved road and follows a trail up Deer Creek Canyon and down scenic Gold Ridge,

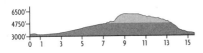

where you'll have 50-mile views of the Mogollon Rim country and the Tonto Basin. Hiking counterclockwise presents a lot of views as you descend Gold Ridge. The Deer Creek area burned in June 2004. Expect eroded trails and deadfall at higher elevations.

Hike northwest on the Deer Creek Trail, which climbs to the crest of a broad desert ridge in 0.2 mile. The Gold Ridge Trail comes in from the left; this will be the return route. Another 0.2 mile on the Deer Creek Trail brings you to the South Fork Trail junction; stay right on the Deer Creek Trail, which continues northwest to Deer Creek. Now the trail turns west and follows Deer Creek toward the mountains. Lower Deer Creek flows most of the time, but may be dry during dry years. As you continue up the canyon, stands of riparian trees such as Arizona sycamore prove that water is never far below the surface. As the canyon walls become steeper, Bars Canyon comes in from the northwest, and the trail and Deer Creek turn southwest. As you ascend the canyon, note the contrast between the dryer southwest-facing slopes, which are covered with a mixture of dense chaparral brush, and the northeast-facing slopes, which are covered with pinyon-juniper woodland, and higher in the canyon with ponderosa pine and Douglas fir. Where the USGS topo shows Windsor Camp, 6.9 miles from the South Fork Trail, you'll enter a meadow with possible campsites and also meet the junction with the Davey Gowan Trail.

Turn left on the Davey Gowan Trail, which climbs east to the ridge above Deer Creek Canyon, then turns south and climbs the ridge to the Mount Peeley Road (Forest Road 201), 1.8 miles from the Deer Creek Trail.

Turn left and walk east on the Mount Peeley Road 0.7 mile to the south

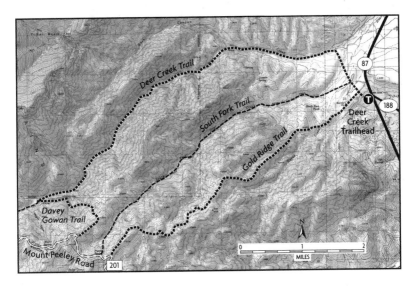

Windmill, Deer Creek, Mazatzal Mountains

end of the South Fork Trail. If you need water, Pigeon Spring is 0.1 mile down this trail. Continue east on the road 0.2 mile, then turn left on the Gold Ridge Road, which descends a ridge northeast just when the Mount Peeley Road turns sharply south. A few yards down the ridge, the road ends at a trailhead; continue on the Gold Ridge Trail. At first, the trail passes through ponderosa pine stands, but it soon comes out onto brushy slopes with ever-expanding views. The trail passes through several saddles as it works its way down the ridge, before making a final steep descent on the ridge crest. As the trail returns to the desert country of the Tonto Basin, the descent moderates. The Gold Ridge Trail ends at the Deer Creek Trail, 5.6 miles from the Mount Peeley Road. Turn right and walk 0.2 mile southeast on the Deer Creek Trail to return to the trailhead.

PHOENIX

42 GO JOHN TRAIL

Round trip ▪	**4.3 miles**
Loop direction ▪	Clockwise
Hiking time ▪	2 to 3 hours
Starting elevation ▪	2130 feet
High point ▪	2560 feet
Elevation gain ▪	780 feet
Seasonal water availability ▪	None
Best hiking time ▪	October through April
Maps ▪	Cave Creek USGS, Cave Creek Recreation Area map
Contact ▪	Cave Creek Regional Park

Driving directions: Starting from Phoenix, drive north on I-17, exit at Carefree Highway, and turn right (east). Drive to 32nd Street, turn left, and drive north to the park entrance. Continue through the park to the Go John Trailhead in the picnic area.

Abandoned mines and prospect holes are common in Arizona and are not always marked.

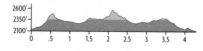

The Go John Trail loops through beautiful Sonoran Desert in Cave Creek Regional Park, near Carefree. This easy loop presents sweeping views of New River Mesa, the East Cedar Mountains, the Bradshaw Mountains, and the Mazatzal Mountains.

From the trailhead, hike north on the Go John Trail (the trail returns from the east). After an easy walk up a small desert valley, the trail climbs a short but steep section to reach a saddle. From here, the desert opens out before you, with views of the wild country around the foot of New River Mesa. Follow the trail north to the junction with the Overton Trail, which joins from the left 0.9 mile from the trailhead.

Stay right to continue the loop. Beyond the Overton Trail, several unnamed trails leave the Go John Trail to the left; stay right at every junction. About 0.3 mile farther, the trail turns east and cuts across the hillside. This area offers some of the best views of the loop. The Bradshaw and East Cedar Mountains dominate the skyline to the northwest and north. Next, the

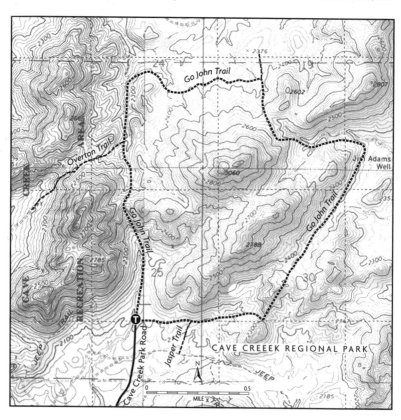

trail turns south and climbs over a saddle. Here you can see a large portion of the Mazatzal Mountains, including the summits made famous by Arizona's license plate, Four Peaks. Below the saddle, the trail drops into a ravine and follows it east before turning southwest up a tributary. A steady but gradual climb brings you to another saddle, where the trail turns west toward the trailhead. The Jasper Trail comes in from the left; stay right to return to the trailhead.

43 PASS MOUNTAIN TRAIL

Round trip ■	**6.3 miles**
Loop direction ■	Clockwise
Hiking time ■	3 to 4 hours
Starting elevation ■	2030 feet
High point ■	2640 feet
Elevation gain ■	1030 feet
Seasonal water availability ■	None
Best hiking time ■	October through April
Maps ■	Apache Junction USGS, Usery Mountain Regional Park map
Contact ■	Usery Mountain Regional Park

Driving directions: Starting on US 60 (Superstition Freeway) in Mesa, exit north on Ellsworth Road, and drive north 7.5 miles to the park entrance. Turn right and drive to the Wind Cave Trailhead.

Starting in popular Usery Mountain Park near east Mesa, this easy loop on a well-graded trail swings around Pass Mountain though fine Sonoran Desert and offers views of Four Peaks, and the Goldfield and Superstition Mountains. Once on the northeast side of Pass Mountain, it's easy to forget that one of the country's largest cities lies just over the ridge.

Walk a few feet up the Wind Cave Trail to the point where the Pass Mountain Trail crosses. Turn left on the Pass Mountain Trail to start the loop. The trail heads north, crossing numerous dry washes and their intervening ridges. After just over a mile of this, the trail turns east and climbs gradually around the north side of Pass Mountain. The trail is in the Tonto National Forest now, and you can look northeast across a vast sweep of open desert, culminating in the rugged crest of the distant Mazatzal Mountains. Turning south, the Pass Mountain Trail climbs gradually toward the unnamed pass east of Pass Mountain. On the far side of the pass, a short, steep descent leads to a switchback, where

the trail resumes its normal, moderate grade. After swinging around the head of the canyon below the pass, the Pass Mountain Trail turns south again, staying along the base of Pass Mountain. Just as the trail turns west along the mountain's base, an unnamed trail goes south toward the nearby subdivision; stay right. The trail follows the boundary between Usery Mountain Regional Park and the Tonto National Forest and climbs over a saddle between the Cat Peaks and Pass Mountain. The Cat Peaks Trail forks left here; stay right on the Pass Mountain Trail. When the trail turns north, a short spur trail goes to the park horse staging area; again, stay right. It's now just 0.5 mile north to the Wind Cave Trail, where you'll turn left and walk a few feet to the trailhead.

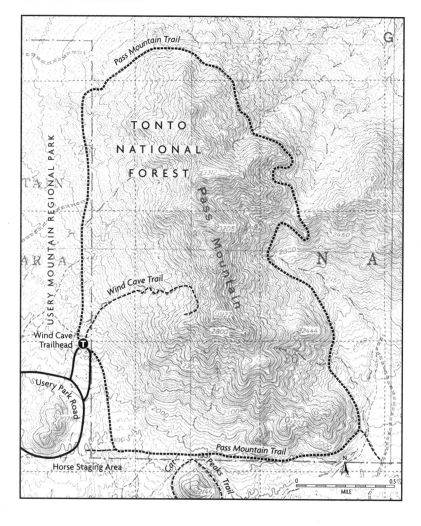

Superstition Mountain and Four Peaks from the Pass Mountain Trail, Usery Mountain Park

SUPERSTITION MOUNTAINS

44 : GARDEN VALLEY

Round trip ■	**8.6 miles**
Loop direction ■	Counterclockwise
Hiking time ■	5 hours
Starting elevation ■	2290 feet
High point ■	2790 feet
Elevation gain ■	1190 feet
Seasonal water availability ■	None
Best hiking time ■	October through April
Maps ■	Goldfield USGS, Superstition Wilderness USFS
Contact ■	Tonto National Forest, Mesa Ranger District

Driving directions: From Apache Junction, drive east on Arizona 88 about 6 miles to First Water Road. Turn right and drive 2.6 miles to First Water Trailhead.

An easy loop, for the Superstition Mountains, this hike starts from the most accessible Superstition trailhead, First Water, and uses the Dutchmans, Black Mesa, and Second Water Trails to loop over Black Mesa and through Garden Valley. Garden Valley is a garden all right—a cactus garden.

Start the hike on the Dutchmans Trail, a broad, easy trail that heads southeast. After about 0.3 mile, the Second Water Trail comes in on the left; this will be the return route. The Dutchmans Trail crosses an open desert valley before heading into the narrower canyon formed by First Water Creek. Leaving First Water Creek on the east, the trail passes over a low saddle, then climbs over Parker Pass. Here the trail turns east along the base of Black Mesa, drops into Boulder Canyon Wash, and meets the Black Mesa Trail 3.9 miles from the trailhead.

Turn left on the Black Mesa Trail, which climbs steeply up a ravine to

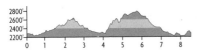

cross a minor saddle and follows a wash northwest onto Black Mesa. After crossing a broad pass on top of the mesa, the Black Mesa Trail

Day-hiking in the Superstition Mountains near First Water Trailhead

follows a drainage northwest for a short distance before coming out into Garden Valley. Garden Valley is a classic Sonoran Desert plain, dotted with cholla cactus, paloverde trees, and creosote bushes. In the middle of the valley, 2.9 miles from the Dutchmans Trail, you'll reach the junction with the Second Water Trail.

Turn left on the Second Water Trail to continue the loop. The trail soon drops off the south rim of Garden Valley, revealing that the "valley" is really part of Black Mesa. Follow the trail as it descends a steep ravine, then turns west and works its way through complex country before emerging into a familiar open valley along First Water Creek. You'll meet the Dutchmans Trail here, 1.4 miles from the Black Mesa Trail. Turn right and walk about 0.3 mile to the First Water Trailhead.

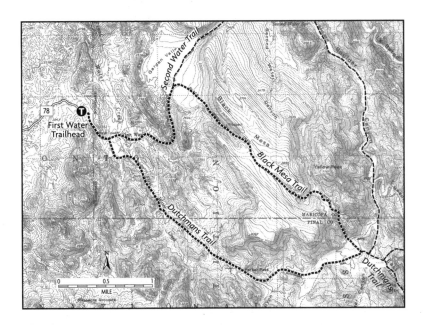

45 LOWER LA BARGE BOX

Round trip	■	**12 miles**
Loop direction	■	Clockwise
Hiking time	■	8 hours or 2 days
Starting elevation	■	1710 feet
High point	■	2490 feet
Elevation gain	■	3600 feet
Seasonal water availability	■	La Barge Creek, Second Water Canyon
Best hiking time	■	October through April
Maps	■	Mormon Flat Dam, Goldfield USGS; Superstition Wilderness USFS
Contact	■	Tonto National Forest, Mesa Ranger District

Driving directions: Starting from Apache Junction, drive east 4.5 miles on Arizona 88 to the Canyon Lake Trailhead, on the left.

Starting from the Canyon Lake Trailhead, the only Superstition trailhead on a paved road, this loop with a cherry stem starts on the Boulder Trail and

then traverses Lower La Barge Box via cross-country hiking. Emerging from the confines of the canyon, the loop continues on the little-used Cavalry Trail and finishes on the Boulder Canyon Trail. Highlights include the awesome narrows of La Barge Canyon and views of Weavers Needle. Hike clockwise to do the cross-country section through Lower La Barge Box near the start of the loop.

The Boulder Trail starts across the highway from the trailhead and climbs steadily up a ridge to the southeast. Don't forget to look back—the views get better as you climb. When the trail turns east, it leaves the ridge crest and contours around the heads of several small side canyons.

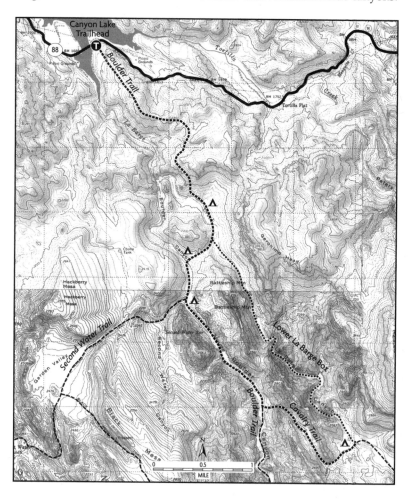

After swinging around a final ridge, the Boulder Trail descends to La Barge Creek. There are campsites on the flats along the creek and seasonal water. The trail crosses the creek, then starts away from it to the southwest. At this point, 2.8 miles from the trailhead, leave the Boulder Trail and hike cross-country up La Barge Creek. The going is easy for a while, but as the canyon walls close in above you, you'll have to do more boulder hopping. There is one slow but short section where you'll have to work your way through huge boulders fallen from the walls above. This narrow section is commonly known as Lower La Barge Box. The term *box canyon* refers to a canyon that becomes impassable because of a dry waterfall forming a barrier, or as in this case, a canyon that becomes too rough for horses and stock.

The narrows come to a sudden end as you emerge into the upper end of Marsh Valley. Watch for the Cavalry Trail on the right side of the wash about 3 miles from the point where you left the Boulder Trail. Turn right on the Cavalry

Hiking the Boulder Canyon Trail, Superstition Mountains

Trail and follow this little-used trail southwest up a nameless canyon. The trail soon turns northwest and climbs over a pass, the high point of the trip, then descends another small canyon into Boulder Canyon where it ends at the Boulder Trail, 1.4 miles from La Barge Canyon.

Turn right on the Boulder Trail and follow it northwest down Boulder Canyon. Usually the trail is distinct, unless recent floods have destroyed it. After 1.3 miles, the Second Water Trail comes in from the left. There are campsites here and usually water in the mouth of Second Water Canyon.

Continue north on the Boulder Trail 0.4 mile, where the trail leaves the canyon on the right. There are campsites here and seasonal water in Boulder Canyon. The Boulder Trail climbs northeast over a saddle, then drops into La Barge Canyon, closing the loop. Continue north on the Boulder Trail 2.8 miles to return to the Canyon Lake Trailhead.

46 | SUPERSTITION CREST

Round trip ■	**19 miles**
Loop direction ■	Clockwise
Hiking time ■	12 to 14 hours or 2 days
Starting elevation ■	2410 feet
High point ■	5057 feet
Elevation gain ■	6510 feet
Seasonal water availability ■	West Boulder Canyon, East Boulder Canyon
Best hiking time ■	October though April
Maps ■	Goldfield, Weavers Needle USGS, Superstition Wilderness USFS
Contact ■	Tonto National Forest, Mesa Ranger District

Driving directions: Starting from Apache Junction, drive about 8.5 miles east on US 60 to Peralta Road (Forest Road 77). Turn left and drive 8 miles to the Peralta Trailhead at road's end.

Starting from the Peralta Trailhead on the southwest side of the Superstition Mountains, this route uses the Peralta Trail for a short cherry-stem section in Peralta Canyon, then heads cross-country along the Superstition Crest, the western ridge of the Superstition Mountains forming the classic skyline seen from the cities in the Valley of the Sun. Dropping off the high ridge, the loop returns on the excellent Dutchmans and Peralta Trails. An option avoids the crest and descends little-traveled West Boulder Canyon. Hike clockwise to get the rugged cross-country portion done near the start of the loop. You'll need the USGS topos for the cross-country portion of the loop.

Start on the popular Peralta Trail, which climbs 1.8 miles northwest up scenic Peralta Canyon through classic Sonoran Desert to Fremont Saddle. Leave the trail here and head south, cross-country. Your objective is the saddle at the head of West Boulder Canyon, 0.9 mile to the southwest (UTM 12S 465460mE 3696570mN). Though the rhyolite pinnacles make the terrain look forbiddingly rough, it is actually easy to make your way between them. Head south, angling for the top of the ridge overlooking the head of Peralta Canyon. Then, turn southwest and follow a drainage toward the saddle described above.

From the saddle, walk southwest up the ridge crest, which soon turns

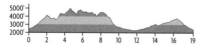

to the northwest and fades out into a terrace well below the main crest. After about 0.6 mile, you'll have to turn southwest again and climb a

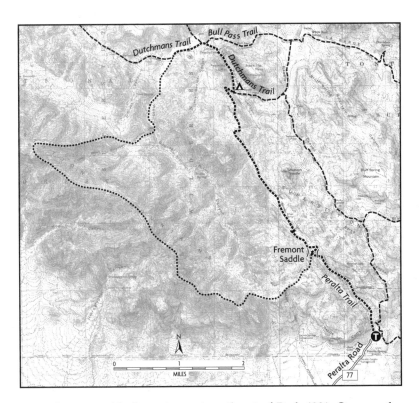

steep slope to reach the main crest southeast of Peak 4301. Once on the crest, stay on it as it heads generally northwest. The walking is fairly easy, though there are ups and downs. The view, especially on a clear day, is dramatic, with the greater Phoenix area spread out to the west and the rugged interior of the Superstition Mountains to the east. You'll pass just below the summit of Peak 5057, the high point of the loop and the highest point of the crest, 3 miles after leaving Fremont Saddle. It's only a few yards to the top of this rocky summit and well worth the effort.

Continue along the crest, which loses elevation as you proceed. There are small places to camp along the crest, if the weather permits and you have enough water. The saddle at the head of Old West Boulder Canyon, 3.1 miles from Peak 5057, presents the only real difficulty along the crest hike. Cliffs force you to descend to the east, slightly below the level of the saddle, then climb back up to it. Continue northwest past Peak 4562, then turn north and contour across to the ridge that descends east just north of Old West Boulder Canyon (UTM 12S 459220mE 3700070mN). Descend this steep ridge to a saddle at about 3000 feet (UTM 12S 461400mE 3700290mN), then turn southeast and drop into Old West Boulder Canyon, right where the Goldfield USGS topo shows a trail. This trail no longer exists but it's

Desert pool, West Boulder Canyon, Superstition Mountains

easy to descend to the bed of the canyon and follow it downstream to West Boulder Canyon. There may be seasonal water in either Old West Boulder or West Boulder Canyons. You'll reach West Boulder Canyon 2.7 miles after leaving the saddle at the head of Old West Boulder Canyon. Turn left and walk down the gravel bed of the canyon 1.2 miles to the Dutchmans Trail, a heavily used trail that crosses the broad, dry wash.

Turn right on the Dutchmans Trail and follow it east past the junctions with the Black Mesa, Boulder Canyon, and Bull Pass Trails. Stay right at each junction. After the trail turns south and heads up East Boulder Canyon, watch for the junction with the Peralta Trail, which is 1.6 miles from the point where you intercepted the Dutchmans Trail. There is seasonal water in East Boulder Canyon near this trail junction, and plenty of campsites.

Turn right on the Peralta Trail, and follow it up a switchback or two over a low saddle south of Palomino Mountain. The well-graded trail heads south, climbing gradually up the basin at the head of Little Boulder Canyon, then crosses a saddle and descends back into East Boulder Canyon. After passing below the triple spires of Weavers Needle, the trail climbs to the head of the canyon at Fremont Saddle, closing the loop 3.7 miles from the Dutchmans Trail. Continue southeast down Peralta Canyon on the Peralta Trail 1.8 miles to return to the trailhead.

47 ┆ BARKS CANYON

Round trip ■	**5 miles**
Loop direction ■	Clockwise
Hiking time ■	4 hours
Starting elevation ■	2410 feet
High point ■	3800 feet
Elevation gain ■	1610 feet
Seasonal water availability ■	Barks Canyon
Best hiking time ■	October through April
Maps ■	Weavers Needle USGS, Superstition Wilderness USFS
Contact ■	Tonto National Forest, Mesa Ranger District

Driving directions: Starting from Apache Junction, drive about 8.5 miles east on US 60 to Peralta Road (Forest Road 77). Turn left and drive 8 miles to the Peralta Trailhead at road's end.

This easy loop from the Peralta Trailhead offers classic views of Weavers Needle in the western Superstition Mountains. The loop uses the Peralta Trail, a short section of crosscountry, and the Bluff Spring Trail to circle through some of the most dramatic scenery in the Superstition Mountains. Hike clockwise because it's easier to find the return trail.

Start the hike on the Peralta Trail, which climbs 1.8 miles up Peralta Canyon to Fremont Saddle. Leave the trail at the saddle and hike east and then north, cross-country (you will probably find an old trail) onto the small plateau 0.3 mile northeast of the saddle. Your objective is the east rim of this plateau, at a point overlooking Barks Canyon. The exact point at which you leave the rim

Weavers Needle in storm,
Superstition Mountains

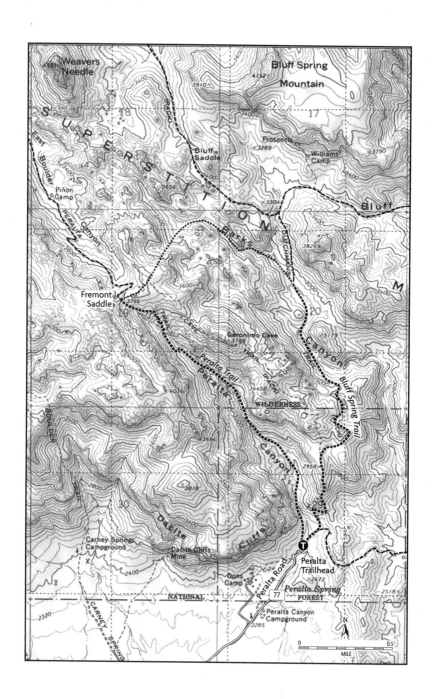

isn't critical because all the drainages lead down to Barks Canyon. Head generally northeast, working your way off the rim of the plateau through the numerous pinnacles until you reach the bed of Barks Canyon about 0.7 mile from Fremont Saddle. Turn right and follow Barks Canyon downstream about 0.7 mile, where the well-used and obvious Bluff Spring Trail comes down the eastern slope to the bed of the canyon. Turn right on the Bluff Spring Trail. The trail follows Barks Canyon for a while, then climbs out on the right and over a ridge to Peralta Trailhead, about 1.8 miles from where you met the trail.

48 ┊ DUTCHMANS TRAIL

Round trip ■	**15.5 miles**
Loop direction: ■	Clockwise
Hiking time ■	9 to 10 hours or 2 days
Starting elevation ■	2410 feet
High point ■	3430 feet
Elevation gain ■	2860 feet
Seasonal water availability ■	Barks Canyon, Needle Canyon, White Rock Spring, Charlebois Spring, Music Canyon Spring, La Barge Spring, Holmes Spring, and Crystal Spring
Best hiking time ■	October through April
Maps ■	Weavers Needle USGS, Superstition Wilderness USFS
Contact ■	Tonto National Forest, Mesa Ranger District

Driving directions: Starting from Apache Junction, drive about 8.5 miles east on US 60 to Peralta Road (Forest Road 77). Turn left and drive 8 miles to the Peralta Trailhead at road's end.

By far the most popular western Superstition hike, this very scenic desert loop starts from the Peralta Trailhead and uses the Bluff Spring, Terrapin, and Dutchman Trails to loop past the base of towering Weavers Needle and through classic western Superstition desert.

From the Peralta Trailhead, start on the Dutchmans Trail, then almost immediately turn left on the Bluff Spring Trail, which climbs over the ridge to the east of Peralta Canyon and then descends to Barks Canyon. The trail follows Barks Canyon north for a while, then climbs out on the canyon's east side, meeting the Terrapin Trail 2.1 miles from the start.

Turn left on the Terrapin Trail and follow it northwest through a confusing

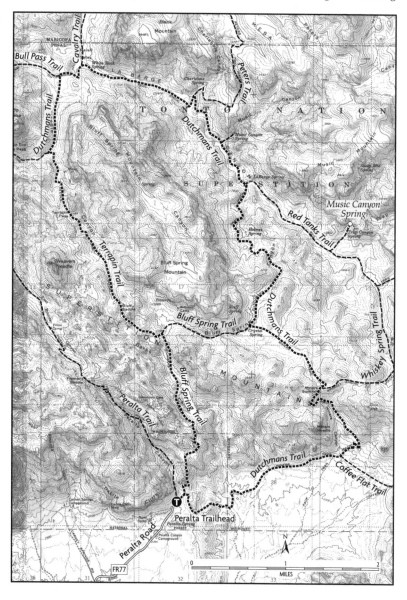

Distant ridges, Superstition Mountains

landscape of pinnacles and huge boulders over Bluff Saddle. Beyond the saddle the trail descends into the headwaters of Needle Canyon, and you'll have some fine views of the sheer east face of Weavers Needle, the most famous Superstition landmark. After passing over Terrapin Pass, the trail descends to the bed of Needle Canyon and ends at the Dutchmans Trail, 2.7 miles from where you left the other end of the Dutchmans Trail.

Turn right on the Dutchmans Trail and follow it north down Needle Canyon. As the canyon opens out into a broad basin, the trail climbs out on the right and meets the Bull Pass Trail 0.9 mile from the Terrapin Trail.

Turn right to stay on the Dutchmans Trail, which now heads east 0.3 mile to the Cavalry Trail and White Rock Spring. Stay right on the Dutchmans Trail and follow it east up La Barge Canyon 1.4 miles to the junction with the Peters Trail. Charlebois Spring is 0.2 mile up the Peters Trail. There are campsites nearby, but the area is seriously overused.

Continue the loop by staying right on the Dutchmans Trail, which continues 1.3 miles up La Barge Canyon past the 0.1-mile spur trail to Music Canyon Spring to the Red Tanks Trail, which comes in on the left. La Barge Spring is 0.1 mile up the Red Tanks Trail, and there are plenty of campsites in the area.

Stay right on the Dutchmans Trail, which leaves La Barge Canyon and heads south up Bluff Spring Canyon. Holmes Spring is below the trail in the bed of the canyon. After 2.1 miles, you'll pass the short spur trail to Bluff Spring.

At Crystal Spring, stay left on the Dutchmans Trail, which heads southeast up an open valley 1.1 miles to Miners Summit and the Whiskey Spring

Trail, which comes in from the left. Stay right and follow the Dutchmans Trail another 1.1 miles past many-summited Miners Needle and down Miners Canyon to the Coffee Flat Trail.

Stay right on the Dutchmans Trail as it heads west across a beautiful open valley forested with stately saguaro cactus. At the west end of the valley, the trail climbs over a ridge and descends to Peralta Trailhead, 2.6 miles from the Coffee Flat Trail junction.

49 FIRE LINE LOOP

Round trip ■	**15.1 miles**
Loop direction ■	Clockwise
Hiking time ■	10 hours or 2 days
Starting elevation ■	3240 feet
High point ■	5470 feet
Elevation gain ■	3480 feet
Seasonal water availability ■	Campaign Creek, Brushy Spring, Black Jack Spring, Pine Creek, Whiskey Spring, Reavis Creek, and Walnut Spring
Best hiking time ■	September through November, April and May
Maps ■	Two Bar Mountain, Haunted Canyon, Iron Mountain, Pinyon Mountain USGS; Superstition Wilderness USFS
Contact ■	Tonto National Forest, Mesa Ranger District

Driving directions: Starting from Globe, drive west about 20 miles on Arizona 88. Turn left on the Campaign Creek Road (Forest Road 449). After 1.9 miles, turn left at a fork onto Forest Road 449A and continue 5.2 miles to the Campaign Trailhead. Forest Road 449A is unmaintained and crosses Campaign Creek several times. A high-clearance vehicle is required, and the road may be impassable after storms. The trailhead is on private land; please stay on the trail and respect private property. There are no campsites at the trailhead.

Named for a trail built to fight a wildfire, this eastern Superstition loop starts from the remote Campaign Trailhead. It follows the Campaign and Pinto Creek Trails up gorgeous Campaign Creek, then crosses the headwaters of Pine Creek on the Fire Line Trail. Joining the Reavis Trail, the loop passes the site of historic Reavis Ranch, then uses the Reavis Gap and a short piece of

the Campaign Trail to return. Hike clockwise to avoid the long, dry climb on the Reavis Gap Trail.

The Campaign Trail skirts Reavis Mountain School, then follows a delightful section of Campaign Creek with a permanent stream. Just 1 mile up the trail, you'll pass the Reavis Gap Trail on the right, which is the return trail. (This trail is mostly not shown on the USGS topo maps—the UTM coordinates of the junction are 12S 491510mE 3709200mN.)

Continue south on the Campaign Trail, which climbs above the creek over a saddle, then returns to creekside. Above the point where the trail leaves the creek, the flow becomes seasonal. Large oak and Arizona sycamore trees dominate the canyon floor, while the slopes above are covered with a mixture of chaparral brush and stubby juniper trees. The Campaign Trail ends 2 miles from the Reavis Gap Trail at the junction with the Pinto Creek Trail, which comes in from the left.

Stay right on the Pinto Creek Trail, which continues south up Campaign Creek. Just after the trail and canyon turn southwest, you may find water

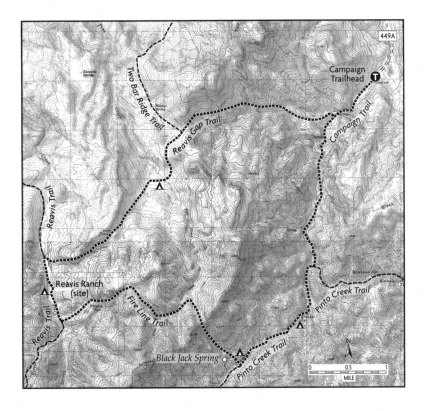

in the bed at Brushy Spring. There are campsites in this area. The Fire Line Trail comes in from the right 1.8 miles from the end of the Campaign Trail. The Fire Line Trail is not shown on the USGS topo map—the UTM coordinates of the junction are 12S 489710mE 3704370mN. Black Jack Spring is located a short distance up a drainage south of the junction. There are several campsites under towering ponderosa pines at this junction.

Turn right on the Fire Line Trail, which climbs steeply out of Campaign Creek's canyon and over a saddle. The trail descends northwest to upper Pine Creek, then turns southwest and follows the creek upstream. When the trail leaves the creek on the west, it makes another steep climb, this time to a nameless saddle east of Reavis Ranch, which is the high point of the loop. A gradual descent leads past Whiskey Spring to Reavis Creek and the Reavis Trail (UTM 12S 485770mE 3705140mN, in case you do the loop counterclockwise), 3.2 miles from the Pinto Creek Trail.

Backpacking the Fire Line Trail, Superstition Mountains

Turn right on the Reavis Trail and follow it north along Reavis Creek. There is seasonal water in Reavis Creek and plenty of campsites in the meadow south of the Reavis Ranch site, and in the apple orchard north of the old ranch area. Reavis Ranch was an operational ranch until the late 1960s, when the Forest Service bought the property. There was an attempt to preserve the ranch house as a historic structure, but careless people burned the building and it was removed. North of the ranch site, you'll meet the Reavis Gap Trail, 0.7 mile from the Fire Line Trail.

Turn right on the Reavis Gap Trail, which is shown on the Iron Mountain USGS topo but not on the Pinyon Mountain and Two Bar Mountain quads. The little-used trail climbs east and northeast over a minor saddle, then descends gradually to cross Pine Creek, where there is seasonal water and a few campsites. On the east side of Pine Creek, the trail climbs north over a saddle and then heads northeast to a second saddle, known as Reavis Gap. Here, 3 miles from the Reavis Trail, the Two Bar Ridge Trail goes north.

Stay right on the Reavis Gap Trail and follow the trail east of the gap, where 2.3 miles of steady descent brings you to Campaign Creek and the Campaign Trail, closing the loop. Turn left and hike 1 mile on the Campaign Trail to the trailhead.

50 : ANGEL BASIN LOOP

Round trip ■	**18 miles**
Loop direction ■	Counterclockwise
Hiking time ■	11 hours or 2 days
Starting elevation ■	4820 feet
Lowest point ■	3280 feet
Elevation gain ■	3060 feet
Seasonal water availability ■	Rogers Spring, Reavis Creek, Plow Saddle Springs, Fish Creek, and Rogers Canyon
Best hiking time ■	September through November, April and May
Maps ■	Iron Mountain, Pinyon Mountain USGS; Superstition Wilderness USFS
Contact ■	Tonto National Forest, Mesa Ranger District

Driving directions: Starting from Apache Junction, drive east about 18 miles on US 60 to the Queen Creek Road. Turn left, drive 1.9 miles, and then turn right on Forest Road 357. After 3.1 miles, turn left on Forest Road 172. Drive north 12.5 miles and turn right on Forest Road 172A. Drive 4 miles to the end of the road at the Rogers Troughs Trailhead. The last 0.4 mile is rough and may require a high-clearance vehicle.

Starting from the remote Rogers Troughs Trailhead in the eastern Superstition Mountains, this loop follows the historic Reavis Trail (the route of the Utah to Mexico Arizona Trail) past the old Reavis Ranch site and its apple orchard. Descending the headwaters of Fish Creek on the little-used Frog Tanks Trail, the loop then follows Rogers Canyon to scenic Angel Basin, where it joins the Rogers Canyon Trail to complete the loop.

From Rogers Troughs, hike northwest on the Reavis Trail. Almost immediately, you'll pass the West Pinto Trail on the right. Rogers Spring is 0.2 mile up this trail. Stay left on the Reavis Ranch Trail,

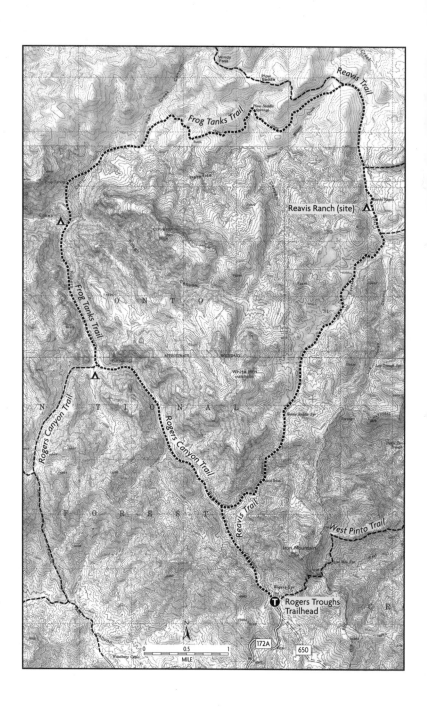

Backpackers in Fish Creek Canyon, Superstition Mountains

which descends Rogers Canyon 1.3 miles to the junction with the Rogers Canyon Trail, which will be the return.

Turn right to stay on the Reavis Trail, which climbs up an unnamed side canyon to the northeast. At the top of the steep ascent, the trail crosses Reavis Saddle and descends gradually down the headwaters of Reavis Creek through pinyon-juniper woodland with occasional stands of ponderosa pines. The Fire Line Trail comes in from the right, 4.2 miles from Rogers Canyon.

Stay left on the Reavis Trail, which soon enters a large meadow. There is seasonal water in Reavis Creek, and plenty of campsites from here past the old Reavis Ranch site. The ranch buildings are gone now, but the apple orchard remains. At the north end of the orchard, the Reavis Gap Trail goes right, 0.7 mile north of the Fire Line Trail.

Stay left on the Reavis Trail, which follows Reavis Creek north for a while, then turns east and climbs away from the creek and over a broad saddle, where it meets the Frog Tanks Trail, 1.2 miles from the Reavis Gap Trail.

Turn left on the Frog Tanks Trail, which descends southwest through high desert grassland into the head of Willow Creek, then turns west and passes Plow Saddle Springs. Descending steadily, the trail stays on the slopes north of Paradise Creek until it finally descends to Fish Creek at the confluence with Paradise Creek. Now, the Frog Tanks Trail turns south and follows Fish Creek downstream into an impressive canyon. As the canyon walls grow higher, the trail veers away from Fish Creek and climbs to Frog Spring. A final steep descent leads to the mouth of Rogers Canyon at Fish Creek, 5.2 miles from the Reavis Trail. There is seasonal water at the confluence and limited camping.

Follow the Frog Tanks Trail up Rogers Canyon, where you'll find a few more campsites and seasonal water. After 1.7 miles, the trail ends at the junction with the Rogers Canyon Trail in Angel Basin, an open flat at the confluence of three canyons. This is a popular campsite, with seasonal water in Rogers Canyon.

Turn left on the Rogers Canyon Trail and follow it southeast up Rogers Canyon. Watch for a cliff dwelling on the north side of the canyon, which is still fairly intact despite careless vandalism. Also look for a huge chock stone high on the west canyon wall. After 2.5 miles, the Rogers Canyon Trail meets the Reavis Trail, closing the loop. Stay right on the Reavis Trail and hike 1.3 miles to Rogers Troughs Trailhead.

51 ⋮ WEST PINTO CREEK

Round trip ■	**17.4 miles**
Loop direction ■	Counterclockwise
Hiking time ■	11 hours or 2 days
Starting elevation ■	3450 feet
High point ■	5540 feet
Elevation gain ■	4070 feet
Seasonal water availability ■	West Pinto Creek, Iron Mountain Spring, Rogers Spring, and Rock Creek
Best hiking time ■	September through November, April and May
Maps ■	Haunted Canyon, Iron Mountain USGS; Superstition Wilderness USGS
Contact ■	Tonto National Forest, Globe Ranger District

Driving directions: Starting from Apache Junction, go east about 46 miles on US 60 to the Pinto Valley Road. Turn left and drive 3.2 miles, then turn left again on a dirt road, just before the mine gatehouse. For the next few miles you'll be on private land in an active mining area; follow the road marked with "Public Access Road" signs. Watch for Forest Road 287, where you'll turn left. Now drive 1.5 miles, turn right, then almost immediately turn left onto Forest Road 287A. Continue 6 miles to the Miles Trailhead. Sections of Forest Road 287A are rough and a high-clearance vehicle is recommended.

Starting from the remote Miles Trailhead on the east side of the Superstition Mountains, this loop follows the West Pinto Trail up West Pinto Creek, over the slopes of Iron Mountain, and along a section of the Arizona Trail on a high, scenic ridge. Return is via the Rock Creek Trail.

Head west on the West Pinto Trail past a large meadow. Just beyond

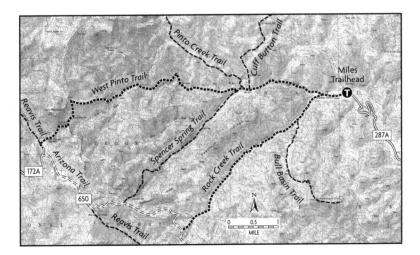

this meadow, at the confluence of Rock Creek and West Pinto Creek and 0.7 mile from the trailhead, the Rock Creek Trail forks left; this is the return route.

Stay right on the West Pinto Trail and follow it west up West Pinto Creek 1.6 miles to the first of several trail junctions. First, the Cuff Button and Pinto Creek Trails come in from the right, then after 0.2 mile the Spencer Spring Trail goes left up Spencer Spring Canyon. Stay on the West Pinto Trail. For a while the trail stays on the south side of the canyon, then it descends to the creek where there is seasonal water. After a section along the creek, the West Pinto Trail climbs onto the north slopes of the canyon. The trail returns to the creek again, only to leave it for a last time and climb steeply west up a brushy ridge. The trail reaches the east shoulder of Iron Mountain, then descends to Iron Mountain Spring before climbing again to cross a pass on the south ridge of Iron Mountain. Descending steeply, the trail passes Rogers Spring, then ends at the Reavis Trail, 5.8 miles from the Spencer Spring Trail.

Turn left on the Reavis Trail and walk less than 0.1 mile to the Rogers Troughs Trailhead. Follow Forest Road 172A out of the parking area for 0.2 mile, and then turn left on Forest Road 650.

This old road, built to fight a forest fire in the 1950s, climbs southeast up the headwaters of Rogers Canyon onto a high ridge with great views. This road is also the route of the Arizona Trail, which leaves the road to the right to follow the Reavis Trail, 1.6 miles from Forest Road 172A. Stay left on the road. After another 1 mile you'll pass the Spencer Spring Trail on the left. Stay on the road another 1.7 miles to the Rock Creek Trail.

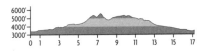

Turn left onto the Rock Creek Trail and follow it down into pinyon-juniper woodland at the head of Rock Creek. There are campsites and seasonal water along the creek. After 3.5 miles, the Bull Basin Trail comes in from the right; stay left on the Rock Creek Trail for another 0.6 mile to the West Pinto Trail, closing the loop. Turn right and walk 0.7 mile on the West Pinto Trail to return to the Miles Trailhead.

Near Rogers Troughs, Superstition Mountains

PINALENO AND GALIURO MOUNTAINS

52 WEBB PEAK

Round trip ■	**3.9 miles**
Loop direction ■	Counterclockwise
Hiking time ■	2 to 3 hours
Starting elevation ■	9490 feet
High point ■	10,030 feet
Elevation gain ■	990 feet
Seasonal water availability ■	Ash Creek
Best hiking time ■	June through October
Map ■	Webb Peak USGS
Contact ■	Coronado National Forest, Safford Ranger District

Driving directions: Starting from Safford, drive south 7 miles on US 191 and turn right on Arizona 366. Drive about 28 miles and park at the Columbine Trailhead, which is just past the Forest Service work center.

This easy loop on the high crest of the Pinaleno Mountains takes you over the top of 10,030-foot Webb Peak through cool aspen, fir, and spruce forest via the Ash Creek and Webb Peak Trails. An optional side hike leads to the brink of 100-foot Ash Creek Falls.

A forest fire burned the Ash Creek area in June 2004. Be prepared for deadfall and trail erosion.

From the Columbine Trailhead, hike north on the Ash Creek Trail, past the summer home community of Columbine, for 0.5 mile to the junction with the Webb Peak Trail. Here you can do a highly recommended 3.7-mile out-and-back side hike to Ash Creek Falls by staying on the Ash Creek Trail.

This option adds 1220 feet of elevation gain on the return from the Falls. The Ash Creek Trail descends Ash Creek past an old lumber mill site. A bypass trail on the left is for horses—stay right and continue on the trail along Ash Creek to Slick Rock, an area of rock slabs too steep for horses but easy for hikers. Just beyond the slabs, the trail veers out on the left side of the

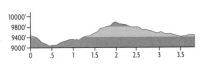

ROUND THE MTN. TRAIL 302
↑ MARIJILDA CREEK   3½
↑ FRYE CANYON TRAIL 36 11
↑ COLUMBINE   17

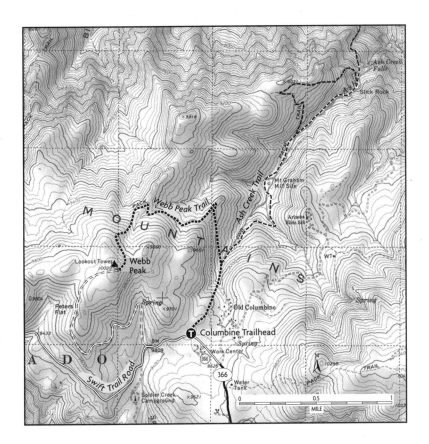

creek, the horse bypass trail rejoins, and you'll hear and see Ash Creek Falls below you.

Back at the junction with the Webb Peak Trail, go northwest on this trail to continue the loop. The trail climbs away from Ash Creek through dense fir and spruce forest, crosses a ridge, then swings around the north side of Webb Peak through a logged area. The final climb is up the north ridge to the gently rounded summit. It is 1.5 miles from Ash Creek to the top. As you would expect from a mountain that rises 7000 feet above its base, the views are stunning in all directions.

To descend, follow the little-used road that leaves the summit to the west. The road descends along the south side of the peak and comes out on the Swift Trail Road after 1.6 miles. Turn left and walk 0.3 mile back to the Columbine Trailhead.

Opposite: *Trailhead in the Pinaleno Mountains*

53 DEER CREEK LOOP

Round trip ■	**25.1 miles**
Loop direction ■	Clockwise
Hiking time ■	3 days
Starting elevation ■	4900 feet
High point ■	7290 feet
Elevation gain ■	7030 feet
Seasonal water availability ■	Limestone Spring, Holdout Spring, Rattlesnake Spring, and Powers Garden Spring
Best hiking time ■	September through November, April and May
Map ■	Kennedy Peak USGS
Contact ■	Coronado National Forest, Safford Ranger District

Driving directions: Starting from Safford, drive west 15.3 miles on US 70. Turn left on Klondyke Road and continue 24.6 miles. Turn left on Aravaipa Road and drive 4.4 miles. Turn right on Deer Creek Road (Forest Road 253). Follow this rough dirt road 6.6 miles to Deer Creek Trailhead.

This loop on the east side of the rugged and remote Galiuro Mountains from the Deer Creek Trailhead starts on the Paddys River Trail and then uses the Rattlesnake Canyon Trail to reach the old Powers Garden ranch site. The loop returns on the Deer Creek Trail. Hike clockwise so that you encounter the fainter trails early in the loop. Return is then on the more heavily used Deer Creek Trail.

Trails in the Galiuro Mountains in general are little-used and may be faint and overgrown with brush. You should have the USGS topo, which shows all the trails on the loop.

From the trailhead, hike 0.9 mile southwest to the junction of the Deer Creek and Paddys River Trails. The Deer Creek Trail will be the return route; turn left on the Paddys River Trail. Follow it southeast across the foothills, through open pinyon-juniper woodland. The trail soon turns south and climbs past Limestone Spring to an unnamed pass south of the

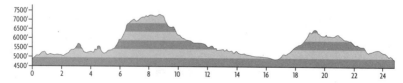

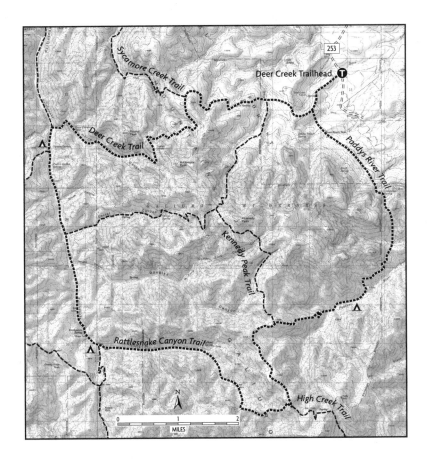

spring. On the far side, the trail descends across a side canyon, then heads into the Paddys River canyon, gradually descending to the bed. Here you'll find seasonal water and possible campsites. After less than a mile along the river, the trail climbs west up a ridge to meet the Kennedy Peak Trail 6.2 miles from the Deer Creek Trail junction.

Stay left on the Paddys River Trail and follow it west along the ridge. The trail dips through a saddle, then turns south along the ridge to pass over the loop high point before meeting the High Creek and Rattlesnake Canyon Trails 1.9 miles from the Kennedy Peak Trail.

Turn right on the Rattlesnake Canyon Trail, which descends west down a ridge, then turns northwest and drops into the head of Rattlesnake Canyon. Where the canyon and trail turn west, watch for a spur trail to Holdout Spring on the right. After 4.3 miles from the High Creek Trail, the trail to Powers Mine comes in from the left.

Turn right to remain on the Rattlesnake Canyon Trail, which follows its namesake canyon north past Rattlesnake Spring. There's seasonal water at the spring and sometimes in the creek, and campsites along the canyon bottom. Pockets of ponderosa pine grow in sheltered spots along the canyon, while the chaparral brush-covered slopes rise above you. You'll reach Powers Garden and the junction with the trail to Grassy Ridge after 3.3 miles. There is seasonal water in Rattlesnake Creek and plenty of campsites near the old ranch.

The Powers brothers were ranching here by the end of the nineteenth century. During World War I, local legend has it that the brothers hid out at Holdout Spring to avoid the draft. The ranch cabin has a fine setting on the edge of a meadow rimmed with ponderosa pine.

To continue the loop, hike north on the Rattlesnake Canyon Trail just 0.4 mile, and then turn right onto the Deer Creek Trail. This fairly well used trail heads east up Horse Canyon, passing Horse Canyon Tank, and then turns southeast to follow the canyon. Near the head of the canyon, the trail suddenly switchbacks left and climbs north to Topout Divide, the pass between Topout and Rockhouse Peaks. Now the trail works its way northeast across the headwaters of Sycamore Creek, meeting the Sycamore Creek Trail 4.4 miles from the Rattlesnake Canyon Trail.

Stay right on the Deer Creek Trail, which now heads east, crossing several tributaries of Oak Creek and passing Mud Spring. The north end of the Kennedy Peak Trail comes in on the right just after the trail crosses Oak Creek, 2 miles from the Sycamore Creek Trail; stay left on the Deer Creek Trail and hike another 0.9 mile to the junction with the Paddys River Trail, closing the loop. Turn left and walk 0.9 mile to the Deer Creek Trailhead.

Desert foothills near Deer Creek, Galiuro Mountains

TUCSON MOUNTAINS

54 COYOTE PASS LOOP

Round trip	■	5.3 miles
Loop direction	■	Clockwise
Hiking time	■	3 hours
Starting elevation	■	2400 feet
High point	■	2630 feet
Elevation gain	■	460 feet
Seasonal water availability	■	None
Best hiking time	■	October through April
Maps	■	Avra, Jaynes USGS; Saguaro National Park Trails Illustrated
Contact	■	Saguaro National Park, Tucson Mountain District

Driving directions: Starting from Tucson, drive west on Ina Road to Saguaro National Park. Stay on the main road as it turns south onto Wade Road, then turns west again and becomes Picture Rocks Road. Just after the road crosses Contzen Pass, it turns sharply right. Park near Contzen Pass, at the first parking area on the right after the pass.

This easy loop through the gorgeous Sonoran Desert of the Tucson Mountains uses the Ringtail, Coyote Pass, Cactus Canyon, Ironwood Forest, and Mule Deer Trails to form a figure eight, double loop with a short cherry-stem section.

Start off by crossing the road to the Ringtail Trail, which heads south down the wash. After just 0.2 mile, the Mule Deer Trail comes in on the right, which is the return route. Stay on the Ringtail Trail as it follows the wash a short distance farther, then wanders off through the open desert to the southeast for 0.8 mile to end at the Picture Rocks Wash Trail. Turn right and follow the trail southwest up Picture Rocks Wash 0.4 mile, and then turn left on the Coyote Pass Trail.

Heading southeast, the Coyote Pass Trail passes the Cactus Canyon Trail after 0.2 mile, which you'll return on; stay left as the trail crosses a saddle, then descends to the east. You'll reach the Cactus Canyon

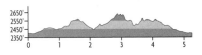

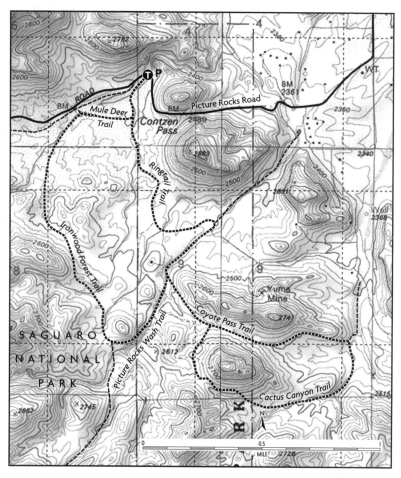

Trail after 0.5 mile; turn right and hike south up the wash on the Cactus Canyon Trail. When the trail reaches a fork in the wash, it chooses the right fork and follows it west, topping out at a saddle. Beyond the saddle, the trail curves north along the base of the hill to the right, closing the first loop after 1.1 miles at the Coyote Pass Trail. Turn left on the Coyote Pass Trail and retrace your steps 0.2 mile to the Picture Rocks Wash Trail.

To start the second loop, turn left and follow the trail southwest up the wash 0.3 mile, then turn right onto the Ironwood Forest Trail. This trail climbs over a low saddle to the northwest, then works its way across several drainages and over another pass. Now the Ironwood Forest Trail turns north and then northeast, meeting the Mule Deer Trail after 1.1 miles. Turn right on the Mule Deer Trail, walk 0.2 mile east to the Ringtail Trail, and then turn left and walk the last 0.2 mile back to the parking area.

Chain fruit cholla cactus, Coyote Pass Loop, Tucson Mountains

55 WASSON PEAK LOOP

Round trip ■	7 miles
Loop direction ■	Counterclockwise
Hiking time ■	5 hours
Starting elevation ■	2900 feet
High point ■	4687 feet
Elevation gain ■	2340 feet
Seasonal water availability ■	None
Best hiking time ■	October through April
Maps ■	Avra, Brown Mountain USGS; Saguaro National Park Trails Illustrated
Contact ■	Saguaro National Park, Tucson Mountain District

Driving directions: Starting from north Tucson, drive west on Ina Road and Picture Rocks Road into Saguaro National Park, then drive south on Sandario Road. Turn right on Kinney Road and drive to the King Canyon Trailhead, which is just north of the entrance to the Arizona Sonora Desert

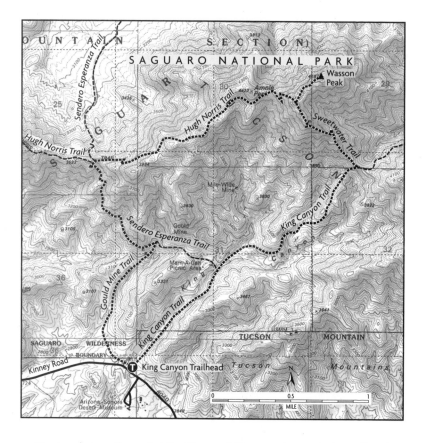

Museum but on the east side of the road. You can also reach the trailhead from south Tucson via Gates Pass Road or Ajo Way (Arizona 86) to the south end of Kinney Road.

Most hikers climb popular Wasson Peak, the highest summit in the Tucson Mountain section of Saguaro National Park, via the long Hugh Norris Trail. Instead, this equally scenic but less-traveled loop uses the King Canyon and Sweetwater Trails to reach the summit, then returns via a short section of the Hugh Norris Trail and the Sendero Esperanza and Gould Mine Trails. The views of the Tucson area and the Santa Catalina and Rincon Mountains from the 4687-foot peak are especially fine.

From the trailhead, hike northeast on the King Canyon Trail, an old road

that used to go to a mine. The trail follows King Canyon and passes the Sendero Esperanza Trail and the Mam-A-Geh Picnic Area after

0.9 mile. Stay on the King Canyon Trail and continue up King Canyon. The trail leaves the canyon for a ridge, which it climbs to a pass and the Sweetwater Trail, which is 1.3 miles from the Sendero Esperanza Trail.

Turn left and hike up the main ridge on the Sweetwater Trail 0.7 mile to the junction with the Hugh Norris Trail and the side trail to Wasson Peak. Turn right and hike 0.3 mile to the summit of Wasson Peak. When you're done enjoying the view, retrace your steps to the Hugh Norris Trail and then turn right to continue the loop. The trail loses altitude quickly via numerous switchbacks, then passes south of Amole Peak. The Hugh Norris Trail then follows the main ridge southwest 1.6 miles to a saddle and the Sendero Esperanza Trail.

Turn left on the Sendero Esperanza Trail and follow it southeast as it descends the desert slopes 0.9 mile past the old mine to the Gould Mine Trail. Turn right and follow the Gould Mine Trail 1 mile south and southeast to the King Canyon Trailhead.

Wasson Peak, Tucson Mountains

56 : BROWN MOUNTAIN LOOP

Round trip ■	3.6 miles
Loop direction ■	Clockwise
Hiking time ■	2 hours
Starting elevation ■	2720 feet
High point ■	3080 feet
Elevation gain ■	820 feet
Seasonal water availability ■	None
Best hiking time ■	October through April
Maps ■	Brown Mountain USGS, Saguaro National Park Trails Illustrated
Contact ■	Pima County Natural Resources, Parks, and Recreation Department

Driving directions: Starting from south Tucson, drive west on Ajo Way (Arizona 86) or Gates Pass Road to Kinney Road. From the intersection of Gates Pass and Kinney Roads, go northwest 1.3 miles on Kinney Road, just past the Brown Mountain Picnic Area, to the trailhead parking on the left.

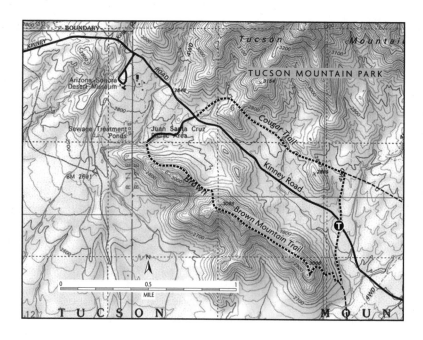

Barrel cactus, Brown Mountain Loop, Tucson Mountains

This easy loop along the crest of Brown Mountain in Tucson Mountain Park uses the Brown Mountain Trail and the Cougar Trail. Views of both the Tucson Mountains and the sweeping Sonoran Desert to the southwest are spectacular. As a bonus, plan to spend some time at the nearby Arizona Sonora Desert Museum which displays plants and animals of this lush desert region.

From the trailhead, walk south on the trail toward the Brown Mountain Picnic Area for 0.3 mile, then turn right on the Brown Mountain Trail. The trail climbs the southeast ridge of Brown Mountain, soon reaching the crest. As it follows the ridge northwest, you're treated to a series of views of the Tucson Mountains and Avra Valley. After passing over the highest point of Brown Mountain, the trail descends through a saddle, contours around the north side of a final peak, and drops down to the Juan Santa Cruz Picnic Area, 1.9 miles from the trailhead. Walk north 0.4 mile through the

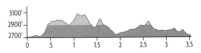

picnic area, cross Kinney Road, and pick up an informal trail that heads northeast toward a powerline. At the powerline, turn right on the Cougar Trail, which follows the powerline across the desert hills to the southeast. When you've walked 1 mile from Kinney Road, turn right on a spur trail and walk 0.3 mile south to Kinney Road and the trailhead.

SANTA CATALINA AND RINCON MOUNTAINS

57 SABINO BASIN LOOP

Round trip ■	**11.7 miles**
Loop direction ■	Counterclockwise
Hiking time ■	8 to 9 hours
Starting elevation ■	2840 feet
High point ■	4840 feet
Elevation gain ■	4410 feet
Seasonal water availability ■	Bear Canyon, East Fork Sabino Canyon
Best hiking time ■	April through November
Map ■	Sabino Canyon USGS
Contact ■	Coronado National Forest, Santa Catalina Ranger District

Driving directions: In Tucson, drive north on Sabino Canyon Road to the Sabino Visitor Center, and park. Travel on the roads beyond the visitor center is by foot or shuttle only. This hike is not quite a closed loop; the trailheads are 1 mile apart on the Bear Canyon Road, but I recommend that you use the Bear Canyon Shuttle to reach the Bear Canyon Trailhead at the start. Keep your shuttle ticket and use the shuttle to return from the end trailhead.

Most of the Santa Catalina Mountains have burned in huge wildfires during recent years, including the north portion of this loop. The trails may be blocked with deadfall or closed outright from time to time; check with the visitor center staff before starting your hike.

From the Bear Canyon Trailhead, follow the Bear Canyon Trail northeast up rugged Bear Canyon. The trail stays near the bed of this seasonal stream for just over a mile. Here you can walk a short distance to a series of

seasonal waterfalls known locally as Seven Falls. Back on the trail, follow it as it climbs out on the south side of Bear Canyon. After passing

Cristate saguaro, a rare form of this common Sonoran Desert cactus

above a sharp bend in the canyon, the trail returns to the bed before climbing out for a final time. Ascending a steep ridge to the north, the Bear Canyon Trail comes out into a sort of hanging valley before climbing over the pass at the north end of the valley. Just beyond the pass, a trail goes right to Sycamore Reservoir and the Arizona Trail. Stay left on the Bear Canyon Trail, which meets the Sycamore Reservoir/Arizona Trail itself in a second saddle, 5 miles from the trailhead.

Turn left on the Sycamore Reservoir Trail, which descends into the East Fork Sabino Canyon. After 0.8 mile, the Palisade Trail comes down the steep slope to the right. Stay on the Sycamore Reservoir Trail and continue down the East Fork 0.4 mile to another junction.

Turn left on the Telephone Ridge Trail and follow it south along the east side of Sabino Canyon. After 1.9 miles, a short spur trail drops down to the end of the Sabino Canyon Road, where you could cheat and catch the shuttle back to the visitor center. Assuming you want to hike the rest of spectacular Sabino Canyon, stay left on the Telephone Ridge Trail and hike

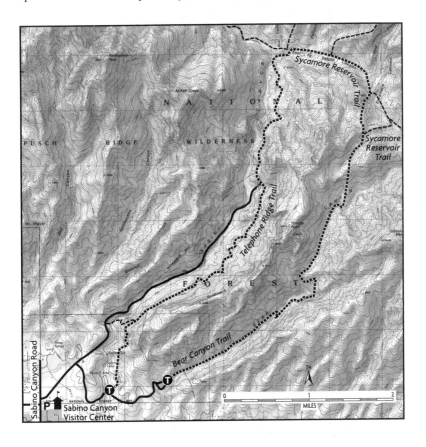

another 3.7 miles to the trailhead, where you can ride the Bear Canyon Shuttle back to the Visitor Center.

58 THREE TANKS LOOP

Round trip ■	**7.7 miles**
Loop direction ■	Clockwise
Hiking time ■	6 hours
Starting elevation ■	2750 feet
High point ■	3960 feet
Elevation gain ■	1320 feet
Best hiking time ■	October through April
Seasonal water availability ■	None
Maps ■	Tanque Verde Peak USGS, Saguaro National Park Trails Illustrated
Contact ■	Saguaro National Park, Rincon Mountain District

Driving directions: In Tucson, drive east on Speedway Road to road's end at the Douglas Spring Trailhead.

Swinging through the foothills of the Rincon Mountains in Saguaro National Park, this loop starts at the Douglas Spring Trailhead and uses the

Garwood Dam, Three Tanks Loop, Rincon Mountains

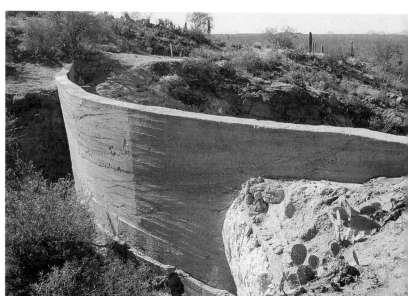

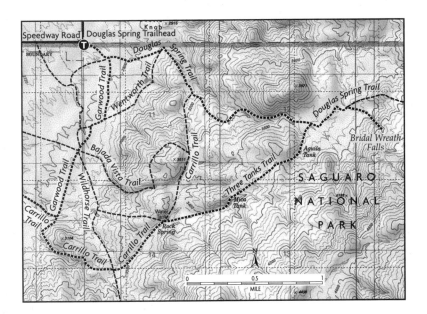

Douglas Spring, Three Tanks, Carrillo, and Garwood Trails to sample this fine piece of Sonoran Desert. An optional side trip leads to Bridal Wreath Falls, a seasonal waterfall.

From the trailhead, hike east 0.2 mile on the Douglas Spring Trail, where the Garwood Trail comes in on the right—this will be the return trail. Continue east across the Sonoran Desert flat 0.4 mile to the base of the hills, where the Wentworth Trail branches right. Stay on the Douglas Spring Trail, which now turns southeast and climbs the foothills 0.4 mile to the north end of the Carrillo Trail. Stay left on the Douglas Spring Trail, which continues southeast for a while before turning east up a canyon. It comes out on a flat and meets the Three Tanks Trail on the right, 1.2 miles from the Carrillo Trail.

The main loop continues on the Three Tanks Trail, but first, take a 1.2-mile out-and-back side trip to Bridal Wreath Falls. Hike 0.3 mile farther on the Douglas Spring Trail, then turn right on the Bridal Wreath Falls Trail and walk another 0.3 mile to the falls. The fall is seasonal, and the best time to see it flowing is during snowmelt, early winter and spring. It may also be running after a heavy summer thunderstorm.

Back at the Three Tanks Trail, hike southwest past Aguila and Mica Tanks, losing elevation gradually. At Rock Spring, 1.3 miles from the Douglas Spring Trail, the Three Tanks Trail crosses the Carrillo Trail. Turn left on the Carrillo Trail and hike 0.8 mile, where the Wildhorse Trail crosses. Stay on the Carrillo Trail west past the old Garwood Dam, where the trail

swings north and drops out of the foothills onto the desert flats once again. The Carrillo Trail meets the Garwood Trail 0.6 mile from the Wildhorse Trail.

Turn right on the Garwood Trail and follow it north past junctions with the Wildhorse, Bajada Vista, and Wentworth Trails a total of 1.5 miles to its end at the Douglas Spring Trail, which closes the loop. Turn left and walk 0.2 mile back to the trailhead.

59 ┆ MICA MOUNTAIN LOOP

Round trip ■	**19.9 miles**
Loop direction ■	Clockwise
Hiking time ■	2 to 3 days
Starting elevation ■	4200 feet
High point ■	8664 feet
Elevation gain ■	5990 feet
Seasonal water availability ■	Miller Creek, Devils Bathtub Spring, Manning Camp Spring, Spud Rock Spring, and Deer Head Spring
Best hiking time ■	April through November
Maps ■	Happy Valley, Mica Mountain USGS; Saguaro National Park Trails Illustrated
Contact ■	Saguaro National Park, Rincon Mountain District

Driving directions: Starting from Tucson, drive southeast about 40 miles on I-10 to the Mescal exit. Turn left and drive 16 miles north on Forest Road 35, and then turn left and go 0.2 mile to the Miller Creek Trailhead.

This is a scenic loop over Mica Mountain, the highest summit in the Rincon Mountains, starting from the east side of the range. A permit is required; it can be obtained in person at the Saguaro National Park Rincon Visitor Center or in advance by mail. Backpackers are required to camp at the designated campsites in the park backcountry.

From the trailhead, follow the Miller Creek Trail northwest up Miller Creek toward the impressive eastern slopes of the Rincon Mountains. The gentle ascent comes to an end after about a mile, when the trail veers west and starts climbing more steeply. After several switchbacks and a lot of

steady climbing through high desert grassland and pinyon-juniper woodland, the trail meets the Rincon Peak and Heartbreak Ridge

Rincon Peak from Miller Creek, Rincon Mountains

Trails on a broad saddle on the crest of the range, 3 miles from the trailhead.

Turn right, and follow the Heartbreak Ridge Trail northwest past Happy Valley Saddle. Another stiff climb up a ridge to the north leads to Happy Valley Lookout. After this, the ascent moderates as the trail follows the crest of a ridge north from the lookout. The Deerhead Spring Trail forks right 3.1 miles from the Miller Creek Trail; stay left on the Heartbreak Ridge Trail. Another steep climb to the north leads to another trail junction where the East Slope Trail goes right. This time turn left on the Devils Bathtub Trail and head west, where you'll soon pass Devils Bathtub Spring. Just 1.6 miles from the Deerhead Spring Trail, you'll meet the Manning Camp Trail.

Turn right on the Manning Camp Trail and follow it 0.9 mile to Manning Camp. This is a designated campsite with a seasonal spring, and a cabin used by the park rangers while on patrol. It's also a trail junction, where the Mica Mountain Trail goes northeast and the Fire Loop Trail goes north.

Leave Manning Camp on the Fire Loop Trail and hike north and northwest past the junction with the Cow Head Saddle Trail. Stay right on the Fire Loop Trail, which now climbs northeast past Spud Rock and over Mica Mountain, the high point of the loop. After enjoying the limited view, continue east on the Fire Loop Trail as it descends the east ridge, passing junctions with the Mica Mountain, Bonita, and North Slope Trails. The Fire Loop Trail turns south along the high east slopes of the mountain to reach Reef Rock, a viewpoint above impressive cliffs. The trail then turns west, passing the south end of the Bonita Trail and Man Head, before meeting the Switchbacks Trail, 4 miles from Manning Camp.

Turn left on the Switchbacks Trail, which descends east 1 mile to the East Slope Trail. Turn left and hike 0.2 mile to another designated campsite, Spud Rock Spring.

From the campground, follow the Deerhead Trail southeast 0.4 miles to the Turkey Creek Trail. Turn left on the Turkey Creek Trail, which passes Deerhead Spring, and then descends the slopes to the east. Eventually the trail comes out on the ridge north of Turkey Creek and the descent moderates. Follow the ridge southeast and south to the Turkey Creek Trailhead, which is 5.2 miles from Deerhead Spring. Follow the road 0.1 mile to Forest Road 35, turn right, walk 0.3 miles to the Miller Creek Road, turn right again, and walk 0.2 miles to the Miller Creek Trailhead.

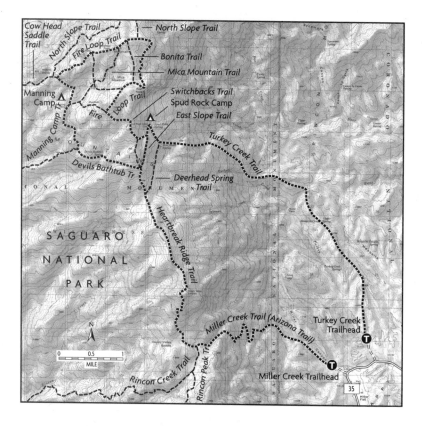

AJO MOUNTAINS

60 : SENITA BASIN LOOP

Round trip ■	**2.6 miles**
Loop direction ■	Counterclockwise
Hiking time ■	1 hour
Starting elevation ■	1670 feet
High point ■	1760 feet
Elevation gain ■	90 feet
Seasonal water availability ■	None
Best hiking time ■	October through April
Maps ■	Lukeville USGS, Organ Pipe Cactus National Monument Trails Illustrated
Contact ■	Organ Pipe Cactus National Monument

Driving directions: Starting from the Organ Pipe Cactus National Monument Visitor Center, drive south 4.3 miles on Arizona 85, and turn right on Puerto Blanco Drive. Continue 5 miles, and then turn right on the Senita Basin Road. Drive 4.3 miles to the trailhead at the end of the road.

This is an easy loop through the southern Sonoran Desert in Organ Pipe Cactus National Monument, starting from the Senita Basin Spur Road.

Senita Basin is named after the rare Senita cactus, also known as old man cactus. Senita resembles the monument's namesake organ pipe cactus, but it is distinguished by its beardlike growth of long gray needles at the tips of the branches. The Senita Basin Trail does a loop around the basin snuggled between the low hills of the Puerto Blanco Mountains, first heading east along the base of the hills. The trail then runs north across numerous small washes and ridges, then turns west and southwest to return to the trailhead.

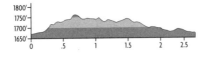

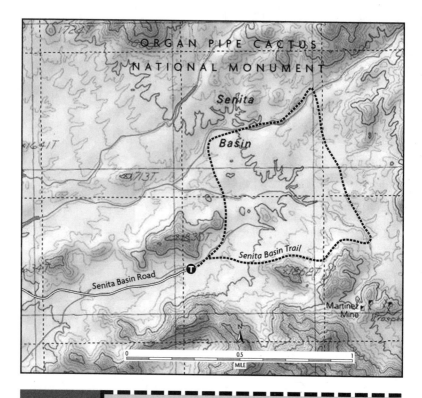

61 ┋ GRASS CANYON LOOP

Round trip	■	**6.3 miles**
Loop direction	■	Clockwise
Hiking time	■	4 to 5 hours
Starting elevation	■	2280 feet
High point	■	3340 feet
Elevation gain	■	1230 feet
Seasonal water availability	■	None
Best hiking time	■	October through April
Maps	■	Mount Ajo USGS, Organ Pipe Cactus National Monument Trails Illustrated
Contact	■	Organ Pipe Cactus National Monument

Driving directions: Starting from the Organ Pipe Cactus National Monument Visitor Center, drive 9.8 miles north on Arizona 85, turn right on the

Alamo Canyon Road, and drive 3.2 miles to the end of the road.

This cross-country loop traverses the foothills of the rugged Ajo Mountains in Organ Pipe Cactus National Monument.

From the trailhead, hike north, cross-country, along the base of the mountains. Note the abrupt transition from the steep mountain slopes to the nearly level desert plain. Stay close to the base of the mountains as you round the north end. Pass a short, steep side canyon, and then turn southeast up Grass Canyon, 2.2 miles from the trailhead. The mouth of Grass Canyon is located at UTM 12S 337770mE 3552400mN.

Climb Grass Canyon southeast to its head at a nameless saddle, staying generally south of the canyon bed on the gentler slopes on the south side of the canyon. From the saddle, descend southeast along a steep, unnamed

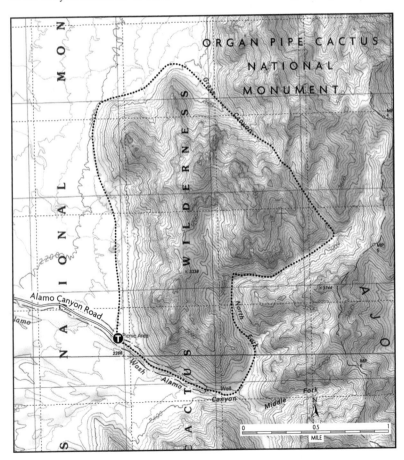

canyon. You will have to negotiate several small dry falls in the bed of this rugged canyon. This canyon drains into the north fork of Alamo Wash; when you reach it, 1.6 miles from the entrance of Grass Canyon, turn right and descend southwest along the north fork. (This confluence is UTM 12S 339270mE 3550640mN.)

Descend the north fork 1.5 miles to Alamo Canyon's main branch, where you can see the canyon opening out onto the desert plain to the west. Turn right again, and follow Alamo Canyon another 0.9 mile to the trailhead.

Natural arches, Organ Pipe Cactus National Monument

62 ■ BULL PASTURE

Round trip ■	**3.1 miles**
Loop direction ■	Counterclockwise
Hiking time ■	2 hours
Starting elevation ■	2360 feet
High point ■	3380 feet
Elevation gain ■	1070 feet
Seasonal water availability ■	None
Best hiking time ■	October through April
Maps ■	Mount Ajo USGS, Organ Pipe Cactus National Monument Trails Illustrated
Contact ■	Organ Pipe Cactus National Monument

Driving directions: Starting from the Organ Pipe Cactus National Monument Visitor Center, cross Arizona 85 onto the Ajo Mountain Drive and drive 11 miles on this one-way loop road to a picnic area and the Bull Pasture Trailhead.

This loop climbs into Bull Pasture, a desert basin perched on the west side of the rugged Ajo Mountains in Organ Pipe Cactus National Monument. Hike counterclockwise to avoid the steep ascent from Estes Canyon.

From the trailhead, the Bull Pasture Trail climbs east up a small canyon, then

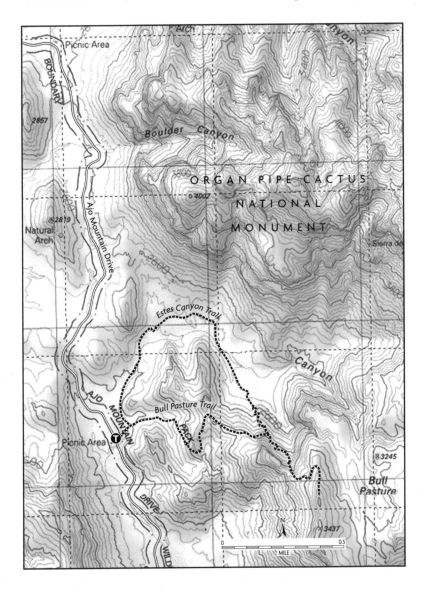

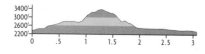

follows a ridge to a saddle. Here the trail swings around onto a northeast-facing slope and meets the Estes Canyon Trail, 0.8 mile from the trailhead. This will be the return route—the rest of the hike is out and back.

Stay right on the Bull Pasture Trail, which climbs up the slope, over the shoulder of a ridge, and east 0.5 mile to a viewpoint on the west rim of Bull Pasture. The ragged skyline of the Ajo Mountains dominates the view to the east, across Bull Pasture, and the summit of Mount Ajo, the highest peak in the national monument, towers to the northeast. Note the numerous clusters of low agave plants, with their stiff, sharp-tipped leaves just waiting to stab hikers. These are appropriately known as shin daggers.

Retrace your steps to the Estes Canyon Trail junction, and then stay right to follow it down a steep slope onto the broad floor of Estes Canyon. The canyon has some particularly fine examples of organ pipe cactus. The trail heads down the canyon to the northwest, then follows it west and southwest 1.3 miles back to the Bull Pasture Trailhead.

Organ pipe cactus, Organ Pipe Cactus National Monument

SANTA RITA AND HUACHUCA MOUNTAINS

63 MOUNT WRIGHTSON

Round trip ■	**10.8 miles**
Loop direction ■	Counterclockwise
Hiking time ■	8 to 9 hours
Starting elevation ■	5440 feet
High point ■	9453 feet
Elevation gain ■	4720 feet
Seasonal water availability ■	Madera Canyon, and Sprung, Baldy, and Bellows Springs
Best hiking time ■	April through November
Map ■	Mount Wrightson USGS
Contact ■	Coronado National Forest, Nogales Ranger District

Driving directions: Starting from Tucson, drive about 24 miles south on I-19, and then exit at Continental. Drive east through Continental and continue on Madera Canyon Road (Forest Road 70) to its end at the Roundup Trailhead.

The classic loop over the top of the Santa Rita Mountains, this hike uses the well-graded Super Trail to ascend Madera Canyon and the southern slopes of Mount Wrightson to Baldy Saddle, where a spur trail can be hiked to the top of Mount Wrightson, the highest peak in the range. From Baldy Saddle, the loop uses the Old Baldy Trail for a fast descent to the trailhead. Views from the summit extend over much of southern Arizona and far into Mexico. In addition, there is the chance of seeing rare bird species in Madera Canyon.

The loop forms a figure eight because the ascent and descent trails cross. Use the well-graded Super Trail for the ascent.

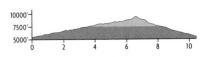

From the Roundup Trailhead, follow the well-named Super Trail up Madera Canyon to the southeast. The trail follows Madera Creek

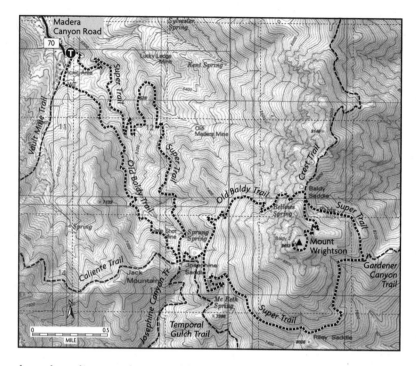

for a short distance, then switchbacks out on the east side of the canyon. There's another short section along the creek before the Super Trail leaves the creek side for the last time and climbs the east side of Madera Canyon through heavy brush in a series of switchbacks. After looping north around the end of a ridge, the trail heads south again and passes through a saddle. The trail now climbs steadily along the east side of the canyon, passing Sprung Spring and reaching Josephine Saddle after 3 miles. Josephine Saddle is also a multiple trail junction. The Old Baldy Trail leaves the saddle to the northwest and will be the return route from this point.

Continue the ascent on the Super Trail, which climbs out of Josephine Saddle to the east. After just 0.3 mile, the upper Old Baldy Trail comes in from the east; this will be the return from the upper portion of the loop. After the junction, the Super Trail heads south along the west slopes of Mount Wrightson. After the trail uses a long switchback to gain elevation, it swings around the south side of the mountain, passing through Riley Saddle. Turning north along the east side of the mountain, the Super Trail passes the Gardener Canyon Trail. On the northeast slopes, the Super Trail passes Baldy Spring, then meets the upper end of the Old

Opposite: *Madera Creek, Santa Rita Mountains*

Baldy Trail at Baldy Saddle, 3.1 miles from Josephine Saddle.

Turn left to stay on the Super Trail, which now heads south and climbs 0.6 mile to the rocky summit of Mount Wrightson, the high point of the hike. The view from this lofty summit encompasses many of the "sky island" mountain ranges of southern Arizona, as well as northern Sonora, Mexico.

Retrace your steps to Baldy Saddle to continue the loop, and turn left on the Old Baldy Trail. The trail descends rapidly via a series of switchbacks, taking advantage of a break in the towering cliffs to either side. Turning southwest, the trail descends past Bellows Spring, then resumes its switchbacking descent. After rounding the end of a ridge, the trail turns south and meets the Super Trail, 1.4 miles from Baldy Saddle. Turn right on the Super Trail and descend 0.3 mile to Josephine Saddle.

Here you have the choice of retracing your steps and returning to the trailhead on the Super Trail, which is a longer but more gradual descent, or using the steeper and shorter Old Baldy Trail.

The Old Baldy Trail heads northwest out of Josephine Saddle and descends rapidly down the west side of upper Madera Canyon for 1.7 miles, ending at the Roundup Trailhead. It is no longer maintained and may be brushy in places.

64 ┊ Bog Springs Loop

Round trip ▪	**4.5 miles**
Loop direction ▪	Clockwise
Hiking time ▪	3 hours
Starting elevation ▪	4890 feet
High point ▪	6690 feet
Elevation gain ▪	1830 feet
Seasonal water availability ▪	Bog and Kent Springs
Best hiking time ▪	April through November
Maps ▪	Mount Hopkins, Mount Wrightson USGS
Contact ▪	Coronado National Forest, Nogales Ranger District

Driving directions: Starting from Tucson, drive about 24 miles south on I-19 and then exit at Continental. Drive east through Continental and continue on Madera Canyon Road (Forest Road 70) to the Madera Picnic Area and Trailhead, 1.1 miles before the end of the road.

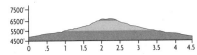

Starting from the Madera Trailhead in Madera Canyon, this loop ascends the Bog Springs Trail to Bog Springs, then traverses high on the west slopes of Mount Wrightson to reach Kent Spring. The descent follows the old Kent Spring Road and trail to rejoin the Bog Springs Trail a short distance from the trailhead. Highlights include close-up views of the steep upper slopes of Madera Canyon and scenic views of the canyon and Santa Cruz River Valley. Hike clockwise to avoid having to climb the steep Kent Spring Road.

From the trailhead, head southeast on the Bog Springs Trail, which climbs gradually up the ridge south of Bog Springs Campground. Stay right where a spur trail goes left to the campground. The trail turns south and meets the Kent Spring Trail 0.8 mile from the trailhead.

Start the loop by staying left on the Bog Springs Trail, which climbs east through the pinyon-juniper and oak woodland. As the trail enters a canyon

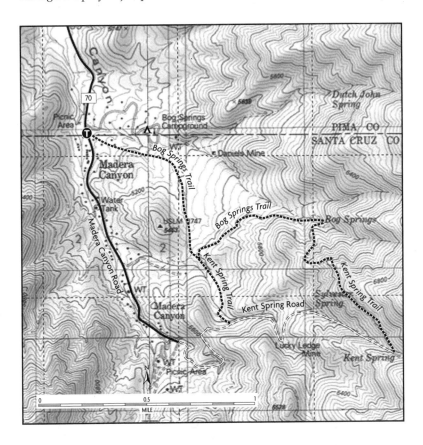

Yucca, Bog Springs Loop, Santa Rita Mountains

on a north-facing slope, ponderosa pines become more common. You'll reach Bog Springs, a trough in the shady canyon bottom, after hiking 0.7 mile from the junction. Beyond the spring, the trail climbs out of the canyon to the south, then climbs steadily southeast across a broad ridge. Openings provide views of Madera Canyon and the rugged ridges descending from Mount Hopkins across the canyon. After 0.8 mile, you'll reach the end of the trail at Kent Spring.

Turn right and descend the Kent Spring Road, a rarely used two-track road that plunges down the canyon. Intermittent flows in the creek at the bottom of the shady canyon add to its charm. After 0.9 mile of this steep descent, turn right on the Kent Spring Trail, which descends north at a more gradual rate. You'll close the loop after 0.4 mile, when the Bog Springs Trail comes in from the right. Stay left and retrace your steps 0.8 mile to the Madera Trailhead.

65 ┊ SONOITA CREEK LOOP

Round trip	■	**1.7 miles**
Loop direction	■	Counterclockwise
Hiking time	■	2 hours
Starting elevation	■	3970 feet
Elevation gain	■	None
Seasonal water availability	■	None
Best hiking time	■	All year
Maps	■	Patagonia USGS, Patagonia Sonoita Preserve trail map
Contact	■	The Nature Conservancy

Driving directions: In Patagonia on Arizona 82, turn northwest on Fourth Street, go two blocks, and turn left. Drive 1.5 miles, and then turn left into the Visitor Center parking area.

This easy loop follows a trail through the Patagonia Sonoita Preserve near Patagonia, where there are opportunities for seeing wildlife, especially birds. Also, pick up a trail map; there are several shorter trails as well as the loop described here.

The Visitor Center, run by volunteer staff from The Nature Conservancy, can fill you in on the history and purpose of the preserve, as well as advise on recent bird and wildlife sightings.

From the Visitor Center, head southeast on the Sonoita Creek. You'll cross the Railroad Grade Trail after about 100 yards; this will be

White-tailed deer, Sonoita Preserve, Patagonia

the return route. Stay on the Sonoita Creek Trail, which now turns east and stays near the bank of Sonoita Creek, a permanent stream. Lush riparian growth fills the valley bottom, including huge Fremont cottonwoods that are some of the largest on record.

When the Sonoita Creek Trail reaches the northeast end of the preserve, it meets the Railroad Grade Trail. Turn left, and take this trail southwest across the flat bottom lands. It meets the Sonoita Creek Trail near the Visitor Center; turn right to return to the trailhead.

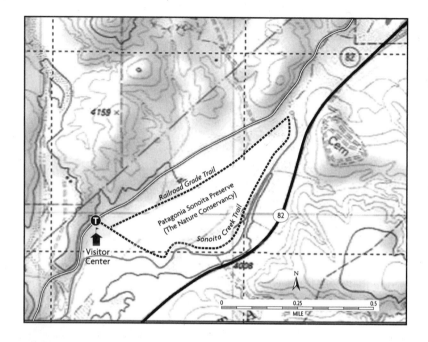

66 ┊ RAMSEY CANYON LOOP

Round trip	■	**8.4 miles**
Loop direction	■	Clockwise
Hiking time	■	6 hours
Starting elevation	■	7400 feet
High point	■	8480 feet
Elevation gain	■	3450 feet
Seasonal water availability	■	None
Best hiking time	■	May through November
Map	■	Miller Peaks USGS
Contact	■	Coronado National Forest, Sierra Vista Ranger District

Driving directions: Starting from Sierra Vista, drive about 8 miles south on Arizona 92, turn right on Carr Canyon Road (FR 368), and drive to the end of the road to Ramsey Vista Campground and Trailhead.

Starting from the Ramsey Vista Trailhead on the east side of the Huachuca Mountains, this loop with a cherry stem takes you into forested upper

Carr Peak from the Ramsey Canyon Trail, Huachuca Mountains

Ramsey Canyon, a world-famous birding site, and around a loop at the headwaters of the canyon.

From the trailhead, the Ramsey Canyon Trail drops southwest to cross Carr Canyon, then contours northwest through an old burn to a nameless saddle between Carr and Ramsey Canyons. Turning southwest, the trail contours into the heavily forested head of Ramsey Canyon. A short distance upstream, 1.9 miles from the trailhead, the trail forks. Turn left and follow the trail south up Wisconsin Gulch. A steady climb brings you to the saddle east of Granite Peak. Follow the trail west and northwest along the crest of the range to the saddle south of Pat Scott Peak. The trail now descends east down Pat Scott Gulch, closing the loop in the bottom of Ramsey Canyon after 4.7 miles. Retrace your steps 1.9 miles to return to the trailhead.

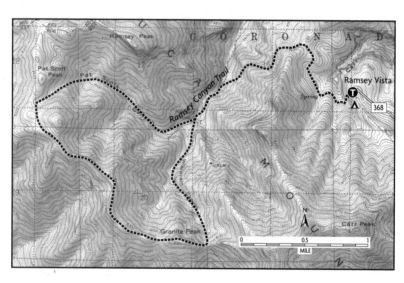

CHIRICAHUA MOUNTAINS

67 : HEART OF ROCKS

Round trip ▪	**7.3 miles**
Loop direction ▪	Counterclockwise
Hiking time ▪	5 hours
Starting elevation ▪	6870 feet
Lowest point ▪	5980 feet
Elevation gain ▪	2200 feet
Seasonal water availability ▪	None
Best hiking time ▪	September through November and March through May
Maps ▪	Cochise Head, Rustler Park, Chiricahua National Monument USGS; Chiricahua Hiking Trails NPS
Contact ▪	Chiricahua National Monument

Driving directions: Starting from Willcox, drive southeast 31 miles on Arizona 186, turn left on Arizona 181, and continue 6 miles to the visitor center. Continue 6 miles on Bonita Canyon Drive to Massai Point at the end of the road.

A classic loop through the volcanic hoodoos of Chiricahua National Monument, the hike starts from the Massai Point Trailhead and uses the southern portion of the Echo Canyon Trail to reach Rhyolite Canyon. Then, the loop follows the Heart of Rocks Trail up Sarah Deming Canyon and into Heart of Rocks itself. A side trail leads to Inspiration Point and a view of upper Rhyolite Canyon. The route finishes with the remainder of the Heart of Rocks Trail and the eastern section of the Echo Canyon Trail.

From the north side of Massai Point, walk a few feet down the Massai Point Nature Trail and turn right on the Ed Riggs Trail. Follow this trail 0.2 mile northeast to the bottom of the canyon and turn left to stay on the Ed Riggs Trail. Already, you are completely immersed in the famous stone hoodoos that assume fantastic shapes. The vegetation along the hike is a pleasing mix of chaparral brush, ponderosa and Apache

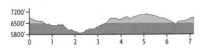

pine, and Douglas fir—with the exact proportions determined by the exposure of the slope you're on. The hoodoos are rhyolite spires, eroded from layers of volcanic rock.

Follow the Ed Riggs Trail south 0.6 mile, where it meets the Mushroom Rock and Hailstone Trails. The Mushroom Rock Trail will be the return route; for now, turn right onto the Hailstone Trail. This trail heads west along the north side of Rhyolite Canyon, giving you a view of hundreds of hoodoos on the south side of the canyon. After 0.8 mile, it meets the Echo Canyon and Upper Rhyolite Trails.

Cochise Head from Heart of Rocks Trail

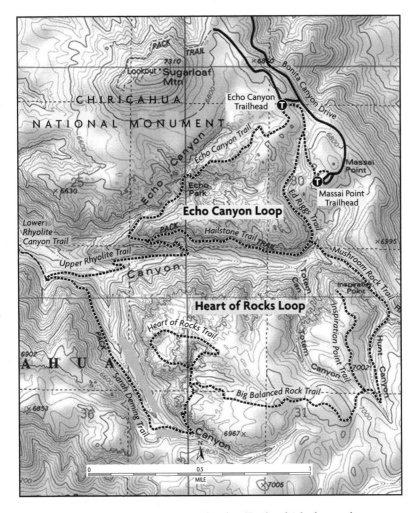

Turn sharply left on the Upper Rhyolite Trail, which descends to cross Rhyolite Canyon, then climbs up the south slopes to the west for 0.9 mile to the Lower Rhyolite Canyon and Sarah Deming Trails.

Turn sharply left on the Sarah Deming Trail, which climbs southeast up the cool, shady depths of Sarah Deming Canyon. Near the head of the canyon, the trail switchbacks north and climbs out of the canyon to meet the Big Balanced Rock and Heart of Rocks Loop Trails, 1.2 miles from the Upper Rhyolite Trail.

Turn left to start the Heart of Rocks loop, which heads north for just a few yards before reaching the start of the loop itself. Turn left and follow the trail through a wonderland of strange rocks. You'll also get views of the high Chiricahua Wilderness to the south. It's 0.8 mile around the loop;

stay left and retrace your steps south the few yards to the Big Balanced Rock/Sarah Deming Canyon trail junction. Turn left to resume the main loop, heading east on the Big Balanced Rock Trail. Just 0.8 mile of gradual climbing brings you to the Inspiration Point and Mushroom Rock Trails.

Here you can optionally hike north to Inspiration Point, which has one of the finest views in the monument. This hike adds 1.1 miles round trip to the hike, and no elevation gain.

Continue the main loop by hiking east on the Mushroom Rock Trail, which immediately descends into Hunt Canyon, then follows it north to Rhyolite Canyon. A sign points out Mushroom Rock, high on the western rim. The trail ends at the Hailstone and Ed Riggs Trails, 1.1 miles from the Inspiration Point Trail, also closing the main loop. Turn right and retrace your steps 0.8 mile to Massai Point.

68 ECHO CANYON

Round trip ■	**2.6 miles**
Loop direction ■	Clockwise
Hiking time ■	2 hours
Starting elevation ■	6780 feet
Lowest point ■	6330 feet
Elevation gain ■	800 feet
Seasonal water availability ■	None
Best hiking time ■	September through November and March through May
Maps ■	Cochise Head, Chiricahua National Monument USGS, Chiricahua Hiking Trails NPS
Contact ■	Chiricahua National Monument

Driving directions: Starting from Willcox, drive southeast 31 miles on Arizona 186, turn left on Arizona 181, and continue 6 miles to the visitor center. Continue 5.6 miles on Bonita Canyon Drive to the Echo Canyon Trailhead, on the right.

This easy but spectacular loop in Chiricahua National Monument follows the Ed Riggs, Hailstone, and Echo Canyon Trails. Hike clockwise to enjoy the great view down Rhyolite Canyon near the start.

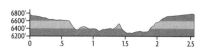

From the Echo Canyon Trailhead, head south on the Ed Riggs Trail. After 0.2 mile, the trail splits; stay right on the Ed Riggs Trail and continue

Rhyolite columns, Chiricahua Mountains

down the canyon another 0.6 mile to the Mushroom Rock and Hailstone Trails.

Turn right on the Hailstone Trail, which heads west along the north slopes of Rhyolite Canyon. As you proceed, you're treated to a stunning view down and across this canyon full of weird rocks. After 0.8 mile of this scenic hiking, you'll meet the Upper Rhyolite and Echo Canyon Trails.

Continue the loop by turning right on the Echo Canyon Trail, which turns northeast into Echo Canyon and soon descends to the dry creekbed. After passing through Echo Park, the trail works its way through the rock formations up a ridge and returns to the Echo Canyon Trailhead, 1.1 miles from the Hailstone Trail.

69 ROUND PARK

Round trip ■	**6.8 miles**
Loop direction ■	Counterclockwise
Hiking time ■	4 hours
Starting elevation ■	8440 feet
High point ■	9645 feet
Elevation gain ■	2140 feet
Seasonal water availability ■	Hillside Spring
Best hiking time ■	May through November
Maps ■	Rustler Park, Chiricahua Peak USGS
Contact ■	Coronado National Forest, Douglas Ranger District

Driving directions: Starting from Willcox, drive east 34 miles on Arizona 186, turn left on Arizona 181, and drive 3 miles to Pinery Canyon Road

Aspens, Chiricahua Mountains

(Forest Road 42). Continue 12 miles to Onion Saddle and turn right on the Rustler Park Road (Forest Road 42D). Drive 3 miles to Rustler Park Trailhead.

This easy loop takes you to a small meadow on the crest of the Chiricahua Mountains via a loop trail from Rustler Park.

Start the hike on the Chiricahua Crest Trail, which climbs southwest above the campground past the Buena Vista Peak Trail, then heads southeast across a steep hillside. Turning southwest as the trail continues around a small peak, the trail passes Hillside Spring and then meets the Long Park Trail in Bootlegger Saddle, 1.3 miles from the trailhead. The Long Park Trail will be the return route; for now, stay right on the Crest Trail. The Bootlegger Trail comes in from the right.

The Crest Trail climbs a short distance as it heads south. A 26,000-acre wildfire burned much of the Chiricahua high country in 1997; this loop alternates between the cool shady depths of the fir, aspen, and pine forest and the surreal forest of sticks left by the fire. The trail drops into another saddle, Flys Park, after 1.1 miles. Several trails leave this small meadow; stay right on the Crest Trail, which now heads around the west side of Flys Peak. The Salisbury Trail merges from the right, and the Crest Trail reaches another saddle and the aptly named Round Park after 0.9 mile.

Several trails leave the perimeter of this little meadow; take the leftmost one, the Flys Peak Trail, to start the return portion of the loop. This trail climbs 0.8 mile north over the rounded summit of Flys Peak, the former site of a fire lookout tower, and drops into Flys Park. Stay right on the Long Park Trail, which stays east of the crest for 1.3 miles to rejoin the Crest Trail in Bootlegger Saddle.

Use the Crest Trail to retrace your steps 1.3 miles to the Rustler Park Trailhead.

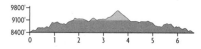

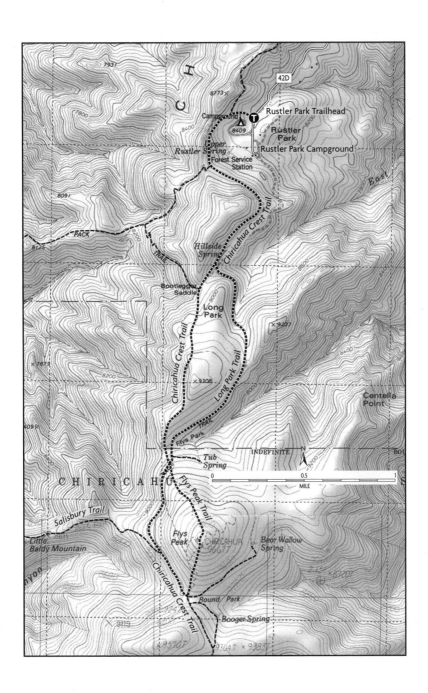

70 ┆ MORMON CANYON LOOP

Round trip ■	**6.2 miles**
Loop direction ■	Counterclockwise
Hiking time ■	4 to 5 hours
Starting elevation ■	6160 feet
High point ■	8760 feet
Elevation gain ■	2660 feet
Seasonal water availability ■	Mormon Spring
Best hiking time ■	May through November
Map ■	Chiricahua Peak USGS
Contact ■	Coronado National Forest, Douglas Ranger District

Driving directions: Starting from Tucson, drive east about 72 miles on I-10, exit at US 191, turn right, and drive south 27 miles to Arizona 181. Turn left and drive east 12 miles, where Arizona 181 turns sharply left. Go straight on Turkey Creek Road (Forest Road 41). Go 9.7 miles and park at the Mormon Ridge Trail on the left side of the road.

Starting from the Mormon Ridge Trailhead on the west side of the Chiricahua Mountains, this rugged loop ascends the Mormon Canyon Trail and returns via Mormon Ridge Trail. You can optionally hike to the top of Chiricahua Peak. Hike counterclockwise to take advantage of the views while descending Mormon Ridge.

The Mormon Ridge Trail will be the return, so walk up Turkey Creek Road 0.3 mile to the Sycamore Campground and the Mormon Canyon Trail. Hike east up Mormon Canyon, where you'll soon pass a spring. Mormon Canyon has a seasonal creek that usually flows after snowmelt, and the canyon floor is covered with a beautiful mix of ponderosa pine, Douglas fir, Apache pine, and quaking aspen. The climb is steady until near the head of the canyon, where the trail climbs up a few final switchbacks to meet the Mormon Ridge Trail, 3.1 miles from the trailhead.

Here you can optionally hike to the top of Chiricahua Peak, the high point of the range. Turn right on the Mormon Ridge Trail and hike south 0.4 mile to the Chiricahua Crest Trail. Turn left, and hike north 0.7 mile to Junction Saddle. Turn right on the Chiricahua Peak Trail, and hike 0.3 mile to the summit. The top of this 9759-foot peak is rounded and heavily forested, so there's no view. This optional hike adds 2.8 miles out and back, and 960 feet of elevation gain.

Back at the junction of the Mormon Ridge and Mormon Canyon Trails, continue the loop by hiking

Mormon Ridge Trail through unburned forest

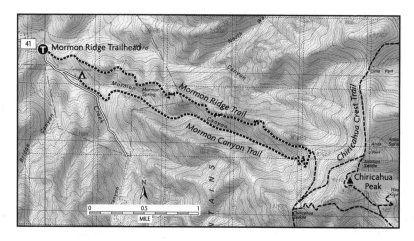

west down Mormon Ridge on the Mormon Ridge Trail, 3.1 miles to the trailhead. The trail tends to stay on the south side of the ridge and passes through an old burn for much of the way. You'll have good views of Mormon Canyon immediately below you, as well as much of the Turkey Creek basin.

71 ┆ CHIRICAHUA CREST LOOP

Round trip ■	**11.5 miles**
Loop direction ■	Counterclockwise
Hiking time ■	8 hours
Starting elevation ■	6160 feet
High point ■	9355 feet
Elevation gain ■	4240 feet
Seasonal water availability ■	Pole Bridge Canyon
Best hiking time ■	May through November
Map ■	Chiricahua Peak USGS
Contact ■	Coronado National Forest, Douglas Ranger District

Driving directions: Starting from Tucson, drive east about 72 miles on I-10, exit at US 191, turn right, and drive south 27 miles to Arizona 181. Turn left and drive east 12 miles, where Arizona 181 turns sharply left. Go straight on Turkey Creek Road (Forest Road 41). Go 9.7 miles and park at the Mormon Ridge Trail on the left side of the road.

Another great hike from Turkey Creek on the west side of the Chiricahuas, this loop ascends to the Chiricahua Crest via the Pole Bridge Canyon and Turtle Mountain Trails. Using the Crest Trail, you climb Monte Vista Peak, an open summit that offers sweeping views, and then continue to Chiricahua Saddle. An optional side trip takes you to the highest summit in the range, Chiricahua Peak. Then the Mormon Ridge Trail is used to descend to Turkey Creek and the trailhead. Hike counterclockwise to face the views as you descend the Mormon Ridge Trail.

From the trailhead, walk 0.1 mile up Turkey Creek Road to the Pole Bridge Canyon Trail and follow this trail as it climbs south up Pole Bridge Canyon through cool, shady pine forest. As the trail grows steeper near the head of the canyon, it starts to switchback, and meets the Turkey Creek Trail 2.2 miles from the road. Stay left on the Pole Bridge Canyon Trail, which follows a ridge southeast toward Johnson Peak, which it skirts on the west. You'll reach the junction with the Turtle Mountain Trail in a saddle after 1.4 miles.

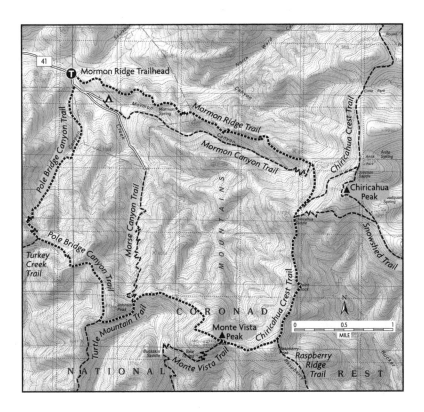

Seasonal creek in Pole Bridge Canyon, Chiricahua Mountains

Turn left on the Turtle Mountain Trail, which contours 0.5 mile across the south side of Johnson Peak to a saddle and the Morse Canyon Trail. Stay right on the Turtle Mountain Trail, which now climbs up a ridge to the east. A broad switchback leads to a trail junction just east of Monte Vista Peak, 1.3 miles from the Morse Canyon Trail.

Turn sharply right on the Crest Trail and hike 0.2 mile to the 9355-foot summit of Monte Vista Peak. Unlike most Chiricahua summits, Monte Vista Peak is open and grassy, and it has a great view. A forest service fire lookout and cabin are used during high fire danger—if the lookout is staffed, ask permission before climbing the tower. To resume the loop, retrace your steps 0.2 mile to the trail junction east of the summit.

Go east on the Crest Trail, which stays more or less on the crest of the range. You'll hike through portions of a large forest fire that burned large sections of the high Chiricahuas in 1997. The Crest Trail is badly in need of maintenance and deadfall will slow your progress. North of Raspberry Peak, the Raspberry Ridge Trail comes in from the right. Follow the Crest Trail north along the crest past Paint Rock, an area that was hit especially hard by the fire. At Chiricahua Saddle, 2.8 miles from the Turtle Mountain Trail, you have the option of an out-and-back side hike to Chiricahua Peak, the high point of the range.

To do this option, turn right and hike 0.9 mile east to the Snowshed Trail, then turn left and walk 0.4 mile to the top of Chiricahua Peak. The rounded, heavily forested summit has no view. This option adds 2.6 miles out and back, and 710 feet elevation gain to the hike.

Back at Chiricahua Saddle, continue the loop by turning left on the Mormon Ridge Trail, which descends along the west slopes of Chiricahua Peak 0.5 mile to the Mormon Canyon Trail junction. Stay right on the Mormon Ridge Trail and follow this trail 3.1 miles down Mormon Ridge to the trailhead.

72 | MONTE VISTA PEAK

Round trip ■	**13.4 miles**
Loop direction ■	Clockwise
Hiking time ■	9 hours
Starting elevation ■	5870 feet
High point ■	9355 feet
Elevation gain ■	3780 feet
Seasonal water availability ■	Sycamore and Bear Springs
Best hiking time ■	May through November
Map: ■	Chiricahua Peak USGS
Contact ■	Coronado National Forest, Douglas Ranger District

Driving directions: Starting from Douglas, drive north 34 miles on US 191, turn right on Rucker Canyon Road, drive 16 miles, and turn left to remain on Rucker Canyon Road. After another 9 miles, turn left on Forest Road 74E. Drive 2.1 miles to the Monte Vista Trailhead on the left.

Starting from Rucker Canyon, this loop ascends scenic Monte Vista Peak in the southern Chiricahua Mountains via the Turtle Mountain Trail, then uses the Monte Vista and Brushy Canyon Trails for the return.

Start the hike on the Turtle Mountain Trail, which heads north up Brushy Peak through pinyon-juniper woodland for 0.7 mile. Here the Brushy Canyon Trail comes in on the right—this will be the return trail. Stay left on the Turtle Mountain Trail, which now climbs up Sycamore Canyon past Sycamore Spring. Near the head of the canyon, the trail switchbacks up to the junction with the trail to Cub Canyon. Stay right and follow the Turtle Mountain Trail north as it climbs steeply up a ridge and passes through a saddle west of Turtle Mountain. Now the grade moderates as the trail climbs across the northwest slopes of Turtle Mountain, then heads north along a ridge. The Pole Bridge Canyon Trail comes in from the left at a saddle southwest of Johnson Peak. Stay right on the Turtle Mountain Trail, which crosses the south slopes of Johnson Peak to another saddle and the Morse Canyon Trail. Stay right on the Turtle Mountain Trail and follow it up the north side of Monte Vista Peak to a trail junction just east of the peak. This junction is 6.1 miles from the Brushy Canyon Trail junction.

Turn sharply right on the Crest Trail and walk 0.2 mile to the grassy top of Monte Vista Peak, which has the best views of all the Chiricahua summits. Retrace your steps to the trail junction and turn sharply right on the Monte Vista Trail. This trail descends across the south slopes of

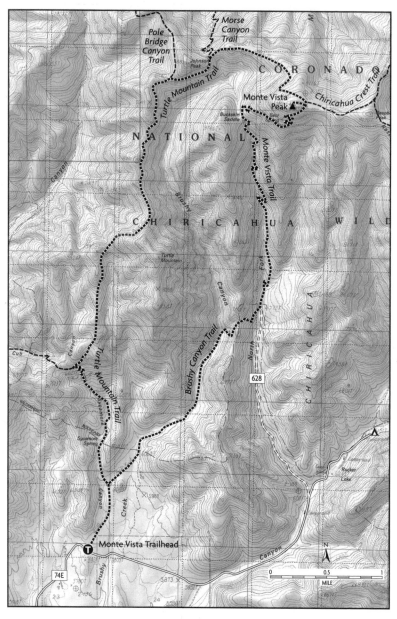

Monte Vista Peak, passing Bear Spring, and drops into Buckskin Saddle before descending steeply down the head of North Fork Rucker Canyon. After 3.6 miles, the Monte Vista Trail ends at the north end of Forest Road 628 and the junction with the Brushy Canyon Trail.

Monte Vista Lookout, Chiricahua Mountains

Turn right on the Brushy Canyon Trail and climb over a saddle into Brushy Canyon. The trail descends this canyon 3 miles to the Turtle Mountain Trail, closing the loop. Turn left and hike 0.7 mile south to the Monte Vista Trailhead.

73 RASPBERRY RIDGE

Round trip ■	**14.7 miles**
Loop direction ■	Clockwise
Hiking time ■	10 hours
Starting elevation ■	6160 feet
High point ■	9580 feet
Elevation gain ■	4610 feet
Seasonal water availability ■	Eagle and Juniper Springs, Rucker Canyon
Best hiking time ■	May through November
Map ■	Chiricahua Peak USGS
Contact ■	Coronado National Forest, Douglas Ranger District

Driving directions: Starting from Douglas, drive north 34 miles on US 191, turn right on Rucker Canyon Road, drive 16 miles, and turn left to remain on Rucker Canyon Road. After another 9 miles, turn left on Forest Road 74E. Drive 5.3 miles to the Rucker Trailhead at road's end.

From the Rucker Trailhead in the southern Chiricahua Mountains, this rugged loop climbs to the crest of the range on the Raspberry Ridge Trail. After traversing a section of the Crest Trail, you return via the Price Canyon and Rucker Canyon Trails.

Large sections of this loop were burned in 1997 and there's little trail maintenance. Expect slow hiking because of deadfall and trail erosion.

From the trailhead, start on the Rucker Canyon Trail and walk 0.2 mile east past the campground to the Raspberry Ridge Trail. The Rucker Canyon Trail will be the return. Turn left on the Raspberry Ridge Trail, which heads northeast and climbs steeply up Bear Canyon. A few switchbacks lead to a saddle at the head of the canyon, and the trail turns northwest and climbs Raspberry Ridge. When the trail reaches

about 8700 feet, the grade moderates, and the trail follows the ridge past Raspberry Peak to end at the Crest Trail, 4 miles from the Rucker Canyon Trail.

Turn right on the Crest Trail, which follows the crest of the ridge north past Paint Rock and an especially devastated portion of the burn. At Chiricahua Saddle, 1.4 miles from the Raspberry Ridge Trail, turn right on the Snowshed Trail and hike 1.1 miles east across the south slopes of Chiricahua Peak to another saddle and the Price Canyon Trail.

Turn right on the Price Canyon Trail, which descends southeast past Eagle and Juniper Springs. After 2 miles, the South Fork Trail comes in on the left; stay right on the Price Canyon Trail, which now plunges southeast into the headwaters of Price Canyon. Another 2 miles brings you to the Red Rock Canyon Trail, where you turn right.

The Red Rock Canyon Trail climbs a bit, then follows a ridge south 0.6 mile to a saddle. Turn right on the Rucker Canyon Trail, which descends

Rucker Creek

west into Rucker Canyon in a series of short switchbacks. Once in the bottom of the canyon, the trail follows the seasonal creek west to the campground and trailhead, which is 3.4 miles from the Red Rock Canyon Trail.

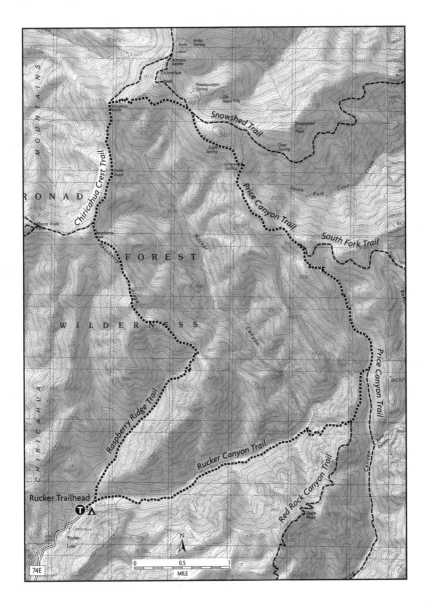

74 SNOWSHED LOOP

Round trip ■	**8.8 miles**
Loop direction ■	Clockwise
Hiking time ■	6 hours
Starting elevation ■	5480 feet
High point ■	7920 feet
Elevation gain ■	3050 feet
Seasonal water availability ■	Cave Creek
Best hiking time ■	May through November
Maps ■	Portal, Portal Peak USGS
Contact ■	Coronado National Forest, Douglas Ranger District

Driving directions: Starting from Douglas, drive northeast about 54 miles on Arizona 80 and turn left on Portal Road. After 7.8 miles, just past the hamlet of Portal, turn left on Forest Road 42. Drive 2.7 miles, turn right on Forest Road 42A, and drive 2.4 miles to the Snowshed Trailhead, which is on the right.

Flowers, Basin Trail

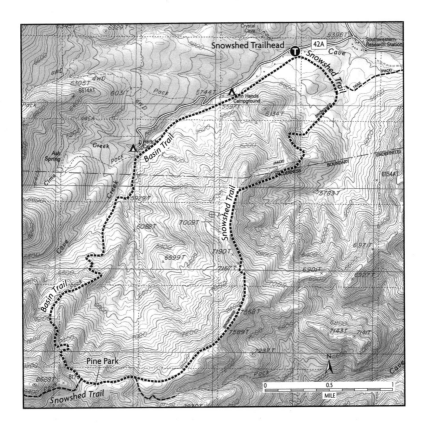

This is a fine loop in the spectacular Portal area of the eastern Chiricahua Mountains. Starting from the Snowshed Trailhead, the loop follows the Snowshed Trail up to Pine Park, then returns on the Basin Trail.

From the trailhead, cross Cave Creek, and walk 0.1 mile to the junction with the Basin Trail, which will be the return trail. Turn left on the Snowshed Trail and follow it southeast through mixed oak and pine forest past the junction with the old Snowshed Trail. Stay right on the Snowshed Trail, which now turns southwest and climbs onto the unnamed ridge between Cave Creek and South Fork Cave Creek. Staying mostly on the east side of the ridge, just below the top, the trail climbs steadily through the 7400-foot contour, then levels out as it follows the ridge eastward, passing the South Fork Trail which comes in from the left in a saddle. At Pine Park, 4.6 miles from the trailhead, you'll meet the south end of the Basin Trail in a fine stand of ponderosa pine and Douglas fir.

Turn right on the Basin Trail, which descends heavily forested

north-facing slopes. After the trail turns northeast, the descent moderates and you'll come out into an old burn, where tall oak brush crowds the trail. The Basin Trail drops down to Cave Creek, crossing to the west bank for a short distance, before passing a short spur trail to Herb Martyr Campground. Herb Martyr Dam, which is silted in but makes a nice waterfall, is visible on the left. The Basin Trail follows Cave Creek southeast, past the spur trail to John Hands Campground, to the junction with the Snowshed Trail, closing the loop 4.1 miles from Pine Park. Turn left and walk 0.1 mile back to the trailhead.

75 GREENHOUSE LOOP

Round trip ■	**13 miles**
Loop direction ■	Clockwise
Hiking time ■	8 hours
Starting elevation ■	5430 feet
High point ■	9520 feet
Elevation gain ■	4640 feet
Seasonal water availability ■	Cave Creek, Deer Spring, Headquarters Spring, Anita Spring, and Cima Creek
Best hiking time ■	May through November
Maps ■	Rustler Park, Portal, Portal Peak, Chiricahua Peak
Contact ■	Coronado National Forest, Douglas Ranger District

Driving directions: Starting from Douglas, drive northeast about 54 miles on Arizona 80 and turn left on Portal Road. After 7.8 miles, just past the hamlet of Portal, turn left on Forest Road 42. Drive 2.7 miles, turn right on Forest Road 42A, and drive 4.1 miles to the Herb Martyr Trailhead at the end of the road.

This is another fine loop out of the Portal–Cave Creek area of the eastern Chiricahua Mountains. The hike starts at the Herb Martyr Trailhead and follows the Basin Trail to the Snowshed Trail, which in turn climbs to the Chiricahua Crest Trail. As you pass Chiricahua Peak, you can optionally hike a side trail to its summit. Return is via the Greenhouse Trail.

Large portions of the Snowshed and Crest Trails were burned in a fire in 1997. There is little trail main-

tenance, so expect slow going due to trail erosion and deadfall.

From the trailhead, follow the Basin Trail 0.1 mile south across Cave Creek, then turn right and head south on the Basin Trail. The trail climbs steadily for 2.5 miles to Pine Park and meets the Snowshed Trail on the crest of the ridge dividing Cave Creek from South Fork Cave Creek.

Turn right on the Snowshed Trail, which climbs 3.2 miles across the slopes of Snowshed Peak, passing Deer Spring, to a saddle west of Snowshed Peak. Another 0.8 mile brings you to another saddle and trail junction southeast of Chiricahua Peak. Turn right on the Crest Trail, which skirts the east side of Chiricahua Peak and heads 1.5 miles north past Junction Saddle and Anita Park to Cima Park, a tiny meadow now almost buried under deadfall from the fire. Turn right on the Greenhouse Trail and follow it east down Cima Creek. Where the trail turns northeast, it leaves Cima Creek and crosses a ridge into another drainage. As this canyon opens out, the Greenhouse Trail meets an old jeep road, 3.7 miles from Cima Park. Turn right and follow this road 1 mile to Forest Road 42A. Turn right on the road and follow it 0.3 mile to the Herb Martyr Trailhead.

Grasslands and oaks near Cave Creek, Chiricahua Mountains

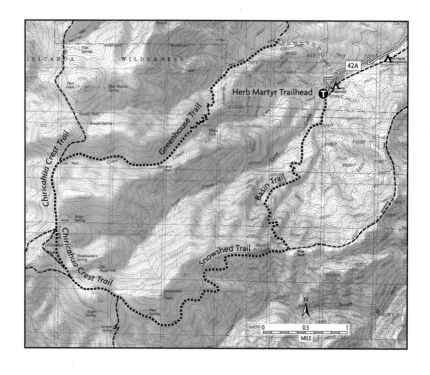

APPENDIX

APACHE-SITGREAVES NATIONAL FOREST

Alpine Ranger District
P.O. Box 469
Alpine, AZ 85920
(928) 339-4384
www.fs.fed.us/r3/asnf

Springerville Ranger District
P.O. Box 760
Springerville, AZ 85938
(928) 333-4372
www.fs.fed.us/r3/asnf

CHIRICAHUA NATIONAL MONUMENT

13063 East Bonita Canyon Road
Willcox, AZ 85643-9737
(520) 824-3560
www.nps.gov/chir/

COCONINO NATIONAL FOREST

Mogollon Rim, Mormon Lake, Peaks,
and Red Rock Ranger Districts
1824 South Thompson Street
Flagstaff, AZ 86001
(928) 527-3600
www.fs.fed.us/r3/coconino/

CORONADO NATIONAL FOREST

Douglas Ranger District
3081 North Leslie Canyon Road
Douglas, AZ 85607
(520) 364-3468
www.fs.fed.us/r3/coronado/

Nogales Ranger District
3081 North Leslie Canyon Road
Douglas, AZ 85607
(520) 364-3468
www.fs.fed.us/r3/coronado/

Safford Ranger District
P.O. Box 709
Safford, AZ 85548
(928) 428-4150
www.fs.fed.us/r3/coronado/

Santa Catalina Ranger District
5700 North Sabino Canyon Road
Tucson, AZ 85750
(520) 749-8700
www.fs.fed.us/r3/coronado/

Sierra Vista Ranger District
5990 South Highway 92
Hereford, AZ 85615
(520) 366-5515
www.fs.fed.us/r3/coronado/

GRAND CANYON NATIONAL PARK

P.O. Box 129
Grand Canyon, AZ 86028
(928) 638-7888
www.nps.gov/grca

KAIBAB NATIONAL FOREST

Visitor Center
200 West Railhead Avenue
Hours: 8 A.M. to 6:30 P.M. Daily
(928) 635-4707
(800) 863-0546
www.fs.fed.us/kaibab

Williams Ranger District
742 South Clover Road
Williams, AZ 86046
(928) 635-5600
FAX: (928) 635-5680
www.fs.fed.us/kaibab

MARICOPA COUNTY PARKS

Cave Creek Regional Park
37019 North Lava Lane
Cave Creek, AZ 85331
(623) 465-0431
www.maricopa.gov/parks/cave_creek/

Usery Mountain Regional Park
3939 North Usery Pass Road
Mesa, AZ 85207
(480) 984-0032
www.maricopa.gov/parks/usery/

THE NATURE CONSERVANCY

Arizona Field Office
1510 East Fort Lowell
Tucson, AZ 85719
(520) 622-3861
http://nature.org/

ORGAN PIPE CACTUS
NATIONAL MONUMENT

10 Organ Pipe Drive
Ajo, AZ 85321-9626
(520) 387-6849
www.nps.gov/orpi/

PIMA COUNTY

Pima County Natural Resources,
   Parks, and Recreation Department
3500 West River Road
Tucson, AZ 85741
(520) 877-6000
*www.co.pima.az.us/pksrec/home2/
   home2.html*

PRESCOTT NATIONAL
FOREST

Bradshaw Ranger District
344 South Cortez Street
Prescott, AZ 86303
(928) 443-8000
www.fs.fed.us/r3/prescott/

Chino Valley Ranger District
735 North Hwy 89
Chino Valley, AZ 86323
(928) 777-2200
www.fs.fed.us/r3/prescott/

Verde Ranger District
P.O. Box 670
(300 East Highway 260)
Camp Verde, AZ 86322
(928) 567-4121
www.fs.fed.us/r3/prescott/

RED ROCK STATE PARK

4050 Red Rock Loop Road
Sedona, AZ 86336
(928) 282-6907
*www.pr.state.az.us/Parks/parkhtml/
   redrock.html*

SAGUARO NATIONAL PARK

Rincon Mountain District
3693 South Old Spanish Trail
Tucson, AZ 85730-5601
(520) 733-5153
www.nps.gov/sagu/

Tucson Mountain District
2700 North Kinney Road
Tucson, AZ 85743
(520) 733-5158
www.nps.gov/sagu/

TONTO NATIONAL FOREST

Cave Creek Ranger District
40202 North Cave Creek Road
Scottsdale, AZ 85262
(480) 595-3300
www.fs.fed.us/r3/tonto

Globe Ranger District
7680 South Six Shooter Canyon
   Road
Globe, AZ 85501
(928) 402-6200
www.fs.fed.us/r3/tonto/

Mesa Ranger District
5140 East Ingram Street
Mesa, AZ 85205
(480) 610-3300
www.fs.fed.us/r3/tonto/

Payson Ranger District
1009 East Highway 260
Payson, AZ 85541
(928) 474-7900
www.fs.fed.us/r3/tonto/

Tonto Basin Ranger District
HC02 P.O. Box 4800
Roosevelt, AZ 85545
(928) 467-3200
www.fs.fed.us/r3/tonto/

INDEX

ABOUT THE AUTHOR

BRUCE GRUBBS is an avid hiker, mountain biker, paddler, and cross-country skier who has been exploring Arizona's mountains and deserts for more than 30 years. Hiking and backpacking are his favorite activities. An active outdoor writer and photographer, he's written seventeen outdoor guidebooks, and his photos have been published in *Backpacker* and other magazines. He is also an active charter pilot and lives in Flagstaff, Arizona.

THE MOUNTAINEERS, founded in 1906, is a nonprofit outdoor activity and conservation club, whose mission is "to explore, study, preserve, and enjoy the natural beauty of the outdoors. . . . " Based in Seattle, Washington, the club is now the third-largest such organization in the United States, with seven branches throughout Washington State.

The Mountaineers sponsors both classes and year-round outdoor activities in the Pacific Northwest, which include hiking, mountain climbing, ski-touring, snowshoeing, bicycling, camping, kayaking, nature study, sailing, and adventure travel. The club's conservation division supports environmental causes through educational activities, sponsoring legislation, and presenting informational programs.

All club activities are led by skilled, experienced instructors, who are dedicated to promoting safe and responsible enjoyment and preservation of the outdoors.

If you would like to participate in these organized outdoor activities or the club's programs, consider a membership in The Mountaineers. For information and an application, write or call The Mountaineers, Club Headquarters, 300 Third Avenue West, Seattle, WA 98119; 206-284-6310. You can also visit the club's website at *www.mountaineers.org* or contact The Mountaineers via email at *clubmail@mountaineers.org.*

The Mountaineers Books, an active, nonprofit publishing program of the club, produces guidebooks, instructional texts, historical works, natural history guides, and works on environmental conservation. All books produced by The Mountaineers Books fulfill the club's mission.

Send or call for our catalog of more than 500 outdoor titles:

The Mountaineers Books
1001 SW Klickitat Way, Suite 201
Seattle, WA 98134
800-553-4453
mbooks@mountaineersbooks.org
www.mountaineersbooks.org

The Mountaineers Books is proud to be a corporate sponsor of The Leave No Trace Center for Outdoor Ethics, whose mission is to promote and inspire responsible outdoor recreation through education, research, and partnerships. The Leave No Trace program is focused specifically on human-powered (nonmotorized) recreation.

Leave No Trace strives to educate visitors about the nature of their recreational impacts, as well as offer techniques to prevent and minimize such impacts. Leave No Trace is best understood as an educational and ethical program, not as a set of rules and regulations.

For more information, visit *www.LNT.org,* or call 800-332-4100.

OTHER TITLES YOU MIGHT ENJOY FROM THE MOUNTAINEERS BOOKS

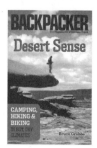
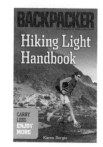